PROBLEMS IN MODERN GEOGRAPHY

J. ALLAN PATMORE

Land and Leisure

IN ENGLAND & WALES

With a preface by Edmund W. Gilbert

David & Charles : Newton Abbot

ISBN 0 7153 4941 4

Set in 10/11 pt Janson
and printed in Great Britain
by Clarke, Doble & Brendon Limited, Plymouth and London
for David & Charles (Publishers) Limited
South Devon House Newton Abbot Devon

*To my mother and father who first
taught me to love and to explore
the land of Britain*

Contents

Illustrations

PLATES

TEXT ILLUSTRATIONS AND MAPS

Preface

THE British Academy awards annually a Research Fellowship, pre-
ferably in social or humanistic studies, from moneys provided by
its newly-established 'Thank-Offering to Britain Fund'. This
generous endowment was given by a group of former refugees
from Nazi oppression, now settled in Great Britain. The holder
of the award is expected to study a subject that has 'some bearing
upon the well-being of the people of the British Isles'. The first Research Fellow, elected in 1967, is the author of this book. The
award has enabled Mr J. A. Patmore not only to take leave of
absence from his university duties as Lecturer in Geography at
Liverpool and devote himself entirely to studying a subject of
very real significance for the well-being of the British people;
but also to travel extensively in the United States and to observe
how that country, with its vast reserves of territory, is meeting
the pressing problems of leisure and land.

The population of the island of Britain is increasing fast, much
faster than was anticipated at the end of the war in 1945. Sir
Christopher Hinton once remarked that 'the United Kingdom is
supporting a population of fifty million people in an island well
designed to accommodate twenty million'. This small and densely
peopled land is becoming ever more crowded. The pressure not
only on good agricultural land, but also on all land now 'protected' in some way by legislation, such as National Parks, Areas
of Outstanding Natural Beauty and Green Belts, will become
continually greater. The increasing population is also increasing
its mobility; and greater mobility inevitably means an increase in
the pressure on the more isolated parts of the country. While

the amount of land remains the same, more and more people are
searching for space on which to live and work and play. Partly as
a result of the technological changes of this century the number
of both hours and days of work decline, thus making more leisure
available for the society of the motor age.

This book deals with the main problems that the new mobility
and the increase of leisure for all have brought to England and
Wales. It treats its subject against both the historical and the geographical backgrounds and makes its points doubly clear by a
lavish equipment of maps. Particular attention is given, as is
natural in considering an island, to the questions which concern
the coast. Over 70 per cent of British holidaymakers go to the
seaside for their annual holiday; over four million people take
their holidays in coastal caravans. It must be remembered that the
coastline is a very limited commodity: England and Wales have
only 2,742 miles of coast and nearly 300 miles of it is substantially
built up. In 1958 it was estimated that the loss of natural coast
had been about 1½ miles a year in the previous twenty. In some
areas high cliffs and limited access have helped to safeguard
against too much development of the coastline, but in other parts
as along the coast of the East Riding of Yorkshire, there is the
problem of clearing extensive pre-war holiday shack development.

It has long been the opinion of the writer of this preface that
far more research should be undertaken into all the complex
problems that concern the use of land for leisure in this small and
crowded island. There are so many competitive claims for the use
of the same land. In making decisions, the case for retaining the
beauty of the scenery can be forgotten so easily because it is impossible to give it a precise value in hard cash. This book provides
the needed material for teaching in schools and universities and
thus for creating an informed public opinion on questions of land
and leisure. It is vital that a greater sensitivity to the beauty of
nature should be developed. Nearly forty years ago that great
pioneer Vaughan Cornish advocated the formation of National
Parks, 'where in times of holiday, the urban population, the
majority of our people, can recover that close touch with Nature
which is needful for the spiritual welfare of a nation'.

                                        EDMUND W. GILBERT

Old Cottage, Appleton, Berkshire
January, 1970

CHAPTER ONE

The Challenge of Leisure

THE FOURTH WAVE

Three great waves have broken across the face of Britain since 1800. First, the sudden growth of dark industrial towns. Second, the thrusting movement along far-flung railways. Third, the sprawl of car-based suburbs. Now we see, under the guise of a modest word, the surge of a fourth wave which could be more powerful than all the others. The modest word is leisure.[1]

THE challenge of leisure, so graphically portrayed in Michael Dower's words, has become of major concern to layman and planner alike. For the layman, that concern is perhaps more implicit than explicit, but in his increased leisure time, with more income at his disposal and with greatly enhanced personal mobility, he can scarcely fail to be aware of the pressures this has generated in the community as a whole. Outdoors, congested roads and crowded beaches seem the inevitable concomitant of the summer weekend, and the lover of rural solitude seeks often in vain for the peace and isolation he values so highly. For the planner, these pressures present an urgent and varied challenge, a challenge bedevilled by the inherent paradox of the need not only to conserve the scarce resources of land and amenity, but also to provide for their fuller use and enjoyment.

The increased demand for leisure facilities is no transient phenomenon: rather it would seem that the most dramatic phases of growth are yet to come. There are two distinct elements in this growth; the time and opportunity available for leisure and the way in which that time is actually used. Precise prediction on either count is obviously impossible, but some indication is given by trends in those social and economic factors which have been shown to influence demand. It can be no more than an indication: as one practising planner recently wrote,

> Our society has endowed, or encumbered itself, with vast numbers of measurable facts, and many planners and others have become preoccupied with the techniques of mathematical forecasting . . . The great weakness in the use of models at the present time lies in our inability to predict cultural changes. Fashions in procreation and migration have constantly confounded the Registrar General: economic productivity has seldom increased at the rate forecast . . .[2]

But this caution is of degree rather than of kind: the indications themselves are clear enough in their general direction for the reasonably foreseeable future.

Estimates of relative changes by the end of the century in some of the more important social and economic characteristics which affect the demand for recreation are shown in Figure 1. The volume of demand is influenced by a variety of factors of which the most tangible are the size and age structure of the population, the time and money available for leisure pursuits and the degree of personal mobility. In 1969 it was predicted that the population of the United Kingdom would be 68,190,000 in the year 2000, an increase of some twelve million in thirty years (but some seven million fewer than had been thought likely in 1965). On the one hand this number will include greater proportions of younger, more active people with more energy for recreation. On the other, there will be larger numbers of retired persons with more leisure time.

Predictions of changes in working hours and of real personal incomes are more hazardous. Rosy visions of automated, computerised production lines providing major increases in income for a three-day working week are probably wide of the mark for the more immediate future, though the thirty-hour, four-day week is a tangible prospect. Hours actually worked still tend

OPPOSITE: *(above)* When towns were small, opportunities for recreation were easily available on their outskirts. Strollers on the banks of the Irwell at Manchester, 1728; *(below)* industrialisation and the railway spawned the urban coastal resorts. Blackpool, with station and separate excursion platforms; tower; promenade and piers.

greatly to exceed agreed weekly hours, with overtime an important part of total pay. At the end of 1967, hours actually worked each week by manual workers still averaged 46·2 for men employed full time.[3] From the point of view of leisure, actual hours worked are less important than their distribution, the availability of longer consecutive periods for recreation. A Bolton textile mill, for example, is able to run new machinery continuously by adopting four-shift working; a 9 am to 5 pm day shift, a 5 pm to 9 pm 'housewives' shift', and two sets of male workers on 9 pm to 9 am night shifts. The night shift workers are on duty for twelve hours on six days and eight hours on one day in a fortnight, and thus do no work at all on seven days in each two weeks. The company acknowledge that 'for the night shifts the problem may be one of increased leisure time'.[4]

The continuing growth in real income gives more people greater sums to spend on leisure activities. Between 1955 and 1967, the average earnings of weekly-paid workers rose by 96 per cent, those of salaried employees by 95 per cent. In the same period, prices rose by about 45 per cent.[5] This general increase in real income by some 50 per cent in thirteen years makes the estimate of an increase of 100 per cent by the end of the century seem almost modest.

Spare time and disposable income are, of course, not necessarily devoted to recreation in any positive sense of the term. Household chores however need no longer take such a high proportion of time, with much drudgery reduced by changes in habits and equipment. Convenience foods, non-iron fabrics, easily-cleaned plastic surfaces and the spread of labour-saving devices all have a part to play. Four households in five now have a vacuum cleaner, over half has a washing machine and more than one in five has completely eliminated open fires. The proportion of income spent on leisure activities is hard to categorise, for there are obvious problems of definition. The pattern will be examined in more detail subsequently, but on highly contrasted activities Britons spent an estimated total of £860 million on holidays in 1967 and some £2,225 million on organised betting and gambling.

One particular item of consumer expenditure, private transport, has a profound effect on recreation habits. In 1967 £1,166 million was spent on the running costs of private cars and motor cycles, but the scale of expenditure is less important in its implications

OPPOSITE: Sport in an urban setting: (above) Hendon golf course, showing the amount of land used compared with housing; (below) indoor climbing wall, University of Liverpool sports centre.

B

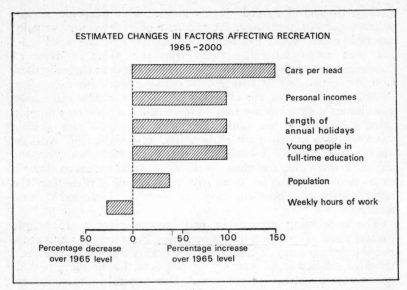

ESTIMATED CHANGES IN FACTORS AFFECTING RECREATION
1965–2000

Cars per head

Personal incomes

Length of
annual holidays

Young people in
full-time education

Population

Weekly hours of work

50   0   50   100   150
Percentage decrease   Percentage increase
over 1965 level   over 1965 level

Fig 1.   Estimated changes in factors affecting recreation, 1965–2000 (data from
A report on recreation and tourism in the Loch Lomond area, Table 1).

than the sheer volume of traffic generated. In 1950 there were
some 2¼ million private cars on the road; by 1960, 5½ million and
by 1970, 12 million. By 1980, the Road Research Laboratory estimates there will be nearly 21¼ million and although the rate of
growth should slacken later in the century as the desire for car-
ownership becomes largely satisfied, there will probably be more
than 26 million by the year 2000.

All these factors—increases in population, personal income,
annual holidays with pay, car ownership, and decreases in hours
of work—suggest at least a doubling in the time available for
leisure in the next thirty years, together with at least twice as
much money to spend on leisure pursuits and personal transport.
But while it is easy to demonstrate the scale of increase in demand,
it is much harder to discern the ways in which increased time and
money will be spent. A variety of factors seems relevant: changes
in occupational structure with a very rapid increase in professional and semi-professional groups; the spread of higher education; much broader curricula at school level; improved housing

standards but continuing increase in the physical extent of urban areas; technological change leading to the development of entirely new forms of recreation.

The demand for leisure is only part of the whole problem: the supply of adequate facilities to satisfy that demand and the allocation of scarce resources of public and private capital and of land in the creation of facilities is of equal moment. Indeed, the impact of Michael Dower's 'fourth wave' is of far more pressing concern than its scale, for many of the consequences of that impact are already present and the problems they pose are acute. The increasing awareness of these problems is reflected in the rapid growth of literature and of research in this field in the last five years[6] and in legislation and government action at national and local levels.

The present book is concerned with only one part of the whole field of leisure activities, outdoor recreation. Its particular purpose is twofold. It examines first the demand for outdoor recreation at the present time, the demand for both formal, organised activities and for informal, individual pursuits. It then reviews the land and water resources which are now available to satisfy that demand. Land in Britain is a scarce and finite resource: over the United Kingdom as a whole there were approximately 585 persons per square mile in mid-1967 while for England and Wales alone that figure rises to 829. Pressure on land is acute, and outdoor recreation is only one of several often competing demands. Knowledge is needed of both the demand and the resource if conflicts are to be resolved in as rational and as equitable a way as possible. This book argues no specific case, but is rather concerned to present a factual account of the situation as it now appears. The emphasis is on the nature and location of outdoor recreational pursuits rather than motivation and direct or indirect financial return: the sociology and economics of leisure are closely related but are rightly the province of other specialists. Consideration is also restricted almost entirely to England and Wales, for in Scotland, pressures differ in degree and in kind.

THE EVOLUTION OF DEMAND

The fourth wave is a mighty force, but its advent has not gone unheralded. Each of its predecessors has played a part in its creation: bleak industrial towns stimulated a desire to seek more attractive vistas, and train and car in turn created and channelled a new mobility.

Man has always had some time for leisure, even when daily hours of labour were necessarily long. Religious festivals were the usual basis, though the 'seventh day' filled as much a physical and a social need as a religious one. Modern leisure is distinguished not only by its range but the degree of movement involved in the search for a change in environment or a new recreational experience. Religious pilgrimages and the search for health at mineral springs gave an early impetus to movement, but such journeys affected only a small proportion of the total population. There was little incentive to travel when journeys were slow and costly, when much of the population was rural and even the largest towns had open fields within easy reach. John Stow, in 1598, echoed the feelings of many when he wrote in his *Survey of London*:

> On May Day in the morning, every man, except impediment, could walk into the sweet meadows and green woods, there to rejoice their spirits with the beauty and savour of sweet flowers, and with the harmony of birds, praising God in their kind.

Industrialisation and its accompanying urbanisation changed all that. By 1851 over half the population of England were urban dwellers; by 1911 over 80 per cent. The environment in which most people passed their days speedily deteriorated as the pressures of rapid industrial expansion, and the need to house large numbers of workers close to their place of work, led to the proliferation of cheap, high-density terrace housing. Speculative builders sought to extract high profits from the seemingly inexhaustible demand for cheap housing. In Birmingham, houses were being built in the 1820s and 1830s for £60 each, houses crowded back to back around dark and filthy courtyards. Between 1840 and 1875, the heyday of the highest housing densities, dwellings were built as many as sixty to the acre.

In reaction, Englishmen romanticised the countryside: 'townsmen though they are, they still think of rural England as home, the countryside as the essential nation'.[7] G. K. Chesterton echoed the thoughts of many when he wrote in 1910:

> 'Every man, though he were born in the very belfry of Bow and spent his infancy climbing among chimneys, has waiting

for him somewhere a country house which he has never seen but which was built for him in the very shape of his soul'. Those who were able fled the city entirely: 'from rustic villas in Surrey and Cheshire the well-to-do moved ever farther from the sight and sound of the advancing town'.[8]

LEISURE FOR ALL

For the majority, escape could only be short-lived. The limitations were of both time and money. The factory system, with its necessary rigidity in working hours, lessened the opportunity for days off. Many working families in the mid-nineteenth century did occasionally get away on day excursions (Figure 2), but these occasions were limited when few public holidays beyond Christmas Day, Easter and perhaps Whitsuntide were recognised. A major change came in 1871 when the passing of Sir John Lubbock's Bank Holiday Act gave four public holidays a year. The Bank Holiday became a British institution and further opportunities for leisure sprang from the gradual spread of a weekly half-holiday, first made compulsory for women and children in factories in 1850.

Throughout Victorian times, recreation for the masses was largely confined to day excursions. The extended annual holiday gradually gained ground but this pleasure was restricted to the thrifty or well-to-do; in 1900 a holiday 'was taken for granted as a luxury which could be enjoyed at a certain level of income but which there was no special hardship in going without'.[9] Between the wars mass holiday-making increased as holidays with pay became more common. In 1925 the Ministry of Labour estimated that about $1\frac{1}{2}$ million manual workers received holidays with pay, whereas by 1937, of $18\frac{1}{2}$ million earning less than £250 per annum, $7\frac{3}{4}$ million had extended holidays with pay of some kind. In the latter year, almost one person in three went away from home for a holiday. In 1938, the Holidays with Pay Act further increased the number of potential holidaymakers by encouraging voluntary agreements for paid holidays. By 1945, 80 per cent of workers received holidays with pay.

Since the Second World War, gains have been consolidated and new habits established. Although holidays with pay have become almost universal, for a variety of obvious reasons holidays away from home have not. Since 1960, the actual number of holi-

NORTH EASTERN RAILWAY

NIDDERDALE FEAST.

CHEAP EXCURSION TO THE SEA-SIDE.

On TUESDAY, Sept. 20th, 1870,

A SPECIAL TRAIN will leave PATELEY BRIDGE, and Stations as under, for

SCARBRO

FARE THERE AND BACK.
COVERED CARRIAGES.

LEAVE	A.M.
Pateley Bridge -	6 0
Dacre Banks :- - - -	6 8
Darley - - - - -	6 12
Birstwith - - - - -	6 17
Hampsthwaite - - - - -	6 21
Ripley - - - - -	6 30
Starbeck - - - - -	6 40
Knaresbro' - - - - -	6 50

3s.

Children under Twelve Years of Age, Half-fare.

The Return Train will leave Scarbro' at 5.30 p.m. same day.

NO LUGGAGE ALLOWED.

☞ The Tickets are only available for Scarbro' in going, and for the Stations at which they were issued on return.

As only a limited number of Carriages can be allotted to this Train, the following Regulations will be strictly observed, in order, as far as possible, to secure the comfort of the public, and to avoid delay :—The number of Tickets supplied for issue will only be equal to the amount of Carriage accommodation, and no persons except holders of Tickets for this Train will be permitted to travel by it, *and any person attempting to travel without a Ticket will be charged the full ordinary fare both ways. The Tickets are at the Stations ready for issue;* and persons who intend to travel by this Train must apply early enough to enable the Station Clerks to procure any additional Tickets that may be required.

YORK, August, 1870.   **W. O'BRIEN, General Manager.**

EDWARD BAINES AND SONS, GENERAL PRINTERS, LEEDS.

Fig 2.   North Eastern Railway excursion handbill, 1870.

daymakers has remained almost stable with annual totals fluctuating between 34 and 36 million, or about three persons out of every five. Of the total, about 5 million holiday abroad, a number which has remained virtually the same since 1963.

But mass recreation is far more than an annual holiday. Shorter second holidays have become increasingly common: the British Travel Association estimates they were taken by over 10 million adults in 1968. Even more important, higher real incomes and more widespread car ownership have released a flood of day excursionists. A British Travel Association survey in 1965 suggested that at least 100 million full-day trips were made in the four summer months of that year.

People are also engaging in a far greater range of outdoor pursuits. The first decade after the war was the heyday of spectator activity. Attendances at association football matches, for example, reached a peak in the 1948–9 season, when something like a million people watched matches each Saturday. Tastes since the mid-1950s have become increasingly active and sophisticated, and Burton and Wibberley have aptly dubbed this the 'age of the participant'.[10] Present trends will be analysed in detail in subsequent chapters but since the mid-50s there has only been decline in one major open-country pursuit, cycle touring. The growth in many others, and in water-based activities in particular, can only be described as explosive,

RAILWAYS AND RECREATION

As opportunities for recreation have increased, so has the mobility which enables those opportunities to be seized. The very nature of the transport available in any period has done much to determine the location, and even the form, of recreational pursuits. Paradoxically, much early escape from the oppressive confines of an urban environment was channelled by the railway to other towns, the nascent resorts. As late as 1927 Albert Demangeon could write that 'British civilisation wears an urban semblance even in its recreation'.[11] Even before the advent of the railway, some coastal resorts had become popular because of their accessibility by water. Margate is a classic instance. By 1802, 'hoys' were bringing over 20,000 passengers a year from London though the voyage lasted eight or nine hours, even in fair weather. With the coming of paddle steamers, numbers rapidly increased: almost

100,000 were landed from London steamers on Margate pier in 1830. Well could Dickens write in *Sketches by Boz* that 'Gravesend was low', Margate was 'worse and worse—nobody there but trades people'.[12]

It was the railway, however, which made the real impact for it could carry large numbers both speedily and cheaply. Its effect on Brighton is an apt illustration. The early growth of the resort had been stimulated by its position (it is the nearest point on the south coast to London) and by the patronage of the Prince of Wales. But, on the threshold of the railway age, its rate of expansion had slackened for existing communications had almost reached the limit of achievement. In 1835, coaches had carried 117,000 persons to the town but the journey was still relatively slow and expensive. The railway arrived in 1841: in 1850, 73,000 were carried to Brighton in a single week; on Easter Monday, 1862, 132,000 in a single day. As E. W. Gilbert sums it up, 'Brighton, once separated from London by a coach ride of six hours, and costing 12s for an outside seat, was now reached by rail in two hours or less at a cost of 9s 6d in a closed carriage'.[13]

For mass recreation, it was not the railway as such but the excursion train with its cheap fares which brought liberation. Excursions date from the earliest years of the railway. Many were extraordinary cavalcades. On the Midland Counties Railway in August 1840, an excursion train from Nottingham to Leicester

... had four engines to drag it forward, and to the beholder appeared like a moving street, the houses of which were filled with human beings ... The number of carriages was 67, and the number of passengers nearly 3,000, most of whom were well and respectably attired.[14]

On the same railway, on 5 July 1841, Thomas Cook organised his first excursion, from Leicester to a temperance demonstration at Loughborough for a fare of one shilling return. Events of varied kinds stimulated the provision of excursions, perhaps none more so than the Great Exhibition of 1851. The railways brought three million people to London from all over Britain, many travelling at absurdly low fares. Fierce competition broke out for the Exhibition traffic from the West Riding between the Great Northern Railway on the one hand and the Midland and London & North Western Railways on the other. The return fare fell first to 15s, and ultimately to as little as 5s.[15]

The success of excursion trains clearly demonstrated the demand for cheap pleasure travel, though they could only satisfy a part of that demand as they ran only on special occasions. But, supplemented by fare concessions on regular trains, they established a taste for the enjoyment of travel. As the railway network spread in the second half of the nineteenth century into remoter rural areas, wide stretches of countryside were opened up for rambling and picnics and on a more extensive scale, tourism developed in such areas as the Lake District. The Cockermouth, Keswick & Penrith Railway built its Keswick Hotel at a cost of £12,000 in the 1860s and introduced through services to Keswick from such diverse places as London, Leeds, Bradford, York and Newcastle.[16] The prime emphasis, however, was still on the seaside resort: the railway by its very nature concentrated rather than dispersed and though it brought greatly increased freedom of movement the channels of that movement were still relatively restricted. The *Railway Chronicle* might aver that in Easter Week 1844 hundreds of thousands were transported to 'the green fields, the smokeless heavens, and the fresh free beauties of Nature', but for most people true countryside was remote and rural peace remained undisturbed.

THE NEW MOBILITY

In comparison with the railway, other forms of movement had for long only limited impact. Prior to 1914, walking and rambling were largely confined to the professional classes and intellectuals. The working man sought rest rather than bodily exertion in his leisure time and generally had little appreciation for the rural scene as such. More important in the latter years of the century was cycling. The bicycle provided a cheap form of travel, and gave far greater personal freedom of movement. Its role in the rediscovery of the countryside can scarcely be underestimated. Its heyday came from the 1880s. The Cyclists Touring Club, founded in 1878, reached a peak membership of 60,449 in 1899: subsequent decline was not an indication of waning popularity, but simply that a craze had become an institution.

In the present century all ideas of mobility have been transformed by the private car. Prior to 1914 motoring was an adventure, the prerogative of the few. Some of those few used their vehicles 'view-hunting', in Carlyle's phrase, as a new and lively adjunct to the appreciation of scenery. Henry James wrote in 1907 that he had 'suffered infiltration' of the motor car which 'contemplatively and touringly used' had brought 'a huge extension of life, of experience and consciousness'.[17] In that year, there were only 32,000 cars on the roads of Britain and the rural landscape remained but little touched by urban intrusion. Between the wars, car ownership rapidly multiplied; 109,000 in 1919, 1 million by 1930 and 2 million by 1939: the real explosion has come since 1945. Above all, the car brought incomparably greater freedom to recreational travel, freedom in the choice of destination, freedom in the timing of journeys, freedom to pause at a moment's whim. Outdoor leisure was no longer limited in location, though that very freedom is the root of so many of the problems with which this book is concerned.

LAND FOR LEISURE

As population, mobility and participation in leisure pursuits have increased, so also have the demands recreation makes on the land. Both area and attitudes have changed—the actual area of land used wholly or partially for recreation, and the attitudes of users to the conflicts which so frequently arise between conservation and the utilisation of land resources. At the present time, it has been estimated that some 3 million acres of rural land in England and Wales are in effective recreational use, about 8 per cent of the total area, though any such estimate can be no more than an approximation because of the lack of data and the problems of definition.[18]

The use of land for recreational purposes is long established. At first, tracts were reserved for the private enjoyment of kings and great landowners. The Norman monarchs created vast areas of 'forest' land, that is land preserved for the king's hunting and subject to forest rather than common law. The term was essentially legal: much forest land was neither wooded nor waste. These forests reached their maximum extent about the middle of the twelfth century when, though neither their numbers nor their size are known with certainty, estimates suggest that they might have covered as much as one-third of England.[19] Even in Tudor times, forest rights were still significant in twenty counties.

Major landowners had their own private preserves. From the early sixteenth-century, castles or fortified houses were replaced by country houses designed for the pleasures of living. These country houses continued to be built for the next 400 years, the last being Castle Drogo, in Devon, between 1911 and 1930.[20] The houses were surrounded by parks, at first tracts enclosed for game, but from the eighteenth century developed in grandiose schemes of landscape design. Such landscape gardeners as William Kent (1685–1748), Lancelot Brown (1715–83) and Humphry Repton (1752–1818) brought order and formality on a grand scale, creating a legacy of continuing importance. Major parks cover several square miles: Woburn has 2,400 acres, Blenheim 2,700 acres and Knowsley 2,500 acres.

Ducal magnificence was little consolation for humbler mortals. Common rights were more important for farming than recreation, giving commoners access to land for grazing, gathering fuel, or fishing. Indeed, there was virtually no demand for land of this type for pleasure purposes: commons were to achieve importance much nearer the present day when many have provided a useful legacy of land with recreation potential. In rural areas the only land of consequence used for recreational purposes was the village green. Most date back to the origins of settlement; some were true commons with grazing rights, but on others there were no such rights. Their exact function is not always clear, though they probably served as a place where the livestock of the village could be protected in emergency.[21] They were certainly, for centuries, the place for play of various kinds. The village butts, for archery practice, were almost invariably set up on the green: as W. G. Hoskins has remarked: 'If the battle of Waterloo was won on the playing-fields of Eton (a very dubious proposition) the decisive battles of Crécy, Poitiers, and Agincourt were certainly won on the village greens of England.'[22] The returns to the Royal Commission on Common Land (1955–8) listed 1,380 such greens, with no records for Nottinghamshire and incomplete records for other counties: the average size of each green was about three acres.

Until the mid-nineteenth century, therefore, there was little general interest in rural land for recreational purposes. Large landowners preserved game and shooting rights over their whole estates, and kept their parks for personal pleasure but there was virtually no demand apart from this. Enclosure extinguished many common rights, causing hardship to many commoners, but concern for the preservation of commons as such came only when urban amenities were threatened.

THE NEEDS OF THE TOWN

It was, scarcely surprisingly, in the towns that the first areas of land devoted wholly to public recreation were established. Prior to the nineteenth century two types were characteristic. The first and by far the more important were areas of common land within or closely adjacent to the urban area. These date back to the earliest days of town development when the majority of inhabitants were still engaged in agricultural pursuits and common rights for grazing and other purposes were restricted to the burgesses. Oxford's Port Meadow, some 350 acres in extent and still an open common, was established by the tenth century: Domesday Book notes that 'all burgesses have in common pasture without the wall, which pays 6s 8d'. Several other major examples survive: Newcastle has its Town Moor of over 1,000 acres, Southampton its Common of 240 acres, Preston its Moor, acquired by the burgesses as a common in 1253 and transformed into a formal park in 1867.

For long, the recreational use of such land was incidental. Open country was not yet an attraction in itself and it was in any case close at hand. Only as towns began to grow in size and population was its worth appreciated by both the speculative builder and the townsman in his growing concern for amenity. Golf was played on Blackheath from the time of James 1, while Epping Forest was so frequented by the denizens of the East End that in their Report for 1793 the Land Revenue Commissioners said it was most important that nothing should be done to enclose it. A century ago a popular song declared 'Hampstead's the place to ruralize', but at this very time the existence of the famous Heath was threatened by the attempts of the Lord of the Manor, Sir Thomas Wilson, to enclose it for building. A bitter legal struggle was waged for over forty years from the 1820s. The Heath was only secured for public access after Sir Thomas died in 1868 and his successor sold his rights as lord of the manor to the Metropolitan Board of Works for £40,000. Out of this, and similar struggles to preserve London's commons for public access and enjoyment, was born the earliest of the amenity preservation societies, the Commons, Open Spaces and Footpaths Preservation Society of 1865.

Not all such struggles were successful, particularly in the Midlands and the north where rapid urban expansion more often saw the enclosure of commons, the extinction of common rights, and the rape of the former heaths by the speculative builder. Birmingham's last areas of heath were enclosed in 1799 and 'eight dreary little red-brick streets shot up where the bracken and the gorse had once flourished—the wonderful English gorse before which the great Swedish naturalist Linnaeus fell on his knees when he first saw it'.[23] In fairness, lack of land for expansion could exacerbate the problems of urban overcrowding. Nottingham is a classic case. Surrounded by some 1,100 acres of open fields over which burgesses held rights of common pasture, the town could not grow outwards until this land was enclosed. Enclosure was delayed until 1845 by 'an unholy alliance of cow-keepers and slum-owners'[24] with the result that the tightly-packed slums of Nottingham were a byword for squalor even by the standards of 130 years ago. There were, even at this time, two sides to the coin of conservation.

The second type of urban recreation area was the precursor of the fun-fairs and other intensive amusement tracts of the present day. Pleasure gardens, a familiar eighteenth-century feature of London and of such resorts as Bath and Cheltenham, varied greatly in kind. Some were merely tea gardens, others surrounded mineral springs where the waters could be taken in pleasing surroundings, while the most famous were complete centres of entertainment with facilities for dining, dancing, concerts and displays. London's Vauxhall Gardens, for example, opened in 1661 and a favourite haunt of Samuel Pepys, extended over twelve acres. Their heyday was the late eighteenth century and they lasted until 1859.

RESORTS AND RECREATION

Pleasure gardens were a direct response to a specific demand for recreation rather than an incidental use of land which happened to be available for the purpose. On a broader scale, this rise in demand was reflected in the growth of whole towns whose function was to satisfy the needs of recreation. The development of spas and their successors, the seaside resorts, has been fully chronicled elsewhere.[25] Both began as centres for the serious pursuit of health, but later became more devoted to pleasure. Spas emerged as true resorts after the Restoration. At this time, there was a conscious seeking after pleasure by the wealthy and leisured classes of society: London was the first resort, but London society sought its own alternatives and patronised the spas in increasing numbers. By 1724, Daniel Defoe could write that 'the coming to the Wells to drink the Waters was a mere Matter of Custom; some drink, more do not, and few drink physically. But Company and Diversion is, in short, the Main business of the Place'.[26] Even in their heyday however the spas catered only for the well-to-do minority. Beau Nash could welcome each visitor to Bath in person, and at this, the largest spa by far in the eighteenth century, the annual total of visitors did not exceed 12,000. The spas developed a distinctive landscape of their own, with not only baths and pump rooms, but libraries, theatres, assembly rooms and parades. The space to promenade, as part of an ordered pattern of exist-ence, was fundamental. At Harrogate this space was provided by the Stray, a former common whose contribution to the life of the spa was recognised in the Act of Enclosure of 1770, when it was preserved as an unenclosed stinted pasture in order that

> all persons whomsoever shall and may have access at all times
> to the said springs, and be at liberty to use and drink the
> waters there arising, and take the benefit thereof, and shall
> and may have use, and enjoy full and free ingress, egress,
> and regress in, upon, and over the said two hundred acres of
> land.

The seaside resorts aped their precursors in many ways. In the latter half of the eighteenth century, the drinking of sea-water was thought to have curative powers, and the early pattern of life at the coastal resorts was modelled closely on that of the spas. In the nineteenth century, both clientele and habits changed. Served by the railway, they offered an avenue of escape for the urban masses. As *The Times* of 30 August 1860 recorded:

> Our seaport towns have been turned inside out. So infallible
> and unchanging are the attractions of the ocean that it is
> enough for any place to stand on the shore . . . Down comes
> the Excursion Train with its thousands—some with a month's
> range, others tethered to a six hours' limit, but all rushing
> with one impulse to the water's edge.

The urban nature of this rush to the coast must again be stressed: of English towns with population exceeding 50,000 one in ten can still be classified as a coastal or inland resort. The three largest,

Brighton, Bournemouth and Blackpool have become the centres of urban agglomerations each containing some 250,000 inhabitants. The focus remains the intensively used foreshore, backed by a promenade and frequently crossed by the spidery ironwork of that Victorian institution, the pier. Emphasis remains on intensity of use. 'Blackpool has been criticised for the apparent harshness of its use of concrete. But how else could one preserve an area, particularly the cliff paths, which so many people wish to use?'[27]

VICTORIAN PARKS

While the seaside resort and the excursion train provided occasional avenues of escape they could do little to alleviate the increasingly stark daily reality of the Victorian urban milieu. Open space was no new element in the urban landscape as we have already seen. Landscaping in the eighteenth century created not only country estates, but Georgian crescents and squares which frequently contained gardens as part of the composition, though such gardens were for the private enjoyment of those living in the surrounding houses. London was a special case. The Royal Parks, which give the West End so much of its character, had long been accessible to the public. Hyde Park, for example, was opened by Charles I about 1635. St James's Park was originally acquired by Henry VIII and laid out as a garden. In 1828, it was landscaped by John Nash and, though remaining Crown property, was designed from the first for public use and in this sense may perhaps be considered the first English public park.

The need for such parks was rapidly becoming evident. As urban growth mushroomed, so living conditions declined. While the death rate in towns had fallen continuously until the 1820s and 1830s, the position was soon drastically reversed. Between 1831 and 1841, the death rate per thousand in the major industrial centres of Bristol, Birmingham, Leeds, Liverpool and Manchester increased from 20.69 to 30.8. Such conditions sparked the Health in Towns movement, associated so closely with the work of the indefatigable Sir Edwin Chadwick. Among the voluminous reports produced, the *Report from the Select Committee on Public Walks* (1833) declared:

It cannot be necessary to point out how requisite some Public Walks or Open Space in the neighbourhood of large Towns must be; to those who consider the occupations of the Working Classes who dwell there; confined as they are during the weekdays as Mechanics and Manufacturers, and often shut up in heated Factories: it must be evident that it is of the first importance to their health on their day of rest to enjoy the fresh air, and to be able (exempt from the dust and dirt of the public thoroughfares) to walk out in decent comfort with their families . . .

It was perhaps typically Victorian to treat the symptom rather than the cause and to rely to a considerable degree on private pilanthropy for such alleviation. Nevertheless, the result was a spate of parks seeking to provide space for recreation where the demand was greatest, within the town itself or on its immediate periphery. For the majority, mobility was limited by time, transport and income: parks were wanted within easy walking distance of the close-packed houses. The first park to result directly from this demand was Derby Arboretum, eleven acres laid out in 1839 by J. C. Loudon, and a gift to the public by Joseph Strutt. It was followed by many others. Liverpool, to name but one example, created the great ring of Stanley, Newsham, Sheil and Sefton Parks in the decade 1864–74. Sefton Park alone cost £264,000 for its 387 acres and £147,000 for landscaping the 269 acres of public park.

Park landscapes offered attractions for residential development, a fact frequently exploited to reduce the effective cost by developing the periphery for high-class housing. Birkenhead Park (Figure 3) is a case in point. The town's Improvement Commissioners obtained powers in 1843 to purchase land for a park, and 226 acres were ultimately bought, 125 acres being dedicated for public use and the remainder around the margins disposed of as house plots at considerably enhanced value. Indeed, when it was opened in 1847, Birkenhead Park was a success financially as well as socially, the whole of the outlay on construction being recouped by the high price received for the fringing land. Land bought for a shilling a square yard was sold between 1843 and 1845 for an average price of 11s 4d.

In layout, Birkenhead Park marks the beginning of a transition from walks and vistas designed solely for 'promenading' to the inclusion of areas reserved for the playing of games. Some eighty years later, the extent of change in concepts is seen in Mawson's

OPPOSITE: A hierarchy of recreational sites in Wiltshire: (top) Inglesham access area on the banks of the Thames at Lechlade; (middle) parked cars on the edge of the downs at Westbury White Horse; (bottom) the Grand Avenue, Savernake Forest.

design of 1922 for Stanley Park, Blackpool. The whole area was conceived as an organised playing space: passive enjoyment is obviously still possible, but the park is not primarily a landscape created for that enjoyment. In one respect, older attitudes remained. Sufficient land was acquired by the Corporation to enable 50 acres to be used for building, and the sale of building plots covered the cost of land purchase and park layout.

COUNTRYSIDE CONCERNS

If urban resorts and urban parks are the major Victorian contribution to facilities for outdoor recreation, the emergence of other pressures had not gone entirely unrecognised. As resources became scarce, concern for conservation increased, though through individual initiative rather than legislation. The first pressures were obviously in urban areas: the formation of the Commons, Open Spaces and Footpaths Preservation Society in 1865 has already been mentioned. But, localised though they were, other pressures attracted attention. In the Lake District, the Lake District Defence Society was created by Canon Rawnsley after he had accepted the living of Crosthwaite, near Keswick, in 1883 and successfully opposed railway penetration into Borrowdale. It was realised, however, that simple opposition did not necessarily result in positive preservation. A major step forward was the founding in 1895 of 'The National Trust for Places of Historic Interest and Natural Beauty', by Rawnsley, Robert Hunter, solicitor to the Commons Preservation Society, and Octavia Hill. Its object was actually to acquire land and buildings by gift or purchase. Many early properties were located in Kent and Surrey or the Lake District, where the founding trinity lived, though the first acquisition was Dinas Oleu, 4½ acres of cliff-land near Barmouth.

Between the wars, mobility rapidly increased and the countryside increasingly came under heavy pressure not only for recreation but from urban and industrial expansion. With drastically decreased housing densities, suburban expansion engulfed large areas with formless sprawl. Physical planning was in its infancy —a separate Ministry of Town and Country Planning was not instituted until 1943—and only around London was positive action taken, with the idea of establishing a green girdle of open space. The London County Council acted to preserve land in 1935 under its own somewhat limited powers and in 1938 the Green Belt

OPPOSITE: Getting away from it all: *(above)* holiday traffic at Minffordd, near Portmadoc; *(below)* equipment for the picnicker, a scene from the BBC TV play *The Gorge.*

C

Fig 3.   Contrasts in park layout; Birkenhead Park, 1844, and Stanley Park,
Blackpool, 1922.

(London and Home Counties Act) was passed by Parliament. These two measures protected some 35,500 acres from encroachment.

Elsewhere it was perhaps more a time for forming opinion than achieving results. In 1926, many local societies were grouped to form the Council for the Preservation of Rural England, that 'conscience of a nation confronted with the increasing disfigurement of its countryside'.[28] The Council early advocated the establishment of National Parks and in 1931 the Report of the National Park Committee under Christopher Addison gave official weight to these arguments. The nation, however, had more pressing concerns in the 1930s than the defence of amenity, though the increasingly widespread use of the countryside for walking was seen in the creation in 1930 of the Youth Hostels Association.

Since 1945, increased mobility, increased incomes, increased leisure time and increased desire to participate in outdoor recreation have sparked not only concern, comment and research, but positive action on a wide front. The detailed results of this action are the concern of subsequent chapters, but two main phases may be distinguished. The first, until the 1960s, was concerned primarily with effective conservation, the second with more positive provision of facilities for recreation, provision designed in part to alleviate pressure in areas of high amenity, in part to acknowledge the vastly increased demand.

Physical planning had its effective charter in the 1947 Town and Country Planning Act. Initially almost entirely concerned with the problems of urban areas, the Act included powers for local authorities to define and propose for the Minister's approval areas of Great Landscape, Historic or Scientific Value, though in practice the protection afforded such areas is flimsy. In 1949 the National Parks and Access to the Countryside Act established a National Parks Commission with the twofold duties of 'the preservation and enhancement of natural beauty' and the provision 'of opportunities for open air recreation and the study of nature by those resorting to National Parks'. Since then ten National Parks have been established, covering some 9 per cent of England and Wales. Powers were also given for the designation of Areas of Outstanding Natural Beauty and for the creation of long-distance footpaths. The formation of the Nature Conservancy in 1949 gave additional protection to areas of particular interest to natural historians with the establishment of Nature Reserves. The situation at

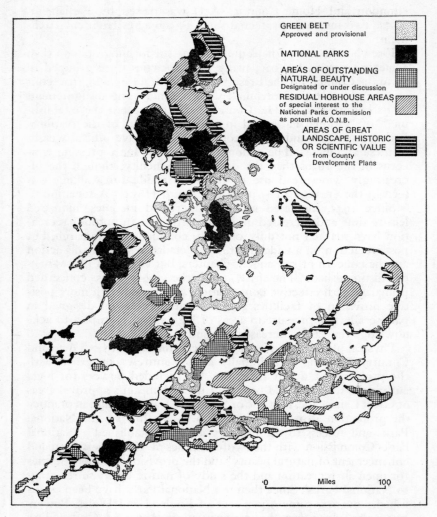

GREEN BELT
Approved and provisional

NATIONAL PARKS

AREAS OF OUTSTANDING
NATURAL BEAUTY
Designated or under discussion

RESIDUAL HOBHOUSE AREAS
of special interest to the
National Parks Commission
as potential A.O.N.B.

AREAS OF GREAT
LANDSCAPE, HISTORIC
OR SCIENTIFIC VALUE
from County
Development Plans

0   Miles   100

Fig 4.   Protected land, 1965 (after *Power and the Countryside*). Minor changes in various categories since 1965 are shown on Figure 62.

the end of the period is aptly summarised by Figure 4, based on a map published in 1965 by the Central Electricity Generating Board[29] to illustrate their problems in siting generating stations transmission lines and in seeking to 'reconcile efficiency with the preservation of amenity'. Over 40 per cent of England and Wales was covered by the various categories of amenity land, but though the negative values of conservation were tolerably well served, more positive co-ordinated action was lacking.

Meanwhile, public pressure on the countryside, and public concern with problems of access and amenity, grew. Interest was focused by the first of the 'Countryside in 1970' Conferences in 1963, under the presidency of the Duke of Edinburgh but associated above all with the energetic advocacy of Max Nicholson of the Nature Conservancy. Attention was drawn to conflicting interests as well as the sheer weight of numbers using facilities. At the second conference in 1965, a series of reports helped to clarify the issues and stimulated a flurry of action and legislation far more positive in intent.

In January 1965, the Sports Council was established 'to advise the Government on matters relating to the development of amateur sport and physical recreation services'. In February 1966, the White Paper *Leisure in the Countryside, England and Wales* (Cmnd 2928) foreshadowed the Countryside Act of 1968, and the replacement of the National Parks Commission by a Countryside Commission with wider powers. Concern for recreation and amenity in a broader sense was established by Section 11 of the Act which laid down the principle that 'In the exercise of their functions relating to land under any enactment every Minister, government Department and public body shall have regard to the desirability of conserving the natural beauty and amenity of the countryside.' This principle already had some measure of wider acceptance. The need for access to reservoirs had been stressed in a circular to all statutory water undertakings and river authorities.[30] In an even more positive vein, the White Paper *British Waterways: recreation and amenity* (Cmnd 3401, September 1967) envisaged the use of the canals as a network of 'cruiseways', subsidised initially to the extent of at least £340,000 a year.

All this, and other legislation in the fields of agriculture, commons registration, town planning and civic amenities marks a new attitude towards resources as a whole, 'the evolution of a new relationship between society and resources, in which the demands of society are becoming more articulate and dominant'.[81] It may point, in the long run, to full public control over the management of rural land despite all the inherent conflicts this would arouse. From the point of view of outdoor recreation, there may now be expected an interim period in which new legislation takes effect (hampered as it may be by economic stringency) and new attitudes evolve. The basis for change must be a full understanding of the existing situation, an understanding which it is the purpose of the present book to foster.

CHAPTER TWO

The Use
of Leisure

THE ANALYSIS OF DEMAND

The demand is surging. Whatever the measuring rod ... it is clear that Americans are seeking the outdoors as never before. And this is only a foretaste of what is to come ... By 2000 the population should double; the demand for recreation should triple. This order of magnitude, in essence, is the heart of the problem. But where will it focus?[1]

AMERICANS not only pose a problem but with massive enthusiasm seek its solution. In 1958 Congress established the Outdoor Recreation Resources Review Commission. Its twenty-seven Study Reports and its final report, *Outdoor Recreation for America* published in 1962, provide an unparalleled body of information and clear guidelines on which future policy could be based. This is particularly the case in analysing demand. On behalf of the Commission, the Bureau of the Census conducted a National Recreation Survey based on interviews with some 16,000 persons, while other workers investigated the effects on outdoor recreation of present and projected changes in income, population, travel facilities and leisure time.

No truly comparable analysis of demand is available for Britain. Until recently most studies were relatively small in scale and focused in particular on demand at its point of satisfaction—the

behaviour of people, for example, where they congregate on day
or half-day trips. Such studies throw light where the problems
are most acute but fail by their inherent nature to provide the
balanced appraisal of the overall pattern of demand which is necessary if priorities for investment, for the creation of facilities and
for the use of land are to be realistically assessed. Lacking such
an appraisal it is all too easy to exaggerate the claims of particular pressure groups, whatever interest they represent, while other
amorphous, inarticulate groups may fail to receive the attention
they deserve.

Recent work has in part at least alleviated these problems. Two
major national surveys have been published based on home interviews with a representative sample of the population. The *Pilot
National Recreation Survey* (1967) of the British Travel Association and the University of Keele was based on a sample of 3,167
interviews carried out in 1965.[2] The Government Social Survey's
Planning for Leisure (1969) was undertaken between September
1965 and March 1966, interviews being obtained with 2,682
people in urban areas, with separate samples for inner London and
the New Towns.[3] On a more local scale, the North Regional Planning Committee's *Outdoor leisure activities in the Northern
Region* (1969) was undertaken in 1967 with a sample of 3,828
persons. Similar surveys have been carried out by the North West
Sports Council and the Greater London Council but the results
are not available at the time of writing.

While these surveys have added immeasurably to our knowledge of leisure activities, there are several problems in their interpretation and use. In each case the sample taken is relatively small
and, though wholly adequate to assess the overall impact of demand,
much less reliance can be placed on results for the necessarily small
sub-samples. In the findings of the survey of the Northern
Region, for example, recreational activities are listed in thirty-
four separate categories: participation levels are such that results
for eighteen of these are subject to considerable sampling error
and 'should be treated with reserve'.[4] This need for caution is
even more relevant when detailed profiles of those taking part
in minority pursuits are sought, and qualitative trends rather than
quantitative values are all that can reasonably be derived. A further
problem is the lack of standard definitions between the various
surveys, making ready comparison extremely difficult. Nevertheless, despite all these reservations, sufficient is now known for

relative levels and patterns of demand to be assessed with some confidence.

LEISURE TIME AND THE WORKING WEEK

Leisure time—far from synonymous with the time devoted to recreation—is that remaining when the demands of work, sleep, eating and necessary chores have been satisfied. The BTA survey sought details of available leisure time and for those in formal employment a typical week was spent in the following way: working 48 hours (comprising 39 hours for the 'official' working week, 3 hours overtime and 6 hours travelling); sleeping 56 hours; eating, cooking and general household chores 15–20 hours; leaving 45–50 hours of 'disposable' time.

This simple average needs qualification when applied to particular groups, whether they are distinguished on the basis of sex, age, occupation or income. The time devoted to sleeping, eating and domestic chores is reasonably constant and the major determinant of leisure time is the number and distribution of hours engaged in work. Distribution must be stressed, for many leisure pursuits require comparatively long unbroken periods of time either in the evenings or at weekends if they are to be followed effectively.

The 'official' or 'normal' working week varies surprisingly little. In the BTA survey, one-third of the total employed had a 40-hour week and another quarter between 40 and 45. The biggest distinction in the sample came with educational background for almost half of those with a university education had a 'normal' week of less than 40 hours (though over a quarter of this group had no fixed hours of employment).

Contrasts are increased when the actual hours worked are considered. Overtime in this sample averaged five hours a week for men even when salaried employees with no paid overtime are included. Certainly, if the sample is a reasonable guide, the effective working week is still in excess of 40 hours for the majority, and over 45 hours for nearly half. Total hours worked varied but little with income—wealth and leisure are far from synonymous —but important for future trends in recreation, varied far more in terms of occupation and education. As the table shows, manual workers put in the longest hours but the executive group also achieved high totals. The shortest week was enjoyed by the third group, largely comprising those in shops, offices and other service occupations.

Occupation	Percentage of total in group working	
	Over 45 hours	Over 51 hours
Manual	45	20
Executive	30	14
Other	17	6

In terms of educational background, the university graduate again came off best: one-third reported they had worked less than 35 hours in the week before the survey.

For some, the time devoted to work was increased by undertaking spare-time or holiday work. The total numbers involved are relatively small (only 9 per cent in the BTA survey) but clearly some reject more leisure time in favour of a higher income. What remains in question is the attitude of such people when real incomes rise.

Another important facet of working habits is the length of the weekend break. On the basis of the BTA survey results, a two-day weekend is still far from universal. Approximately one-third of those in employment worked every Saturday, one-third occasionally or on alternate Saturdays. Many obviously have another day, or half-day, free instead but as the report acknowledges 'many people who have both the means and the enterprise to take up recreations which are both sophisticated and time-consuming may not do so because their participation at weekends is restricted to a single day'.[5]

The final component of the weekly working routine is the time taken in the journey to and from work. On average, this occupies the equivalent of an additional full working day each week. It varies but little in length with the size of community in which a person lives, but there are wide deviations away from the mean, too wide for generalisations to be particularly meaningful. As with the effective working week, while many are prepared to work long hours to achieve a higher income, so others accept the penalty of the loss of leisure time which a long daily journey brings in order to live and bring up their families in what they conceive as congenial surroundings.

HOLIDAYS

If the time devoted to work is the major restraint on leisure, the annual holiday is the major opportunity. Chapter 5 deals with the use made of holidays, but the time available for them merits brief mention here. Paid holidays have now become a right rather than a privilege and their incidence is illustrated in Figure 5. The apparently high proportion of those who had no paid holiday (24 per cent) needs some explanation. While it almost certainly includes many self-employed people and pensioners who do not have formal holiday periods, in addition many non-employed persons (including housewives) have probably answered for themselves rather than for the employed head of the household as asked. This value is therefore almost certainly overstated and others relatively understated.

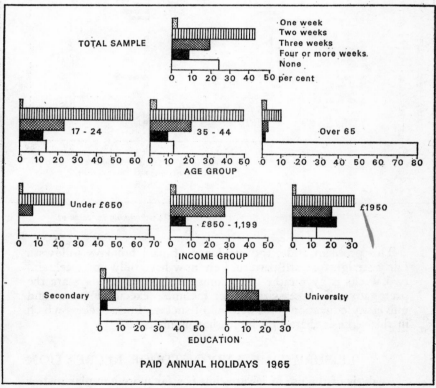

Fig 5. Paid annual holidays, 1965 (data from *Pilot National Recreation Survey Report No 1*).

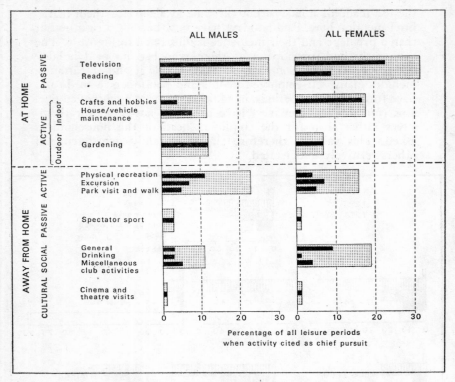

Fig 6.   The use of leisure time, 1965–6 (data from *Planning for leisure*).

This problem aside, the incidence of paid holidays follows a fairly straightforward pattern. Few now have only one week and two weeks is by far the most common. Longer holidays are the prerogative of those with higher incomes, 'executive' status and university education—one symbol of success, but a success which in this sense is shared by increasing numbers.

LEISURE TIME AND OUTDOOR RECREATION

Analysis of the use of leisure time is a far more complex matter than an assessment of its extent. As we have seen, the average Briton has something like 45–50 hours a week, and two or more full weeks a year, of 'disposable' time to devote to leisure pursuits, but there are wide differences in the ways in which the time is used. To some, the very possession of leisure is not an unmixed blessing: in the BTA survey almost half the sample felt they had enough leisure though 45 per cent wanted more. The greatest demands for more leisure came from the 35–44 age-group (59 per cent) and from those with a reasonably high income (56 per cent in the £1,200–1,949 income bracket), while advanced education and car ownership also stimulate a comparatively high desire. Indeed, while only 39 per cent of those without cars wanted more leisure, the proportion was 52 per cent for those with them. If these figures are a fair reflection of attitudes, they indicate a more positive demand as opportunities increase.

This book is not concerned with the total use of leisure time but only that proportion devoted to outdoor recreation beyond the confines of the home. This is very much a minority use, for all the evidence points to activity in and around the home, and passive activity in particular, as occupying the bulk of 'disposable' time.[6] This was clearly highlighted in *Planning for Leisure* (Figure 6). Even excluding general social activities and uncategorised pursuits, well over half the leisure time of both men and women was spent at home. Watching television was the most time-consuming pastime, followed by gardening for men and crafts and hobbies (primarily knitting) for women.

Nevertheless, outdoor recreation as a whole still occupied a substantial amount of time. Although individual activities might not achieve high totals, when combined together they amounted to 23 per cent of all leisure periods for men and 16 per cent for women.[7] These proportions are, of course, not constant throughout the year nor throughout the life cycle. Outdoor activities naturally reach their peak at summer weekends (Figure 7). In terms of age and domestic circumstance, the effects are more varied (Figure 8). Physical recreation declines with age, and more drastically—for women in particular—with marriage. On the other hand, more passive pursuits such as excursions and park visits show far less marked fluctuations.

In so far as they affect outdoor recreation, these fluctuations will be examined in more detail later: suffice for the moment to note the general level of participation, and the range within which fluctuations occur. The overall proportion of time devoted to outdoor activities may seem relatively low, as indeed it is if activities at any one period are considered. Cumulatively, the picture is very different, and even more important from the planning point of view is the potential for growth. At present, many facilities for recreation, though often appearing to be under pressure, are used only by a small minority, even at peak periods of demand. Quite small increases in the frequency of use will generate an inordinate increase in that demand. The BTA survey showed clearly that the higher the income level, occupational class and educational status, the greater the number of activities pursued, particularly those of an active nature: it is people with these very characteristics who

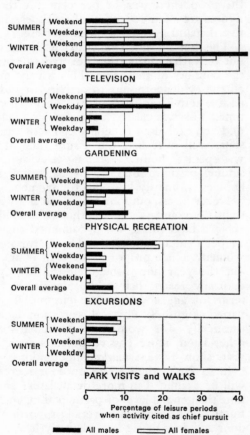

Fig 7. Seasonal variation in major leisure activities, 1965–6 (data from *Planning for leisure*).

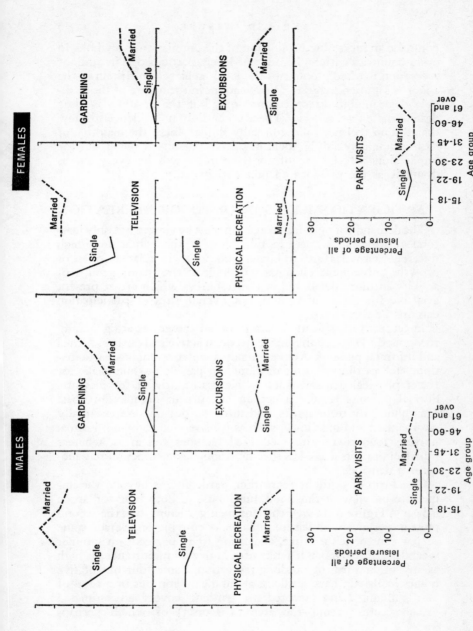

Fig 8. The effect of age on participation rates in major leisure activities, 1965–6 (data from *Planning for leisure*).

comprise an increasing proportion of the population as a whole. In other countries with higher income levels, participation in outdoor recreation markedly outstrips the levels achieved in Britain in the 1960s as Figure 9 suggests. Qualifications in the nature of the available data inhibit direct comparisons, but the contrast is clear despite these reservations.[8] There is certainly no evidence to show that Britain will not follow broadly similar lines: the majority of leisure time may still be spent in passive pursuits at home, but the implications of the use of the remainder will be every bit as dramatic as the previous chapter anticipated.

PARTICIPATION RATES IN OUTDOOR RECREATION

The demand for outdoor recreation must be viewed not only in its total relationship to leisure time, but in the extent to which different activities are followed and in their relative rates of growth. Subsequent chapters will look at the major groups of activity in more detail and at the resources which are at present available for their satisfaction, but overall rates of participation can first be considered.

In terms of classification certain broad categories are generally recognised.[9] Distinction is made between active and passive, formal and informal pursuits. Active pursuits involve strenuous participation, such as football, golf or climbing; passive pursuits make far fewer physical demands such as picnics or driving for pleasure. Formal pursuits require a certain measure of organisation, best exemplified by team sports, and informal pursuits are essentially unorganised and individual, such as walking and camping. Formal pursuits tend to require specialised facilities and areas, whereas informal pursuits make less specific (though sometimes more widespread) demands.

One form of outdoor recreation, gardening, is beyond the immediate purview of this book, but its use of both time and space is heavy. Figure 6 showed that for men gardening was the second most important of all leisure pursuits, occupying on average some 12 per cent of leisure time, and rising to 22 per cent on summer weekdays. For women it ranks fifth in overall importance, as high as any other form of outdoor recreation. Some four out of five homes in Britain have gardens, about 14 million out of a total of 18·3 million. Land devoted to gardens covers an estimated 620,000 acres (about the area of Dorset) of which perhaps

OPPOSITE: Coastal concentrations: *(above)* caravans at Ingoldmells, Lincolnshire; *(below)* Butlin's holiday camp at Filey, Yorkshire.

500,000 acres is devoted to lawns.[10] At the end of the second world war, there were marked distinctions between different parts of England and Wales as to the proportions of households with cultivated gardens, ranging from 75 per cent in the South East to as little as 11 per cent in the North West.[11] These distinctions, a legacy largely of nineteenth-century housing conditions, are now much less evident due to the more uniform standards of post-war housing. Little is known of the role of the garden in recreation as a whole beyond the most simple generalisations, and more needs to be discovered of the effect of a garden on participation in other forms of outdoor recreation.

Outside the home, the dominant form of outdoor recreation in terms of both the total time involved and the frequency with which it is undertaken is pleasure driving. This is equally the case in other countries with comparable standards of car ownership (Figure 9): the average American, for example, went driving for pleasure on more than twenty days a year in 1960–1, and 58 per cent of Swedes went for an outing by car at least six times a year in 1963.

Precise information on the total pleasure use of cars in Britain is not easy to derive, but the indications are plain enough. The BTA survey showed that 89 per cent of car owners used their vehicles for pleasure purposes at some time, though only 44 per cent had actually made pleasure outings in the month prior to the survey. Forty-five per cent of all households possessed a car in this study.[12] Other evidence is fragmentary, but all points in the same direction. A BTA survey over the Whitsun weekend in 1963 showed that 56 per cent of the total population undertook some pleasure travel over the three-day period, of whom 60 per cent travelled by car. Since then, further increase in car ownership has increased potential and the total incidence of car-based recreation is under-represented by these figures. One further indication must suffice: of the 30 million who took holidays away from home in Britain in 1968 66 per cent travelled by car, compared with 40 per cent in 1960, and 60 per cent in 1965.

Patterns of car-based activity will be discussed in Chapter 4 but, in addition to the sheer volume of travel it generates, car ownership also has the effect of increasing relative participation in outdoor recreation as a whole and in certain activities in particular (Figure 10). Car ownership is not the only factor involved (possession of a car itself implies a relatively high level of income), but

OPPOSITE: Problems of access: *(above left)* limited time, Plas-yn-Rhiw, Caernarvonshire; *(above right)* limited welcome, coastal footpath at Porth Oer, Caernarvonshire; *(bottom)* limited area, in the Nantlle valley, Snowdonia National Park.

D

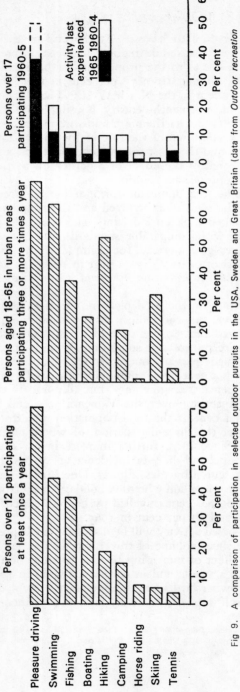

USA 1959-60

Persons over 12 participating at least once a year

Pleasure driving
Swimming
Fishing
Boating
Hiking
Camping
Horse riding
Skiing
Tennis

Per cent

SWEDEN 1963

Persons aged 18-65 in urban areas participating three or more times a year

Per cent

GREAT BRITAIN 1965

Persons over 17 participating 1960-5

Activity last experienced
1965 1960-4

Per cent

Fig 9. A comparison of participation in selected outdoor pursuits in the USA, Sweden and Great Britain (data from *Outdoor recreation for America*; *Outdoor Recreation in Sweden*; and *Pilot National Recreation Survey Report No. 1*).

These figures indicate trends only rather than direct comparisons because of differences in definition of activities and in the periods concerned. Swimming, for example, refers to outdoor swimming in the USA and Sweden, all swimming in Great Britain. Hiking in Sweden is simply 'walking for pleasure', in Britain 'walking 5 miles or more, excluding hill and fell walking'. For pleasure driving in Britain, the solid portion of the column represents those persons in households which have cars and who use them however occasionally for day or half-day trips. Other evidence suggests that the total for the whole population is nearer that shown by the broken lines. The figure for tennis in the USA is an estimate based on 1968 levels of participation.

these figures are underlined by the results of a survey in Birmingham, also carried out in 1965, where it was again shown that having a car encouraged more frequent participation in outdoor recreation, even in the use of sites within ten minutes' walking distance of the survey area.[13]

Percentage of persons using local recreation areas at least once a week

	Winter	Summer
Car-owning households	30·6	59·3
Non-car-owning households	19·6	54·9

After the use of the car (and often associated with it) come other informal passive pursuits such as picnicking, strolling or playing simple family games. These activities are hard to define precisely or to quantify, but their importance must not be underestimated. In the American ORRC study, 'walking for pleasure' was undertaken on average some eighteen days a year, only two days less than 'driving for pleasure' and three times the rate for swimming. In Sweden walking not only had a very high rate of participation but was at least the equal of driving.

Sweden 1963
Percentage persons 18–65 in urban areas

	At least once a year	Six or more times a year
Driving for pleasure	80	59
Nature walks, bilberry or mushroom picking	85	61
Other walking for pleasure	75	65
Outdoor swimming	67	59
Indoor swimming	19	11

Directly comparable figures for rates of participation are not available for Britain, but the BTA survey recorded that on the previous Saturday or Sunday afternoon 5 per cent of those interviewed had been for a drive of two hours or more and 4 per cent for a walk of at least three miles. Recorded participation would undoubtedly have been much greater if less rigorous definitions had been used, but was still high in relative terms. More specific information is given in the Northern Region survey, but applies of course to that area alone:

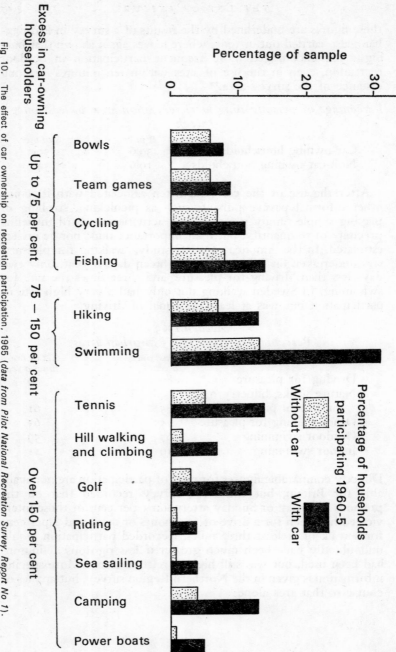

Fig 10. The effect of car ownership on recreation participation, 1965 (*data from Pilot National Recreation Survey, Report No 1*).

Per cent of population participating

	On average Saturday	On average Sunday	Within last three months
Trip to coast	4	7	38
Trip to country	2	5	35
Going for walk	7	11	43
Swimming	1	2	17

Data refers to July 1967

The relative extent to which people engage in more active kinds of outdoor recreation is illustrated in Figure 11. Direct comparison between the varied surveys is made difficult by the differing form of the questions asked; by the differing ways the results are tabulated; by the differing activities for which information was collected; by the different definitions used and by the fact that for many minority pursuits the numbers obtained in the samples are very small and liable to considerable sampling error. Nevertheless, a reasonably clear picture emerges both of the relative popularity of the various activities and of some of the major factors influencing the extent of participation.

In terms of the total recreation experience of an individual over his whole life-span, three clear groups can be distinguished (Figure 11A). Those in the first group, followed by 30 per cent or more of the population, are all cheap to undertake, needing only simple skills taught in childhood or at school. Such facilities as are required, sports pitches and swimming baths for example, are readily available in most communities. The next group of activities are still fairly common, from skating to youth-hostelling, though the values for both sea- and inland-sailing may be a little overstated here because of some possibility of double-counting the various types. After these come the true minority pursuits with, in addition to the four shown, such activities as ski-ing, go-karting, pony-trekking, gliding and water ski-ing. Apart from various motor sports all these have been experienced by less than 5 per cent of people.

While to an individual the fact that he has at some time in his life experienced a particular activity may be of prime importance, for the planning of recreation facilities the total incidence of outdoor recreation at one given period is of far greater significance (Figure 11A and B). The comparatively small proportion of the total population engaged in any single activity is most striking, a fact underlined by Figure 11C which again emphasises the much greater importance of such informal 'passive' activities as strolling and excursions to the countryside and coast.

On any count, swimming is by far the most actively pursued sport, for it is one of the very few sporting skills learned early in life which is not later abandoned. No other single sport approaches even half the number of swimming's adherents, particularly when indoor and outdoor swimming are combined: it is popular with both sexes and through a large age range. Succeeding it are a number of activities which claim some 4 or 5 per cent of the population as adherents. Team games are largely a masculine preserve, and are dominated by soccer and cricket. Tennis is the one sport which attracts almost equal numbers of men and women. Hiking and camping are also popular, though information about them is confined to the BTA survey. In this context, hiking was defined as 'hiking, walking 5 or more miles, excluding hill- and fell-walk-

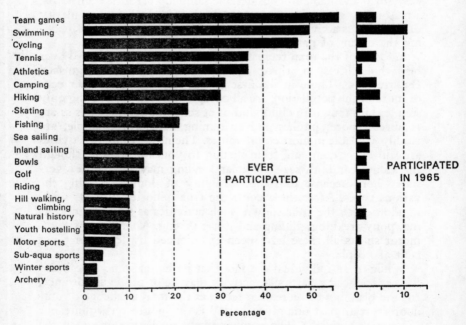

Fig 11.   Rates of participation in major outdoor activities.

A. Participation throughout the life cycle, and in a given year (data from *Pilot National Recreation Survey, Report No 1*).

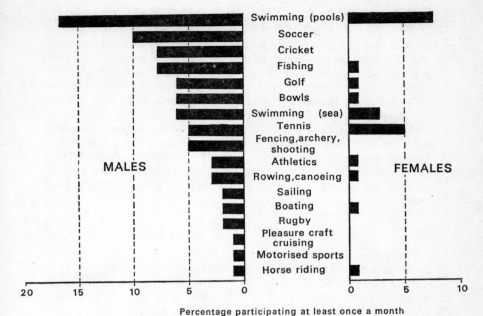

MALES · FEMALES

Swimming (pools)
Soccer
Cricket
Fishing
Golf
Bowls
Swimming (sea)
Tennis
Fencing, archery, shooting
Athletics
Rowing, canoeing
Sailing
Boating
Rugby
Pleasure craft cruising
Motorised sports
Horse riding

20 15 10 5 0   0 5 10

Percentage participating at least once a month

Fig 11.   Rates of participation in major outdoor activities.
B.   Differences between the sexes (data from *Planning for leisure*).

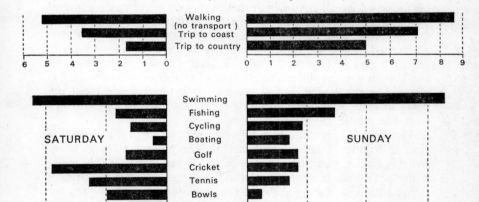

Walking (no transport)
Trip to coast
Trip to country

6 5 4 3 2 1 0   0 1 2 3 4 5 6 7 8 9

SATURDAY · SUNDAY

Swimming
Fishing
Cycling
Boating
Golf
Cricket
Tennis
Bowls
Athletics

1.0   0.5   0   0   0.5   1.0   1.5

Percentage participating on an average summer weekend
(Northern Region)

Fig 11.   Rates of participation in major outdoor activities.
C.   Differences between Saturday and Sunday participation in the Northern Region
(data from *Outdoor leisure activities in the Northern Region*).

ing': such a definition excludes the more passive forms of strolling and short-distance walking. In this sense it is far more of a young person's recreation, with three times as many people under 17 as adults participating. Camping ranks surprisingly high in terms of recent participation, but the term itself is broad and covers both the simple, cheap and arduous form most practised by the young and single, and family camping of later years often associated with car ownership. Fishing is not only popular, but is characterised by frequent participation: the BTA survey showed that 72 per cent of fishermen had been out fishing in the month prior to the survey, a rate only surpassed by golfers with 80 per cent.

AGE AND PARTICIPATION

Participation rates closely reflect the proportion of the population as a whole to which a particular activity appeals. Age and sex are the most obvious limiting factors, but others such as the availability of facilities and of time, car ownership and income level, and the dictates of fashion condition opportunity.

Those activities which span the greatest age range record the highest rates of participation. It is indeed the fact that they can be followed by all ages which makes the appeal of such informal pursuits as pleasure driving, walking and picnicking so widespread. In this sense, four main groups of outdoor activity may be distinguished. They are illustrated in Figure 12A from Swedish experience and in Figures 8 and 12B from Britain. The details of the British pattern differ for reasons of tradition, climate and income, but the available data are not only less reliable from the point of view of possible sampling error, but they are not uniform over the whole range of activities.

The first group comprises vigorous pursuits ('physical recreation' in Figure 8) and is dominated by the youngest age-groups: for this reason, total participation is comparatively low. There are many variations in the age at which interest declines. In Britain, participation in skating and athletics largely disappears by 30, but some team games survive more strongly to a later age. In tennis, only about 5 per cent of those who have played continue their interest into the thirties.

The second group consists of sports which still demand a reasonably high standard of physical performance, but where

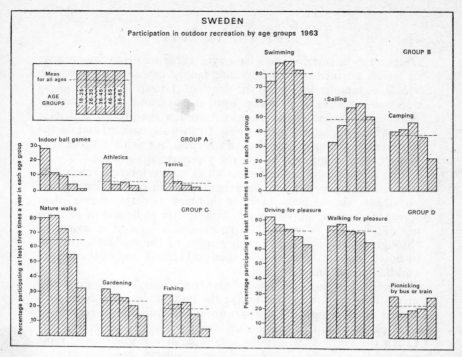

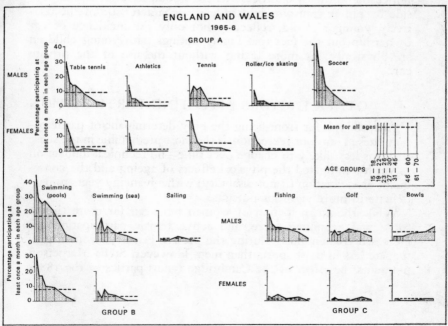

Fig 12. The effects of age on participation in differing types of physical recreation in Sweden (A) and England and Wales (B). No directly comparable data are available for activities in Group D in England and Wales, though some indications are given in Figure 8 (data from *Outdoor recreation in Sweden* and *Planning for leisure*).

interest can be sustained to a later age: these are often the pursuits in which all members of a young family can take part. In the Swedish examples shown on the diagram (Group B) the participation rate remains above average until after 45, and only drastically declines below half the average in the oldest age-group. In Britain also swimming, sailing (particularly fresh-water sailing) and camping persist strongly into the mid-forties, but with a somewhat greater relative interest among the youngest age-groups.

The third group comprises activities where interest reaches its peak in later years. They are generally more contemplative, less physically demanding—outdoor hobbies perhaps rather than sports in a true sense. This is particularly true in Britain of gardening (Figure 8), of golf, a sport in which interest is sustained through middle age rather than a sport of the middle-aged, and of bowls, a sport of the middle-aged and elderly and of the lower-middle income range.

The final group ('excursions' and 'park visits' in Figure 8 and group D of Figure 12A) is by far the most widespread both with regard to age range and, for motoring and walking, in respect of total participation as has already been seen. The difference between the various age-groups is comparatively small: it is most noticeable in the Swedish case where an outing into the countryside by public transport is particularly characteristic of the relatively young and old, reflecting not only the incidence of car ownership but the fact that family outings with young children are physically far more taxing without the use of the private car.

OTHER FACTORS AFFECTING PARTICIPATION

Age, though far from being the only determinant of participation rates in outdoor recreation, is the most predictable in the sense that it is least likely to change over time—no technical innovation as yet has mitigated the physical effects of ageing and the consequent disinclination (if not disability) with advancing years to participate in more vigorous pursuits.

While the emancipation of women has been far more than a social and economic force, and active female participation has increased tremendously during the present century, women participate less in most sports than men. However, Stella Margetson pinpoints the effect of the Cambridge tennis parties of the 1880s and 90s: langorous croquet gave way to a passion for tennis which 'brought the sexes together on the courts in a wave of exciting activity' though movement for the fair sex can scarcely have been easy in dresses tied back by an apron with pockets in it for spare balls. Nonetheless, Richard Jebb's American wife could write 'it is certainly livelier movement than I have indulged in for many a day'.[14] Today tennis is a sport which, among adults, is played as much by men as women, but by more girls than boys at school. Other active sports are more specifically a male preserve (Figure 11B), but so far as informal outdoor pursuits are concerned there is little distinction in rates of participation (Figure 8).

The time factor is of increasing importance. Many activities need a relatively long uninterrupted period of time if they are to be enjoyed to the full. Figure 11C highlights the distinction in this respect between 'Saturday' and 'Sunday' activities. The former are typically team games or other pursuits where participation can be confined to quite brief spells: the latter, such as trips to the countryside and coast, fishing and boating, need more continuous periods of time which for the majority is still found more readily on Sunday. The spread of a five- and even a four-day working week will greatly increase the time which can be spent away from home and thus the potential opportunities for these more wide-ranging activities.

Of other factors, the effects of car ownership in increasing outdoor recreation as a whole have already been discussed. Similarly, studies in America and Britain have shown that high income and high levels of education also stimulate participation—indeed, the effect of all these is almost inextricably interlinked as a comparison of Figures 10 and 13 suggests. The impact of such advantages however seems not so much in increasing opportunity as in increasing awareness and desire. Swimming, for example, is a cheap pastime which is relatively unpopular among the lower income groups and the less well-educated: about a quarter of those enjoying a high income and a university education mentioned swimming as an activity in the BTA survey, but only 5–10 per cent at the other end of the scale. Hiking again requires little special equipment or expense, but is much more frequently pursued by those with more money and an advanced education. More predictable are fishing, whose importance increases less with income than most, and golf, which is of negligible significance at incomes much below £1,200 per annum.

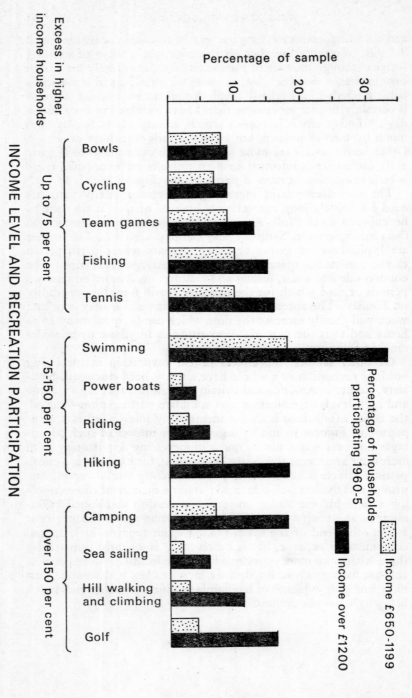

Fig 13. Income level and recreation participation, 1965 (data from *Pilot National Recreation Survey*, Report No 1).

INCOME LEVEL AND RECREATION PARTICIPATION

Percentage of sample

Percentage of households participating 1960-5

Income £650-1199

Income over £1200

Excess in higher income households

Up to 75 per cent
- Bowls
- Cycling
- Team games
- Fishing
- Tennis

75-150 per cent
- Swimming
- Power boats
- Riding
- Hiking

Over 150 per cent
- Camping
- Sea sailing
- Hill walking and climbing
- Golf

ACTIVITY GROWTH RATES

Participation in outdoor recreation is not only growing overall but, as already inferred, some activities are increasing far more rapidly than others. Relative rates of growth as well as present levels of involvement must be identified, for both are important in considering the actual provision of facilities. In this last connection, it is also useful to distinguish between those activities which are normally carried out close to where a person lives, in an urban setting in the majority of cases, and those which involve a journey away from home into open country.

Present evidence suggests that the following patterns of growth will be characteristic of the remaining decades of the twentieth century.[15]

Growth rate	Urban	Open country

More rapid than population growth (relative increase)	Athletics
	Golf
		Motoring
		Mountaineering
		Ski-ing
		Camping
		Horse riding
		Fishing
		Most water
		  sports
		  (canoeing,
		  sailing, etc)
		Nature study

Similar to population growth (relatively, little change)	Gardening Major team games Swimming	Walking Hunting

Slower than population growth (relative, though not necessarily absolute, decline)	Major
	  spectator
	  sports
		Youth hostelling
		Cycling

Substance is given to these general predictions when recent trends are examined more closely. It is almost impossible to establish precise rates of growth for adequate indices rarely exist. This

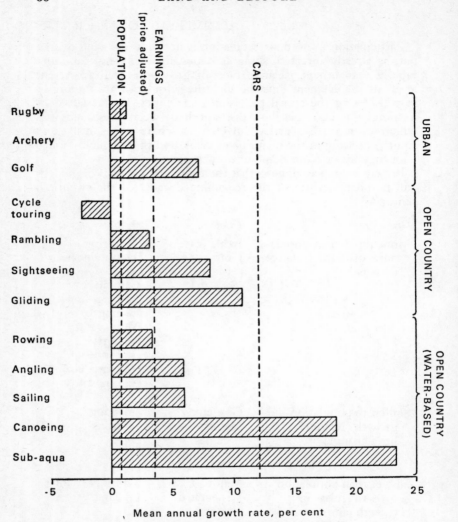

Fig 14. Growth rates in outdoor activities. See text for note on sources and their interpretation.

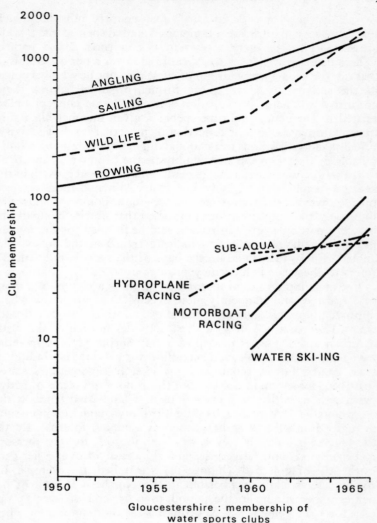

Fig 15. Membership of water sports clubs in Gloucestershire, 1950–66 (after Gloucestershire CC, *Outdoor Water Recreation* Figure 3). Note that club membership is plotted on a logarithmic scale, so that a given rate of growth is shown by a line of the same inclination anywhere on the graph.

is notably the case with informal, open-country pursuits, which by their very nature are unorganised and dispersed over wide areas; indeed their very attraction lies in their casual nature. Where data are available for a specific site over a period, trends at that site (or even a whole group of sites) may not be wholly typical of the activity. Even for more formal, organised sports, there are many problems. Participation is itself a vague concept unless related to frequency and time spent: a given membership figure for a club may be a poor reflection of its actual level of activity. Equally, club affiliations to a national organisation are not a wholly reliable guide: increases may simply be the product of improved organisation, while apparent stagnation may conceal growth in the average membership of individual clubs. With all these reservations, however, the trends are clear enough. Some are shown in Figure 14, though it must be emphasised that precise comparisons between particular growth rates would be illusory for the reasons just discussed. The aim is to indicate trends in the 1960s: the annual growth rate stated on the basis of the specific index used[16] refers to the years immediately prior to 1966–7.

The most rapid rates of increase are in those activities of a more sophisticated (and frequently more expensive) nature, those where improved mobility is an asset and above all, those associated with water. Comparatively few of these activities normally take place in urban areas. This is perhaps scarcely surprising, for facilities have long been available, and accessible, for playing the traditional team games, bowls, tennis and the like. It is sometimes stated that these sports are in decline, but this is not so in terms of active participation, with a few exceptions of which lawn tennis is the most notable.[17] Most are holding their own and in some, such as rugby football and archery, there is a modest increase. By far the biggest growth, however, has been in golf. By any measure its expansion is impressive: the annual increase of over 7 per cent in the sale of golf balls (Figure 14) is matched, for example, by an increase in club membership in the Northern Region of 6.8 per cent per annum in the period 1956–65, and of over 15 per cent for 1964–5 alone.[18] Such growth is the more important when the game's large land requirements are kept in mind.

In open country, most pursuits have registered large increases. Cycling is an exception, for it has much less attraction with more widespread car ownership and rampant road congestion. For most water-based pursuits, growth can only be described as ex-

OPPOSITE: National Park intrusions: *(above)* Trawsfynydd nuclear power station and overhead cables, Snowdonia; *(below)* Lime works at Rylstone, Yorkshire Dales.

plosive. The situation in terms of one county, Gloucestershire, is illustrated by Figure 15. All clubs have at least doubled their membership in the period, and the 1960s have seen the dramatic impact of such active and noisy sports as water ski-ing and motor-boat racing which, though still minority interests, pose acute problems in the use of limited water resources.

In almost all activities, future growth rates must depend to a large extent on the availability of suitable facilities: simple projection of existing trends can be very misleading. Equally, many of the most rapidly growing pursuits are still in the early stages of development when the most dramatic impact is made. Their present expansion may be impressive, but as yet their total effect is comparatively small. Some may be but a passing fashion, though technological change will undoubtedly lead to the development of further new forms. Thus fibreglass, nylon and terylene have revolutionised sailing and there are already some forty ski instruction centres using artificial surfaces.

Widening opportunities and increased participation are the prime characteristics of the use of leisure. The actual pattern is complex, the details often unclear, but there can be no mistaking the implications for outdoor recreation. In the remainder of this book, implications for both demand and supply will be examined, not least in those cases where the satisfaction of demand raises such severe problems in the use of land and water that the enjoyment of leisure is seriously impaired.

OPPOSITE: Solitude and concentration, a contrast in intensity of use: *(above)* windswept fells at Fleet Moss in the Yorkshire Dales National Park; *(below)* Bank Holiday Monday on New Brighton beach.

E

CHAPTER THREE

Urban Outdoors

A NATION OF TOWNSPEOPLE

'GOD made the country, and man made the town': though William Cowper's familiar dictum is manifestly untrue, his words still echo English disdain for the surroundings in which the vast majority live. 'The English are town-birds through and through', wrote D. H. Lawrence, 'yet they don't know how to build a city, how to think of one or how to live in one'.[1] Though much out-door recreation may take place in the open country, four-fifths at least of all leisure time is spent in or near the home,[2] that is, for most, in an urban environment. The problems—and the opportunities—of outdoor recreation in an urban setting have not always received the attention they deserve.

By any standards, England and Wales are the most urbanised of countries. It is hard to distinguish between town and country dwellers in any meaningful way when the two are so closely intermingled and interrelated. The Registrar General counts as rural those living in Rural Districts, some 10 million out of a total population of over 48 million, but the Rural Districts themselves incorporate many small towns and suburban communities. Agriculture now occupies only 3 per cent of the employed population and at least nine people out of ten are urban in habit if not in formal address.

Nevertheless, although we are a nation of townspeople (indeed

[handwritten margin note: USE AS HYPOTHESIS]

of city-dwellers, for one person in three lives within the immediate confines of the six great conurbations alone), towns still cover a comparatively small proportion of the land as a whole. We may at times feel that 'having made our towns with such careless incompetence' we '. . . are now proceeding with the same recklessness to disperse ourselves over the countryside, destroying and dishonouring it with our shoddy but all-too-permanent encampments',[3] but truth is rather less dramatic. It has been estimated that towns occupied 10·8 per cent of England and Wales in 1960, having exactly doubled in area since the turn of the century.[4] Regionally there are wide variations as Figure 16 indicates: the urbanised South East stands in strong contrast to Wales where towns are still an alien and often a remote growth.

The erosion of agricultural land for town-building continues, but no longer at the rate prevalent between the wars when Clough Williams-Ellis sounded his timely warning in *England and the octopus* (1928). Then, in reaction to the tightly-packed Victorian city, towns sprawled in an amorphous and often wasteful way, untrammelled by the rigid controls of post-war planning and with housing densities of twelve or less to the acre. With agriculture depressed, land was relatively plentiful and cheap and on average some 60,000 acres a year were absorbed for urban use. At present the annual rate is less than 40,000 acres, averaging 36,300 between 1956 and 1965. Land has been clearly recognised as the scarce resource it is, and even though more liberal densities are now being encouraged for housing schemes,[5] towns should still only cover 15–16 per cent of the total land area by the end of the century. To keep such figures in perspective, the amount of land lost from agriculture for urban development may be compared with the amount transferred to woodland and forests:

Land transferred from agricultural use, annual average 1961–5 in thousand acres[6]

	To urban use	To allotments, woodlands and forestry developments
England and Wales	38·2	16·2
Scotland	6·1	44·2

For Britain as a whole, forests exceeded towns in their demands on agricultural land, and even in England and Wales consumed more than two-fifths of the urban total.

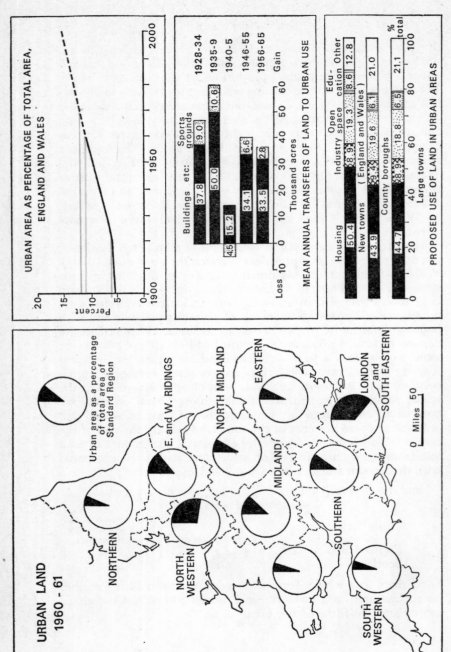

Fig 16.　The extent and use of urban land. Sources of data are indicated in the text.

OPEN SPACE IN TOWNS

Urban areas are far from continuously built up. Apart from land devoted to private gardens, considerable tracts are private or public open space. The exact proportion of open space fluctuates between differing settlements, but the following table shows the mean percentage of the total area occupied by each major land use for a sample of towns in 1950: [7]

	Housing	Industry	Open Space	Education	Other
London	42·0	5·0	15·0	2·0	36·0
County Boroughs	43·4	8·1	18·7	2·8	27·0
Large towns	43·5	5·3	21·5	3·0	26·7

These figures may be compared with those on Figure 16 for the *planned* use of land in New Towns and other types: outside London, open space accounts on average for about 19 per cent of the total area in each case.[8]

Within the town, open space fulfils two main functions: firstly it provides opportunity for recreation of both active and passive, and formal and informal kinds; secondly, and less tangibly, it has a visual and psychological role in enhancing the whole quality of the urban environment. These functions are not mutually exclusive. Trim lawns designed to heighten the setting of an office block may also serve for typists to laze in the sun during the lunch break: equally, the open green swathe of a cricket pitch may add much visually to adjoining housing. The present concern is primarily with recreation, but the wider importance of open space must not be forgotten in considering its provision.

To fulfil its role, open space takes many forms. Playing fields, sports and recreation grounds cater for active sport. More passive needs are served by parks in varied guises, whether ornamental gardens, informal open spaces or areas of woodland and common. Children's playgrounds, allotments and golf courses fulfil more specific needs, while areas of water may enhance amenity and provide further opportunities for recreation.[9]

In addition to form, questions of ownership and access must also be considered. Publicly-owned land may only be available to restricted groups—school playing fields are a particular case in point—while privately-owned tracts may be available to the public at large or to club members or works employees only.

VARIATIONS IN OPEN SPACE PROVISION

With such complexity of form and ownership, and with all the individual accidents of history, it is not surprising that the actual provision of open space should differ widely between towns and sharply diverge at times from the general average of just under one-fifth of the total urban area. Urban planners have been concerned to establish standards of provision, but in assessing standards many complex factors are involved and decisions have been made all too often on 'crude assumptions and arbitrary assertions in place of established facts'.[10] Development plans record widely different thinking: Liverpool, for example, envisaged a standard of 4 acres per thousand population and Hatfield 14, and these were by no means extremes. Variations are found between different types of town, between towns of very similar type and, in some ways most important, between different parts of the same town.

One problem has been the lack of knowledge of existing provision in comparative terms in any more detail than the generalised category of open space. In August 1964 a joint circular from the Ministry of Housing and Local Government (49/64) and the Department of Education and Science (11/64), *Provision of Facilities for Sport*, suggested inter alia that local authorities should review their areas to determine what provision existed for sport and physical recreation and what future requirements would be. Close on the heels of this circular came the creation of the Sports Council in January 1965 and the establishment of regional Sports Councils: these regional councils were used to co-ordinate surveys of facilities within their respective areas.

The surveys, 'initial appraisals' as they were termed,[11] were not exclusively urban or outdoor in emphasis, though they were directed particularly towards such capital intensive facilities as swimming pools, indoor sports centres, athletics stadia and golf courses which by their very nature are located most often within or adjacent to towns. The material collected permits useful comparisons to be made within each region, but it is unfortunate that no attempt was made to standardise the terms of reference between the regions to enable an accurate national picture to emerge. Variations exist both in topics covered and in basic definitions. In the Southern Region, for example, indoor sports centres were defined as 'community sports halls, purpose built' and only two recorded in an area of almost 3 million people: in Lancashire the requirement was 'halls of 1,800sq ft or over used for physical recreation'—249 in all!

For the present purpose the appraisals are neither as uniform in their treatment nor as wide-ranging in the topics they cover as could be wished, although they have made available much material hitherto inaccessible. In the North West, where work began before the regional Sports Council was established and was the responsibility of the county planning authorities, parks and gardens and children's playgrounds were among the items included in the initial brief and as a result a reasonably comprehensive picture of open space provision over the whole region can be derived (Figure 17). The pioneer survey was carried out in Lancashire in 1964–5 and that for Cheshire, modelled closely on it, in 1965–6. Even here, where co-ordination was close, there are problems beyond those of survey dates in directly comparing results from the two counties. Lancashire, for example, did not include golf courses in the return of sports ground acreages whereas Cheshire did. Nevertheless, the maps are an apt illustration of the variations of open-space provision which occur on a regional scale.

Detailed analysis would be of parochial concern alone, but it is worth noting the extent of variation. The region comprises rural as well as urban areas, of course, but those classed administratively as urban are distinguished by shading on the first map and their boundaries are picked out with a heavier line on the remainder. On each of the maps of specific facilities, the shadings are such that the denser the shading the more lavish the provision of that facility in relation to the number of people living in the area.

Contrasts are well illustrated by the provision of parks and gardens, defined as all types of land over one acre in extent used for general open-air recreation. Public parks are the most familiar form, whether formal floral displays or 'natural' mown grass and trees. Privately-owned gardens or estates to which there is public access are also included. For the counties as a whole, the average provision is 2.7 acres per thousand persons in Lancashire and 4.6 acres in Cheshire. The variation between individual authorities is great, ranging from places such as Carnforth and Haydock with no provision at all, to Wigan Rural District in Lancashire with 21.5 acres per thousand persons and Bucklow Rural District in Cheshire with 40.9. The last two illustrate the individual anomalies

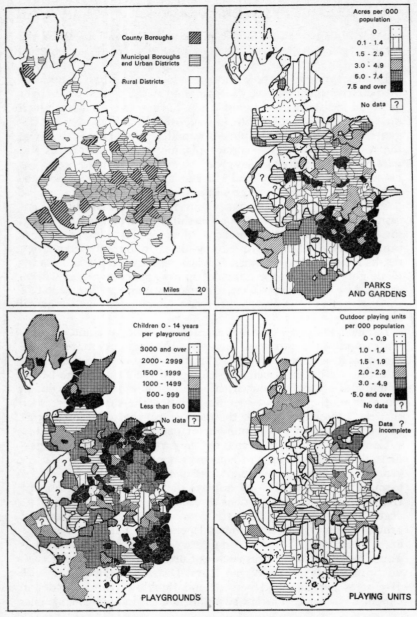

Fig 17. Parks and gardens, playgrounds and playing fields in Lancashire and Cheshire, 1965–6 (data from Lancashire CC *Survey of existing facilities for sport and physical recreation, Preliminary report* and *Recreation in Cheshire: Survey of existing facilities for sport and physical recreation — 1. Preliminary report*).

which inevitably arise, for Wigan RD includes within its boundaries Haigh Hall (241 acres) which is owned by the County Borough of Wigan, and Bucklow the 854 acres of Tatton Park gardens, a county-owned park of wide regional importance.

Leaving obvious anomalies aside, some results are still surprising, for it is not always the towns usually considered to have the most attractive environments which have the most generous provision. On the Lancashire coast, for example, Morecambe has only 1·8 acres per thousand persons and Formby 0·5, whereas such industrial centres as Liverpool, Manchester and St Helens have 2·5, 3·4 and 4 respectively. The distribution of levels of provision is not however as random as the map at first glance might suggest. There is a close relationship between the total population of a local authority and its acreage of parks and gardens, for generosity of provision tends to be directly proportional to the size of population. Thus, in general terms, large towns have higher levels of provision than smaller towns. In part, the explanation for this lies in the relative accessibility of open countryside. The Rural Districts have in general the lowest levels of provision for settlements are small with little need for artificial substitutes for closely adjacent rural vistas. Conversely, in the larger towns, the need to preserve areas of open space became evident in the last century as true countryside became increasingly remote for the average citizen.

Variation in the provision of children's playgrounds and play-streets has a different basis, for playgrounds serve a highly localised need: location is more important than size or numbers. Though there are many anomalies, there is a tendency for the number of children per playground to increase the larger the child population of the local authority, as much a reflection of high densities of population as of unsatisfied demand.

The third map depicts 'playing units'. As mentioned already, it is not possible to map the recorded acreages of sports grounds as the two counties used different definitions, Lancashire excluding golf courses on the grounds that individual golf clubs frequently serve a much wider area than that of the local authority in which they happen to be situated. In Lancashire, 7,958 acres of sports grounds were recorded, representing 1·6 acres per thousand population: the 111 golf courses add another 9,110 acres, and raise the average level of provision to 3·7 acres per thousand persons. The comparable figure for Cheshire is 5 acres per thousand population. 'Playing units' emphasise the facilities themselves rather than the area they occupy, each individual pitch, court, green or course being counted as a single unit regardless of its size. The result is a crude measure of the opportunities for playing organised outdoor games in any area: as the map shows, the range of variation is much less than for parks and playgrounds, 59.6 per cent of all authorities having between 1 and 1.9 playing units per thousand population. Nevertheless, as with parks, local authorities with large populations tend to have higher levels of provision of sports facilities. Perhaps equally important, the larger authorities can also offer facilities for a much wider range of minority sports.

The case of Lancashire and Cheshire forcibly illustrates the wide variations in the provision of differing kinds of open space which can occur between contrasting types of settlement on a regional scale. Such variations occur also between towns of similar type, as the following table shows for ten of the established post-war New Towns: [12]

Acres of open space per thousand population, mid-1966

	Within designated area	Freely available for use within designated and adjoining areas
Basildon	5.9	10.77
Bracknell	11.7	12.38
Corby	10.9	13.45
Crawley	20.3	22.25
Harlow	21.1	21.22
Hemel Hempstead	17.0	15.79
Newton Aycliffe	12.5	13.82
Peterlee	39.2	27.89
Stevenage	13.5	12.22
Welwyn Garden City	24.0	23.51

Within the designated areas, total provision ranges from some 6 acres per thousand persons at Basildon to 39 acres at Peterlee, though the other towns fall into two groups, one with some 11–17 acres, the other 20–24. When the nature of open space is examined more closely, the reasons for the anomalies become clear. At Peterlee, 67 per cent of open space is woodland, for within the designated area is the major natural feature of Castle Eden Dene and tracts of land liable to mining subsidence where woodland is the obvious form of land use. In contrast, Basildon has only

1 per cent of its open space in woodland, though there are large areas of farmland and of agricultural smallholdings not technically classed as open space. The whole problem of classification, of function and location, is highlighted by the second column of figures. This includes land which is not simply 'open space' in a technical sense, but freely available for use 'by residents of the town, either as members of the general public, as members of sports associations, or as forming a particular section of the community such as schoolchildren'.[13] It ignores to some extent the arbitrary boundary of the designated area, including all adjacent sites used by residents though the majority of such sites either directly adjoin the boundary or are within half a mile of it. At Basildon, for example, the woodlands of Westley Heights are included, some 300 acres lying just to the south of the boundary itself. But while these may be more realistic figures of open-space provision, they still show a very considerable range, and emphasise the variations in provision which occur.

So far, the emphasis has been on variations between towns, but in some ways even more important are internal differences. In London, for example, the former London County Council adopted in 1945 an open-space standard of 4 acres per thousand population within the administrative county (together with a further 3 acres per thousand outside, in the Green Belt). At present, the old LCC area of Inner London has only 2·5 acres per thousand, Lambeth, Southwark, Newham and Tower Hamlets all less than 1·6 acres, while Islington has only 0·47 acres. London's central parks are rightly famed and add immeasurably to the quality of its environment, but 'the great built-up area stretching from Park Lane to the Mile End Road has virtually no proper open space; Stepney and Shoreditch are particularly bare'.[14]

It is most frequently the inner areas of tightly-packed Victorian terraces where both deficiency and need is greatest, but even when redevelopment takes place it is often not possible to provide sufficient open space by normally accepted standards without too drastic a drop in the number of dwellings built. Liverpool's inner area of Everton illustrates the dilemma. At present 18 acres of recreational open space serve a population of over 70,000— approximately a quarter of an acre for every thousand persons— and only 11 more acres are planned. To bring the area up to a standard of 6 acres per thousand would mean reducing the population to 50,000, unacceptable in terms of the city's housing needs as a whole. Present thinking suggests a compromise population of some 62,000 served by 195 acres of open space, much of it in the form of a new central park.

OPEN SPACE STANDARDS

These illustrations of variations in the provision of open space in towns, and the recognition of almost bewildering variety in its form and function, lead back to the problem of determining how much such space is required and where it should be located.

For over forty years, thinking in Britain has been conditioned by the standard formulated by the National Playing Fields Association soon after it was founded in 1925, and most recently confirmed in 1955.[15] This recommended 6 acres of permanently preserved playing space per thousand population, but expressly excluded school playing fields (except where these are available for general use out of school hours and during holidays), woodlands and commons, ornamental gardens, full-length golf courses and 'open spaces where the playing of organised games by the general public is either discouraged or not permitted'. This standard has been commended as a general guide by successive governments together with one acre of ornamental public open space per thousand population. It was derived initially in a rather arbitrary fashion. It assumed that active games playing was limited largely to the 10–40 age-group, comprising exactly half the total population in the mid-1920s, and that within this group about 30 per cent would not for a variety of reasons wish to play games and a further 30 per cent would be catered for by their own school or college facilities. This left some 200 potential players for every thousand population, and their basic needs could be accommodated on a 6-acre site, with just room for a senior football pitch, a junior football or hockey pitch, a cricket square, a three-rink bowling green, two tennis courts, a children's playground and a pavilion. By 1955, national changes in population structure meant that there were only 415 per thousand in the 10–40 age-group and, assuming the same proportion still interested in active sport, only 166 per thousand to be catered for. Nevertheless, the NPFA argued that the 6-acre standard was still valid as rising standards meant that better facilities were needed and a greater proportion of older people were enjoying active recreation.

The NPFA standard, valuable though it has been as a rough

yardstick, is now of rather limited worth. The initial assumptions on which it was based were arbitrary, particularly in determining the numbers likely to need games facilities[16] and the rates of participation in particular sports. Habits have also changed in fundamental ways since the 1920s and greater prosperity and mobility mean that people are willing and able to travel much greater distances to satisfy some leisure needs. But perhaps the greatest weakness of the standard lies in its emphasis on the total provision of open space, with no guidance as to its location. Distribution is fundamental to effective use, though in fairness the NPFA itself recognises that

> an assurance that the total space for recreation . . . is not less than 6 acres per 1,000 is not, on its own, the complete answer. It is also important to see that the playing space is situated where it is most wanted. If it is so far away from the centres of population, or is so inaccessible that it is not used, the purpose of its provision is largely defeated.[17]

Location must also be allied to function. For some types of activity, such as golf, people will be prepared to travel quite considerable distances—indeed many activities can be carried on completely beyond the built-up area and it is important to identify those which are truly urban in nature—whereas for others, such as children's play, close proximity to the place of residence is of paramount importance. A hierarchy of open-space uses can be conceived, varying from those of purely local significance to those with regional importance serving the town or city as a whole. Three broad categories may be recognised, though they are far from being mutually exclusive.

At the most local level, the needs of those lacking time, ability or desire to travel far must be considered. Small, easily accessible spaces are needed for children of pre-school age to play and at the other end of the age range for old people to stroll, or sit and watch the world go by. Such spaces should be sited not more than a quarter of a mile from the place of residence and in such a way that access is not barred by busy roads. These needs are overlain by the weekday requirements of other age-groups wanting somewhere to sit and walk either near home or near their place of work. The lunch-hour needs of workers can often be catered for by open spaces which enhance visual amenity as well as fill a recreational need. Most cities have such spaces in their business districts—St John's Gardens and Pier Head in Liverpool, or Park and City Squares in Leeds, for example. Even half-an-acre can be of real value in such circumstances.

The intermediate stage in the hierarchy satisfies local needs of a more general nature. Bigger spaces for the more adventurous play of older children, grass kick-about areas, hard porous play areas, facilities for such games as tennis or bowls played fairly frequently but for comparatively short periods and an area big enough for adults to walk or stroll. Such spaces should be within reasonable walking distance of home—perhaps three-quarters of a mile to a mile away at most. Studies in London suggest that spaces of less than 50 acres in extent are not very effective at this distance if all facilities are to be included in a single park.[18]

More specialised demands are less restricted by time and accessibility, and are satisfied at the topmost level of the hierarchy. Team games or other sports played for longer periods justify time spent on travel, though demand for the most popular such as football or cricket may be sufficient to warrant the provision of pitches at relatively close-spaced intervals. Parks must be large enough or possess adequate amenities to attract families at weekends. Access in all these cases (except for the fortunate few living in close proximity) will be by car or public transport rather than on foot: once people are prepared to travel a couple of miles or more, needs may be satisfied beyond the confines of the town rather than within it and facilities once thought of traditionally as urban may be better provided in a rural setting: the Victoria Park of the 1870s is being replaced in role by the country park of the 1970s. Indeed, present mobility is such that the distinction between outdoor recreation in an urban as opposed to a rural setting is one of degree rather than of kind and urban open space cannot be viewed in isolation from a rural hinterland. It is as true of the country as of the town that 'we have got used to thinking of the public space as something apart from the town and its life: we must bring it back and interweave it with the other threads of living, working and moving'.[19]

URBAN OUTDOOR SPORTS

Nevertheless, limitations of time or mobility do mean that many outdoor activities necessarily retain a purely urban flavour. In terms of active recreation, participation in many sports is only

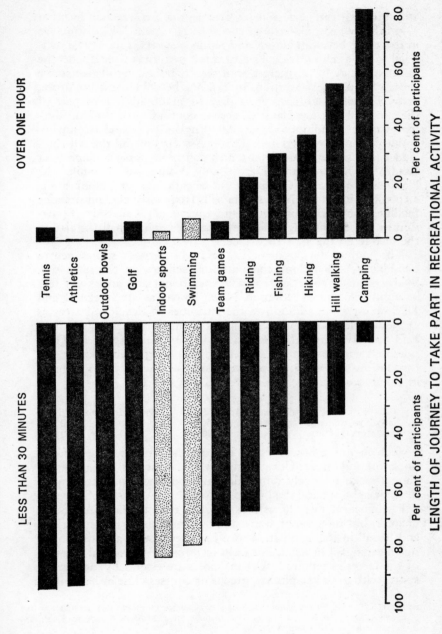

Fig 18. Journey times and recreational activities (data from *Pilot National Recreation Survey, Report No 1*).

attractive if it can be reasonably frequent in a convenient location
—in other words, close to the place of residence. The distinction
in this sense between indoor and outdoor sports is somewhat artificial so far as an individual's recreation pattern is concerned: the
difference may be of interest or of season, but all involve an active
regard for physical exertion. Indeed, in the fickle British climate,
many basically outdoor sports may be practised at least part of
the time indoors especially to ensure continuity of training during winter conditions. The All England Ground Company
(jointly owned by the Lawn Tennis Association and the All England Club) has built covered tennis courts of porous concrete at
Bradford, Birmingham, Derby and Manchester,[20] while the
National Equestrian Centre at Stoneleigh has an indoor arena
20,000sq ft in extent. New sports halls frequently contain practice
facilities for cricket and golf, and Liverpool's University Sports
Centre has a climbing wall built into the sports hall simulating
the characteristics of a rock face.

The logical development is the multi-purpose sports centre
combining both indoor and outdoor facilities on the same site.
Such centres involve large capital investment and are as yet few
in number,[21] but whether in New Towns as at Bracknell and
Harlow, or as an addition to the amenities of developed areas as
at Newcastle-upon-Tyne's Lightfoot Centre or Stockton's North-
End Sports Centre, they fill an obvious community need. Their
potential attraction can be seen in the following attendance figures
for Harlow's Sportcentre, applying to typical weekly programmes
in summer and winter, not to special events:[22]

	Summer		Winter	
	Grounds	Sports Hall	Grounds	Sports Hall
Active participants	1,400	1,050	900	2,300
Spectators/visitors	2,250	2,200	1,600	3,850

Such facilities, however, are beyond the strict confines of this
book for indoor activities though often voracious consumers of
capital make relatively minor demands on land, but their impact
must be kept in mind if a balanced overall view is to be obtained.[23]

Participation rates in various sports were discussed in the last
chapter, but no attempt was made to distinguish between 'urban'
and 'rural' in this context. As we have seen, such a distinction is
not meaningful in itself, but only in terms of the actual location
of the facilities required. 'Urban' sports are essentially 'accessible'
sports with grounds, pitches, greens or courses close at hand. This

OPPOSITE: Subsidised recreation: *(above)* cabin cruisers crossing Chirk aqueduct on the
Llangollen Canal; *(below)* the site of Thurstaston station, to be developed as a car park
and picnic area on Cheshire's Wirral Way.

is graphically illustrated by Figure 18 where for the first seven activities listed over 70 per cent of participants spent less than half an hour in travelling to take part and no more than 7 per cent at most had journeys exceeding an hour. All seven, with the exception of swimming, are formal, organised activities and all require formal provision of facilities. They are followed by an intermediate group of informal activities, riding, fishing and hiking, which need open space or unpolluted water but may be pursued close to the built-up area rather than in more remote stretches of countryside, in green belt as much as in truly rural conditions.

Team games have previously been shown as the most frequently pursued outdoor sport: they are overwhelmingly dominated by the two codes of football, by cricket and bowls—all largely male bastions (Figure 19). In terms of the provision of space, demands for football and cricket pitches may first be considered. Association football remains by far the most popular with some 750,000 regular adult and post-school players in Great Britain.[24] Rugby Union, the other major winter sport, musters some 115,000 players in England and Wales other than those playing at school. Cricket is more regional in its impact, but it has been estimated that about 310,000 would be playing cricket on a fine summer weekend.[25]

Figures for gross participation give little idea of actual land requirements. The Sports Council has published estimates based on a survey carried out in the New Towns in 1964, from which the following table is taken:[26]

Male age group	Soccer	Percentage participants in Rugby	Cricket
15–19	13·7	1·0	3·0
20–29	11·5	1·5	4·9
30–44	3·1	0·2	2·8
45–59	—	—	0·7

When these proportions are applied to a hypothetical town of 60,000 inhabitants, the following requirements emerge:

	Participants	Pitches required
Soccer	957	22
Rugby	93	2
Cricket	467	11

OPPOSITE: Dillon Reservoir State Park, Ohio, USA: *(above)* holiday cabin overlooking the wooded slopes of the reservoir; *(below)* marina on an inlet of the reservoir, with hinged gangways to allow for changes in water level.

F

To these major sports must be added provision for tennis, hockey, bowls and netball. Based on observed rates of participation, the Sports Council suggests the following overall provision in a town of 60,000 as a realistic fulfilment of existing needs: [27]

	Number of playing units (pitches, courts, greens)	Size of playing unit (acres)	Acreage
Soccer	22	2·25	49·50
Rugby	2	2·78	5·56
Cricket (exclusive use)	6	3·60	21·60
Cricket (joint use)*	5	0·75	3·75
Lawn tennis	30	0·15	4·50
Hockey	2	1·52	3·04
Bowls	10	0·60	6·00
Netball	1	0·15	0·15
Ancillary facilities (Pavilions, car parking, practice areas, landscaping, etc, at 50 per cent of playing area)			47·00
			141·10

* These pitches are also used for winter games: each would be 4·75 acres in extent, but only the amount shown, for the cricket square itself, would be for exclusive cricket use.

This acreage represents about 2·4 acres per thousand population, but it is the availability of playing units in the right proportion and the right location which is important. The popularity of individual sports varies with regional traditions and overall requirements with the age structure and social and economic patterns of the community. No provision is included either for expansion of existing sports or for minority sports: it must also be remembered that sports grounds are only one component of total open space.

A highly important element in the provision of sports facilities that has not so far been considered is that of ownership. Many existing sports grounds are privately owned for the exclusive

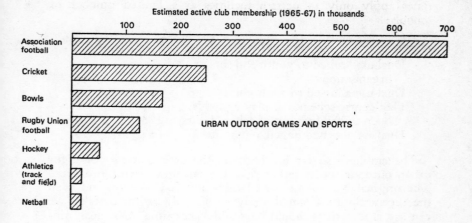

Fig 19. Active club membership of urban outdoor sports (after D. D. Molyneux).

use of club members or works employees: in Lancashire, for example, 42 per cent of all sports grounds are in private hands. While this implies some restriction on availability, it may not be at all serious, for many sports naturally develop club structures and have an important social element.

Far more significant is the use made of playgrounds and playing fields owned by education authorities. These frequently cover virtually as much land as other sports facilities—Lancashire for example has 7,958 acres of sports grounds, and an additional 7,655 acres of school playing fields of which only 726 acres are available for casual recreation by the general public or children out of school hours. The dual use of such facilities raises real problems of supervision and additional wear though too often 'the criterion used in making this land available appears to be the attitude of some governing bodies of education authority and not [the] amount of use the educationally owned playing fields may take'.[28] The picture in England and Wales as a whole was examined by the National Playing Fields Association in 1964[29] though the following table is only a rough (and perhaps optimistic) guide to the situation because of the equivocal nature of many of the replies received and the fact that dual use practices some-

times apply only to certain facilities at a limited number of
schools:

	County Councils (out of 59)	County Boroughs (out of 50)
Dual use limited to youth and similar organisations	38	34
Dual use allowed to adult clubs	21	17
Play-centre schemes or playing fields open to children out of school hours	6	10
Dual use not encouraged or permitted	23	16

The emphasis so far has been on the extent of provision for
urban outdoor sports rather than the location of that provision.
The original NPFA standard largely ignored location and even
the recent Sports Council study could only affirm that 'all we
can say is that they should be readily accessible'. Obviously, individual circumstances vary far too greatly for any but the most
general guidelines to be of practical value. Earlier sections have
indicated the time taken in travel to varying facilities and the
place they might occupy in a hierarchy of provision. Accessibility, however, must not be confused with centrality for improved mobility may make sites on the fringe of the built-up area
more attractive. The case may be instanced of Manchester Rugby
Club and Cheadle Hulme Cricket Club. The former had a 9-acre
site north of the city at Kersal but was in some economic difficulty. The club therefore sold the site for development for
£57,000 and purchased for £51,000 a new site of 22 acres of
green belt land in Cheadle Hulme where planning permission had
been refused for building. They were joined in the venture by the
cricket club, for their activities were seasonally complementary,
and the former cricket ground was sold for £25,000. Total
development of the new site at Grove Lane will cost near
£100,000 before completion in 1970, but the vastly improved
facilities will include four Rugby grounds (instead of two), two
cricket pitches (one completely independent and with a 75-yard
radius boundary) and provision for tennis, bowls, badminton and
social activities.[30] The whole scheme is an object lesson in making
the maximum use of land by grouping complementary activities,
and in using the benefits of contemporary mobility by choosing
a location where land values are comparatively low because the
site is unavailable or unattractive for other urban uses.

GOLF

One sport merits separate consideration because of its voracious hunger for land and its rapid growth. In Lancashire, golf courses occupy 9,110 acres, 1,360 acres more than that occupied by all other forms of outdoor sports facility, and 55 per cent of the recreational land for some 0·8 per cent of the population. Golf is, indeed, still a minority sport, though golf courses occupy some 94,000 acres of England and Wales.[31]

As a sport, golf has many advantages. It requires little organisation, it can be played through all seasons and be enjoyed by players with a wide range of skill and of age. There are no precise figures for the total number of active golfers in the country: the Golf Foundation has suggested there were about one million in 1967, or approximately twenty per thousand of the total population.[32] More specific figures usually relate to club membership rather than all actively taking part: in Lancashire this was the equivalent of eight members per thousand population, in the Northern Region 10·5. There are undoubtedly quite wide regional variations. Though beyond the direct scope of this book, it is interesting to note that in Scotland there are some 400 golf courses for five million people; in England just over 1,000 for 46 million. Within England itself, a rough measure of regional differences is given by membership affiliations to the English Golf Union, though the Union does not include all clubs. For England as a whole there were 4·5 such members per thousand population, and this varied on a regional scale from 4 in the South East and the West Midlands to 4·7 in the South West, 5 in East Anglia and 5·1 in Northern England.[33]

There is no mistaking the rapid growth of the sport. The Golf Foundation estimates that the number of active players doubled between 1954 and 1967 and more specific corroboration is given by the North Regional Planning Committee's survey which showed an increase in club membership of 61 per cent in nine years.

Comparatively little is yet known about the characteristics of the golfing population, though the available evidence largely supports the traditional assessment of this as a middle-class sport.[34] In a study of the members of seven clubs in the North Region, over three-quarters were in non-manual occupations. The proportion classed as company directors, employers and managers, professional and self-employed persons varied from 43 to 81 per cent of the 'economically active' members, though these figures are not wholly representative as the less affluent could be expected to play far more on works courses or on local authority courses where payment is made for each round. Few people travel very far to play: the North Region's study showed that the majority of members lived within five miles and less than one-tenth more than ten miles from the urban clubs, though in rural areas with fewer courses, much greater distances may be travelled. In this connection, of course, it must be remembered that few parts of the country are really remote from a golf course: as Figure 20 indicates, only very small areas of the South East are more than six miles from a course, and all these areas are within ten miles.

Distance alone is no measure of the adequacy of provision of golf courses. Many existing courses are closed to new members and at some public courses in the South East queues may form by 4 am at weekends, with the morning's allocation taken by

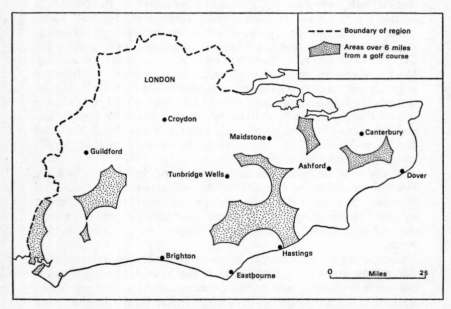

Fig 20. Golf course provision in south-east England (after Greater London and South East Sports Council, *Sports Facilities — Initial appraisal, Volume 1, Map 5*).

dawn.[35] The Golf Development Council suggests a maximum of
40,000 rounds per annum as the maximum use which should be
made of a course: for a playing membership of 600, this means
the equivalent of a little over five games a month for each member. Many private clubs would consider 40,000 rounds a year
excessive, but the figure is often surpassed on municipal courses.
Beckenham Place, for example, easily accessible to central and
south-east London, records 86,000 rounds a year, perhaps the
most intensive use in the country. At this course on Sunday 'when
the gates are opened at 7.30 there is a Brand's Hatch sprint to the
club house and a final race to buy a numbered ticket for the
round'.[36] Although pressures are greatest at the weekend, golf has
neither the extreme weekly or seasonal peaks of many other
sports. In the North Region survey it was shown that, during a
six-week summer period, morning and afternoon play from Monday to Friday accounted for 39 per cent of total play recorded
as against the 48 per cent possible had play been evenly spread
throughout the week.

Figure 21 records the provision of golf facilities at county level
on a national scale. This can be viewed against the Sports Council's recommended standard of one eighteen-hole course for
20,000–30,000 persons. Provision is lowest in the heavily populated
areas, the industrial 'core' of England from London to Lancashire.
It is higher in rural areas (where a single course may only be
accessible to a comparatively small population), in 'residential'
counties and those with a coastal location which attract both non-
resident holidaymakers and retired people. These trends can be
seen more clearly in Figure 22, which records the situation in
London and the South East in more detail. The second and third
maps attempt to distinguish courses on which there is pressure
from those with spare capacity, though the measure used is necessarily crude. The major pressures are obviously in and adjacent
to London itself, where additional provision would be difficult
from the point of view of available land: there is also some
evidence of pressure in West Sussex.

Golf, therefore, is a sport for which there is increasing demand,
with acute pressures arising close to the major urban areas. It is
not perhaps so much an 'urban' sport as one undertaken within
reasonable distance of home. Most golf courses originally had a
country location, where land was cheaper,[37] though many are
now engulfed by expanding towns. As a form of land use, they

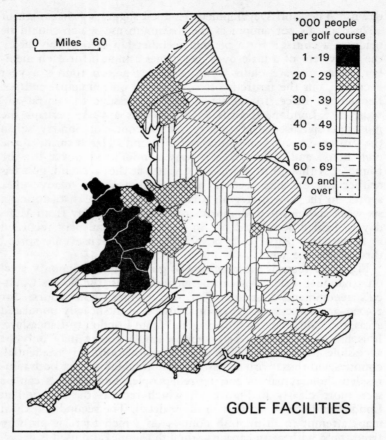

Fig 21. Golf facilities in England and Wales. No distinction is made between 9 and 18 hole golf courses.

would seem to belong still to locations beyond the built-up area though, even with present mobility, at only a short distance from it. They can be developed on undulating and agriculturally poor land but their fundamental problem is their low intensity of use, with something like 100 acres required to satisfy the needs of 600 people. More account must be taken of the wider opportunities they provide, not only as a visual amenity, but for other forms of

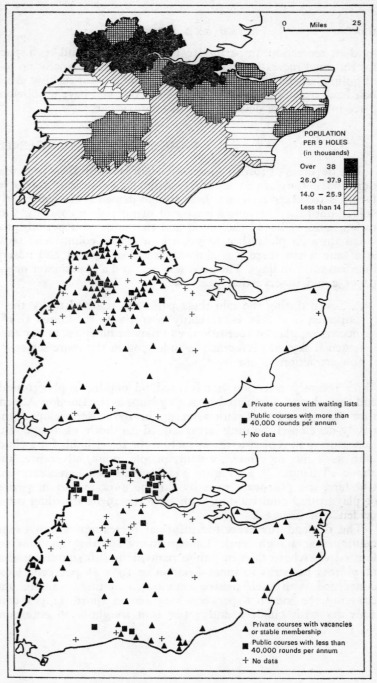

Legend on first (top) map:
POPULATION
PER 9 HOLES
(in thousands)

Over   38
26.0 − 37.9
14.0 − 25.9
Less than 14

Legend on second (middle) map:
▲ Private courses with waiting lists
■ Public courses with more than 40,000 rounds per annum
+ No data

Legend on third (bottom) map:
▲ Private courses with vacancies or stable membership
■ Public courses with less than 40,000 rounds per annum
+ No data

Fig 22. Golf facilities in south-east England (based on Greater London and South East Sports Council, *Sports Facilities − Initial Appraisal, Volume 1*, maps 4 and 6).

outdoor recreation. In particular, public footpaths and even space for informal recreation can be incorporated with virtually no loss of golfing amenity. They are eminently suitable for making green belt land visually and functionally attractive and have an obvious place in the future development of country parks.

PARKS AND PLAYGROUNDS

The devotees of formal sports are adept through their organisation and enthusiasm at securing adequate, or at least tolerable, facilities for their activities. Less formal demands are less clearly voiced until they become a matter of major public concern. Victorian parks reflected the mood and the mode of a period, provided through philanthropic gesture or sound commercial sense at a time when there was almost unrelieved squalor and misery in urban surroundings. The need was real, and a Manchester newspaper could observe that

> . . . even during the rain these parks are resorted to by the workmen . . . It is certainly something to know that mechanics, glad of recreation, will play at ninepins, under an ungenial sky, in preference to indulging in the more seasonable attractions of the tap.[38]

More recently attention has focused on children's playgrounds and their design, stimulated by such groups as the London Adventure Playground Association set up in 1962. Redeveloped and newly-developed housing areas added to both challenge and opportunity in replacing the attraction the street holds for a child, with its 'light, movement, colour, people, noise, adventure, and above all danger'.[39] As Figure 23 illustrates for Lancashire and Cheshire, the post-war era is by far the most important period of playground construction, with only the 1930s affording other evidence of real zeal.

The demand for areas for informal recreation within towns continues at a high level. Though many sporting facilities are located elsewhere than in public parks, it is still significant that of visitors to parks in inner London in 1964 86 per cent were concerned with such passive activities as sitting, walking and enjoying the view: 6 per cent engaged in sport, 12 per cent activities with children and 3 per cent sought such entertain-

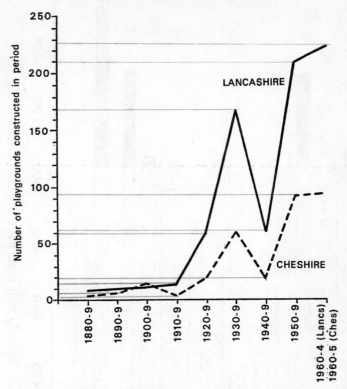

Fig 23.   Playground development in Lancashire and Cheshire.

ments as concerts, art galleries, fun-fairs or the zoo.[40] In Masser's study of a part of Birmingham, which included visits to all types of outdoor recreation facility, only 17·6 per cent of such visits in winter and 21·7 per cent in summer were for the purposes of active sport.[41]

The London study gives a very useful insight into the present functions of an urban park system, even when the special circumstances of the metropolis are borne in mind. Parks in inner areas are sometimes thought to have outlived their usefulness, except in terms of visual amenity, but this is very far from the case. Of the population aged 15 and over, 70 per cent had visited

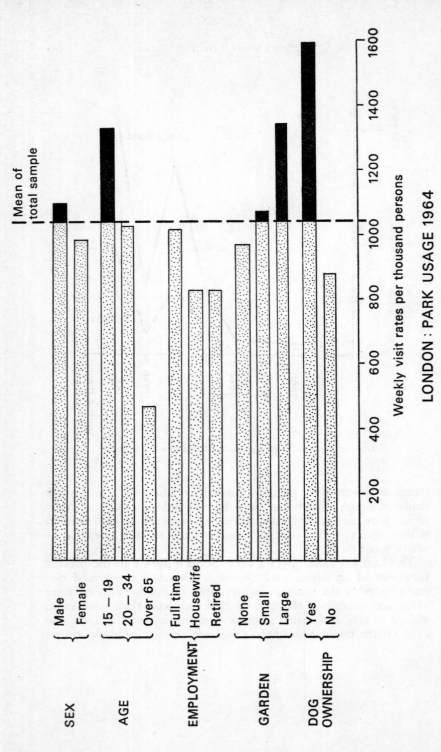

Fig 24.   Park usage in London, 1964 (data from GLC *Survey of the use of open spaces*).

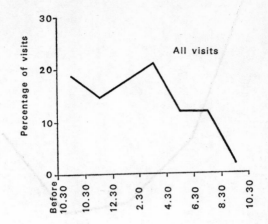

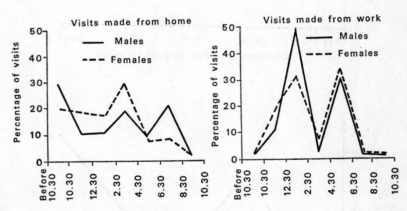

PARK VISITS : TIME OF ARRIVAL

Fig 25.   Park visits in London: time of arrival (data from GLC *Survey of the use of open spaces*).

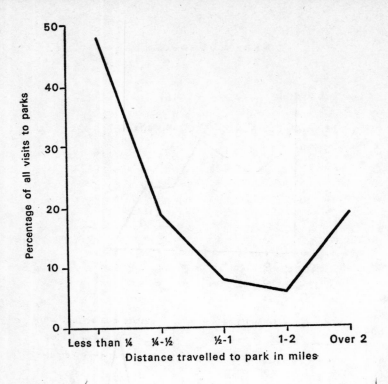

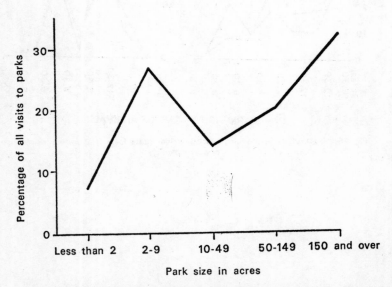

Fig 26. Park visits in London: distance travelled and park size (data from GLC *Survey of the use of open spaces*).

at least one open space in the month prior to interview, 39 per cent in the previous week.

Figure 24 illustrates the relative use of parks by different groups. The average weekly visiting rate was 1,040 for every thousand persons. Small differences between particular groups must be viewed with caution because of the total size of the study sample, but there were particularly high rates for teenagers, those with dogs and rather surprisingly those with large gardens. Proximity to a park is obviously important: those living in areas exceptionally well provided with open space made 1,490 visits per thousand, those in areas less well provided 1,060 and those in an intermediate category 710. This suggests that both opportunity and lack of opportunity may stimulate, with least effort made where facilities are adequate but not outstanding.

The pattern of use of parks in London is shown on Figures

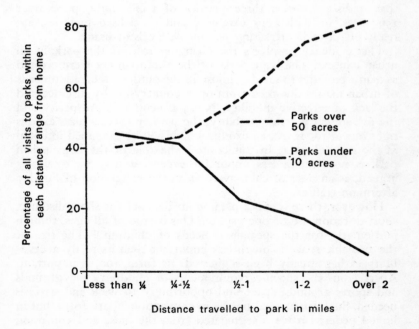

Fig 27   Distance travelled to small and to large parks in London (data from GLC *Survey of the use of open spaces*).

25–28. Visits from home (Figure 25) show morning, afternoon and evening peaks, the presence of young children accentuating the afternoon peak for women and conversely tying them to the home in the evening. In parks associated with workplace rather than home the peaks are, as expected, in the luncheon break and immediately after work.

More important is the evidence that emerges of a hierarchy of park use and function. Frequent short visits are made to parks close at hand. Seventy-eight per cent of all journeys to parks in the week prior to survey were made on foot, and 70 per cent between Monday and Friday. Quite small parks can satisfy this need, for accessibility rather than size is obviously important (Figures 26–7). At weekends there is time and opportunity to be more selective (Figure 28). Car or public transport is more likely to be used and a much longer stay made: when the visit involves more effort far better facilities are demanded and analysis shows that at distances over three-quarters of a mile only spaces over 150 acres, or with very extensive and specialised facilities, are really effective in attracting reasonable levels of usage

This evidence emphasis the changing role of the park in an urban context. The large parks of the Victorian era were created as major facilities to satisfy almost all the outdoor recreation needs of urban masses divorced from open countryside by distance and the lack of effective mobility. Now, as economic prosperity and the private car increase mobility, the weekend sees a mass exodus right out of the town, an exodus which will be examined in detail in the next chapter. In this context the role of the large urban park is now much less important except, it may be cynically argued, as an oasis of calm away from the congestion of Sunday afternoon traffic.

However, there is still a paramount demand for short-distance, short-duration use of open space. This is true of all ages, though particularly for the specialised needs of children.[42] The size of the available space is much less important than its ready accessibility as has already been suggested. Its form, too, is important. Apart from the specific requirements of children's playgrounds and sports grounds, space and opportunity to walk and stroll is needed. Such space need not be in conventional park form, but in linked pedestrian ways segregated from the noise and confusion of traffic. The need is linear, rather than nuclear, a true promenade whether the vista is urban or pseudo-rural. Georgian England,

OPPOSITE: Forest recreation: *(above)* picnic site created by the Forestry Commission in the Ceiriog Forest; *(below)* 'Zandenplas' or 'playing pond' in the Dutch Forest of Nunspeet. Four thousand people can be accommodated here, in an area not much greater than that occupied by the road interchange in the background.

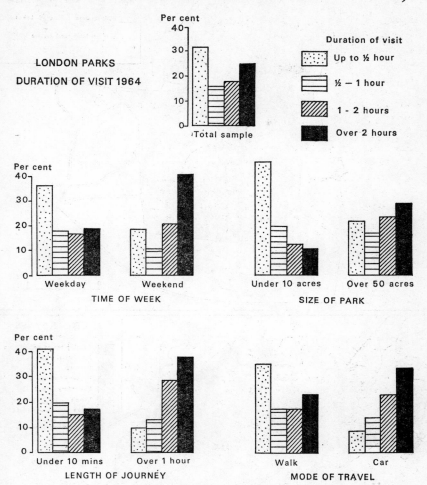

LONDON PARKS
DURATION OF VISIT 1964

Fig 28. Duration of visits to London parks, 1964 (data from GLC *Survey of the use of open spaces*).

OPPOSITE: Huron-Clinton Metropolitan Authority parks, Detroit, USA: *(above)* gravel extraction on a site at Island Lake which will subsequently be developed as a park; *(below)* Kensington Metropolitan Park, the largest park in the system, with Martindale Beach in the foreground and Maple Beach in the background across the artificial Kent Lake.

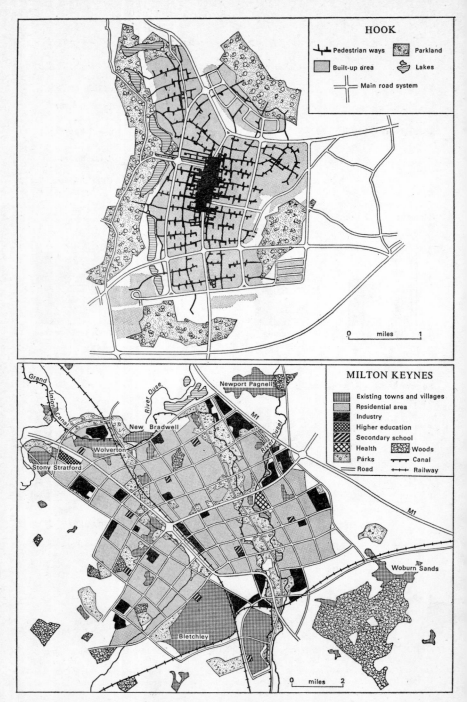

Fig 29. Contrasts in parkland location in planned New Towns. The abortive scheme for Hook had a compact urban nucleus set within a ring of parkland reached by pedestrian ways, while the interim plan for Milton Keynes envisages a much lower density of development with linear parks penetrating the built-up area along the canal and river valleys.

where urban living was perhaps first recognised as having distinctive qualities and opportunities but where the countryside was rarely yet debarred to the urban dweller, provides a useful prototype. In 1785, Leicester Corporation resolved 'to form a promenade for the recreation of the inhabitants ten yards wide from the North End of St Mary's Field next the town to the gate opposite the turnpike leading to London'. The New Walk remains as a very pleasant way from the city centre to Victoria Park through a number of small open spaces.

The need, it must be reiterated, is obviously to view open space as part of the whole functioning of the town as a place in which to both work and live, rather than simply space left over after other needs have been met. Existing towns have but little chance for radical change though there are opportunities in the legacy of existing parks, in the redevelopment of both commercial and residential areas and in the creation of pedestrian precincts and ways. Oxford's High Street would be an incomparable place for an urban promenade shorn utterly of traffic's danger and distraction. New Towns can provide exciting examples of creative possibilities, whether the compact urban nucleus set in an accessible matrix of open space, as in the abortive Hook scheme, or the penetration of linear parks to the very heart of the settlement in the interim proposals for Milton Keynes. Such schemes emphasise the false dichotomy between rural and urban in a recreational sense: the concern is rather with space and the time and manner of its use.

CHAPTER FOUR

Countryside and Coast

THE URBAN IMPACT

Whatever changes may come in leisure habits, and however much our towns may be made more fit for living, a very large number of people will probably continue to spend a large part of their free time in their motor cars, visiting the countryside and the coast . . . This movement away from the towns in leisure time is constantly growing; and it is taking place in mid-week as well as at weekends, and in spring, autumn and winter as well as summer. No one would want to halt the process.

THE new dimension given by the new mobility, accorded this formal recognition in the 1966 White Paper *Leisure in the Countryside England and Wales* (Cmnd 2928), has been constantly stressed in preceding chapters. Urban man has burst from urban confines and although it may be optimistic to suppose that 'no one would want to halt the process', its reality and its implications are profound. Again in the words of the White Paper,

Given that townspeople ought to be able to spend their leisure in the country if they want to; that they will have more leisure; and that in future they will be able to buy cars and boats and otherwise spend money on their weekends and holidays, the problem is to to enable them to enjoy this leisure without harm to those who live and work in the country, and without spoiling what they go to the countryside to seek.

The lineaments of the problem are the concern of the remainder of this book. It has engendered much heat (and, fortunately, not a little light) as interests inevitably conflict. Preservationists are acutely concerned by the rude shattering of rural calm, by the wanton erosion of rural quality: 'the danger comes from caravans and camping in the unspoilt dales and daleheads, from the noise of motor boats on hitherto quiet lakes, from mass tourism on the fells, and from the congestion of motor traffic'.[1] Drastic remedies are advocated:

The Lake District by an accident of geography escaped the full effects of the earlier [industrial] revolution. But it is far from certain that it can escape the effects of the technological age. The happy isolation which formerly protected it from industrial spoilation has been ended by the coming of the motor-car and the motor road. It may well be that only by definite and planned intervention can its ruin be averted. To do virtually nothing to improve the roads within the Lake District may serve to defend it; but any such attempt would be ineffective if the roads leading directly into the Lake District were to be upgraded. For to up-grade these roads would be tantamount to extending an open invitation to more and more vehicles to come in their thousands.[2]

Riposte comes in the sheer volume of the weekly outpouring from the towns, with pent-up frustration in such claims that

There is NO real shortage of amenity land in this country. It is only that far too much of it is in the hands of the very few, and ordinary people are kept out by wire fences and gamekeepers. The millions are herded into barracks whilst the few are not obliged to give up any of their traditional amenities.[3]

Debate at a more rational level has been informed by numerous recent investigations into the mass recreational use of the countryside and though many gaps in knowledge still remain to be filled, a reasonably clear picture emerges. In this chapter, the existing pattern of demand for day and weekend use will be analysed, and in subsequent chapters the impact of holiday-makers, the supply of land and other facilities and the problems and opportunities which emerge in the relationship between demand and supply will be considered. Inevitably, discussion must focus on the existing situation, but it must never be forgotten that this is far from static and that we have not really seen as yet the full effect of mass recreation in the countryside. One measure of potential increase was that derived in a study of the New Forest which showed that, as compared with 1965, visitors would more than treble in number by 1981 and increase almost five-fold by the end of the century.[4]

CAR AND COUNTRY

The sheer volume of pleasure motoring was emphasised in Chapter 2: the present concern is where, when and in what ways its impact is felt.

There is little reliable evidence to estimate the total volume of recreational travel out of towns. At national level, the BTA *Pilot National Recreation Survey* recorded only 5 per cent of all contacts as going for a drive of two hours or more the previous Saturday or Sunday afternoon, but interviewing was spread over several weeks of late September and early October 1964, and in this context the figure must be regarded as 'tentative in the extreme'.[5] More significant was the fact that 44 per cent of all car owners recorded at least one day trip the previous month (though not necessarily to the countryside). For London alone, the LCC survey showed that in June 1964, 7 per cent of all adults had visited the country the previous Saturday and 12 per cent the previous Sunday. For those possessing a car, the proportions rose to 14 and 23 per cent respectively.[6] Over a holiday weekend, figures are naturally higher. For Whitsun 1963, a BTA survey suggested over half the population engaged in some pleasure travel during the three-day period and of these 60 per cent travelled by car.[7] Such data are isolated and lack comparability but it is perhaps not unreasonable to suggest that between one in four and one in three of car-owning households undertake some pleasure travel during summer weekends, and perhaps one in eight of those without cars. Since 49 per cent of all households owned cars in 1968,[8] such proportions would give a summer weekend volume of perhaps nine million day trips in England and Wales.

Day trips and visits to the country are, of course, far from synonymous. The attractions of towns, and of seaside resorts in particular, remain very strong, especially when holidays are considered (Chapter 5), but they still retain a very real appeal for more casual excursions. Among car owners, the *Pilot National Recreation Survey* found the following proportions for the three basic types of destination:

Destination	Per cent of day trips	Per cent of half-day trips
A town	17	20
The country	29	47
Seaside	32	19

For day trips, the three types of destination were of roughly equal importance, but the countryside almost equalled the other two combined for excursions of shorter duration. It must not be forgotten that even within the country, towns have an attraction of their own. They provide catering and other amenities and may well be of high visual quality. In the Lake District on a typical summer weekend, Ambleside and Bowness each attract more than 40 per cent of all day visitors to the National Park.[9]

National figures give little idea of local conditions. Towns and coastal resorts can by their very nature absorb large numbers of people and cater for those of gregarious intent. On a peak day in 1965 Brighton attracted 100,000 day visitors (compared with 20,000 staying visitors and a resident population of 163,000)[10] Rhyl and Prestatyn claim a peak of 110,000[11] and Southport 300,000 day visitors[12] and even though these are estimates only and must be viewed with some caution, they emphasise the high potential capacity of beaches and promenades. The countryside in contrast can only absorb comparatively small numbers. The Peak District National Park received an estimated 5½ million day visitors in 1963,[13] but it covers 542 square miles: Brighton accommodated some 6½ million day visitors in 1965, with a coastal frontage 5½ miles long, 60 acres of corporation-owned beach and 250 acres of foreshore between high and low water-marks.

Information about the extent to which a given stretch of countryside absorbs visitors at any one time is difficult to obtain for two basic reasons. In the first place, the countryside is used in quite different ways by different groups. At the one extreme there are those who pass through without pausing, their pleasure derived from the drive itself and from seeing the scenery while on the move; while at the other there are those who make directly for one particular location as the prime object of their journey and remain there for as long as possible. The first group contribute to the volume of traffic using the road system, but unlike the second group make no specific demands on land. In between these extremes are many possible permutations, and the whole concept of a trip is a complex and individual one. In a study of the Forest of Dean, for example, it was found that 57 per cent of all visitors to the Forest Park stopped at more than one point in the Park and at one large picnic area, Speech House, 40 per cent of visitors did not intend to make a specific stop there when they set out on their journey. Again, the role of the drive itself as part of the purpose of the trip is emphasised by the fact that over 70 per cent of visitors to the Forest from Bristol, Newport, Cardiff and Birmingham did not take the shortest route there on either outward or return journeys, and most trips were either partial or complete circuits rather than making the return journey by the same route as the outward one.[14]

The other difficulty relates to the sheer problem of gathering information virtually simultaneously over a wide area, where distances may be great, many trippers continually on the move and many others parked in ones or twos, or walking as individuals or in small family parties. In an attempt to obtain a more adequate and reliable picture, East Sussex County Council has used helicopters, with aerial observers linked by radio to interview teams on the ground. By this means, 250 square miles of coast and countryside, and 148 major parking locations were examined in one day.[15] There is an obvious case for the further development of such techniques, but surveys on this scale are expensive and need many observers. Most existing surveys have been undertaken with more modest resources of labour and finance, and have tended to concentrate on traffic counts at specific locations and interviews at well-used sites. This does not invalidate their results, but means some caution must be used in their interpretation.[16]

Despite these problems, some evidence does exist of the total number of visitors in particular areas of countryside. The New Forest, for example, some 145 square miles in extent, was visited by 58,005 people on Bank Holiday Sunday, 1965, with a total of 20,002 cars.[17] The peak was between 4 and 5 pm when 16,771

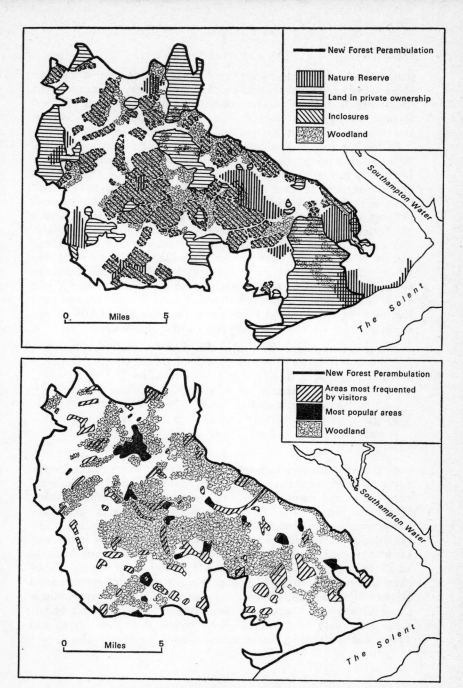

Fig 30. Land use and intensity of recreation activity in the New Forest (based on maps 8 and 9, *South Hampshire Study, Supplementary Volume 2*, and used with the permission of the Controller of HMSO).

people and 5,766 cars were recorded. The previous Sunday there were 40,318 people and 13,967 cars. In very different types of surrounding, the East Hampshire Area of Outstanding Natural Beauty (151sq ml) contained about 1,600 car-borne picnickers at the peak period of an August Sunday afternoon in 1966.[18]

In neither case is land used exclusively for recreation. In the New Forest, private land and the productive woodlands of the Inclosures cover some 47,000 acres of the total of 93,000 acres (Figure 30) and further areas are designated as Nature Reserves. On the remaining areas of woodland, heath and grassy 'lawns', grazing and recreation co-exist, with public access traditionally unrestricted and vehicular access tolerated though not a right. Even so, areas of real pressure are comparatively limited and closely related to the road pattern. East Hampshire is a rural area where the recreational use is incidental, and in that sense more typical of Britain's countryside in recreational terms. Of the 1,600 visitors, about 900 were at actual picnicking sites (and over half of these were at Old Winchester Hill and Butser Hill alone), the remainder parked on road verges and in gateways.

> The most apparent feature is the relative unimportance of recreation in terms of actual exclusive land use compared with the acreage of agricultural land and woodland. The recreational uses and activities are scattered in a diffuse pattern on sites surplus to agricultural needs, where pressure has been so great that the agricultural use has been relinquished or occasionally where dual use operates with agriculture or forestry.[19]

This theme is one to which we shall return at much greater length, for it is fundamental to any consideration of land use and recreation in the countryside. The low density of much existing leisure use, but also the low capacity of most rural areas in absorbing recreational demands must be continually stressed. The crowded countryside is a relative concept at best. Even in areas of evident pressure, the actual numbers involved are comparatively small. In the Lake District on Bank Holiday Sunday 1966, Grasmere had 10,000 visitors, Coniston Water 6,000, Derwentwater and Borrowdale 5,650 and Langdale about 2,000. These totals include those who stopped for only a short time as part of longer excursion: they may be compared with totals of 19,500, 18,950 and 15,800 for Ambleside, Bowness and Keswick respectively.

RANGE, TIME AND SEASON

To the car-borne excursionist, the relative attraction of potential destinations is powerfully conditioned by their accessibility in terms of both distance and time. All available evidence suggests that the majority of day and half-day trips range comparatively short distances from home (though the deliberate choice of circuitous routes may add much to the overall mileage). During August Bank Holiday 1965 the average one-way distance travelled on half-day excursions was twenty-nine miles, and on all-day trips fifty miles (Figure 31).[20] These findings are corroborated by the *Pilot National Recreation Survey* with 38 per cent of all day and half-day trips in the previous month covering less than twenty-

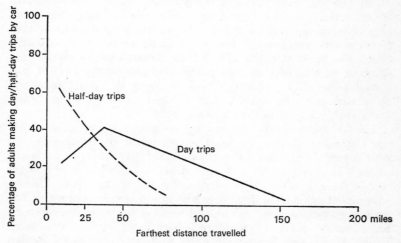

Fig 31.   Distance travelled on day and half-day trips by car (data from British Travel Association).

five miles in one direction, and with another 35 per cent travelling between twenty-five and fifty miles.[21] Averages all too often mask reality: longer trips are of course made—at Whit weekend 1963, one in seven of all holidaymakers travelled to points more than 100 miles away, and in the *Pilot National Recreation Survey* one in ten had travelled more than seventy-five miles. More adventurous journeys in terms of distance might be expected at holiday weekends: equally, these figures undoubtedly under-represent the volume of short-distance mid-week and evening travel.

More specific evidence is yielded by the various site studies. The characteristics of the site itself, and its location in regard to major urban centres, will influence the results, but the dominance of short distances is striking in every case. The importance of location is emphasised in the Lindsey study (Figure 32), carried out in early July 1967. The principal towns lie along the coast, and at sites close to them (A, B, C, and G) 80 per cent or more of all visitors had travelled less than ten miles.[22] Even the presence of smaller towns influences the pattern: at Hubbards Hill (site F) almost half the visitors had come from nearby Louth,[23] though the attraction of this Wolds site was sufficient to bring one-third of all visitors from between ten and twenty-five miles, nearly all from the coastal towns. Site E (Belmont TV mast) is more remote from any town and not only was the total number of visitors comparatively small but most came from the 10–25-mile zone. The remaining site (D) is more anomalous: a picnic area adjacent to one of the main roads to the coast (A 631), it had considerable use by visitors travelling along this route from the West Riding to the resorts, over one-quarter of the total having come from more than fifty miles away.

The Wiltshire study (Figure 33) suggests the importance that the character of the site itself exerts when the proportion of people travelling from more than twenty-five miles away is examined. Least attractive to longer distance travellers is Inglesham Access Area, a twenty-acre meadow on the banks of the Thames adjoining Lechlade bridge. It is basically a simple, open area for picnics, games, boating, fishing and bathing but without even such amenities as toilets. In an intermediate category are Westbury White Horse and Pepperbox Hill: at both, one person in five had come from over twenty-five miles away. Both areas are striking viewpoints with easy car access and ample open space (63 and 73 acres respectively) but no toilets or other organised facilities. Savernake Forest exercises the greatest long-distance attraction. Public access is permitted to 2,300 acres, and at the picnic area are toilets, a water supply, hearths for open fires and the starting point of a self-guided Forest Walk.

The evidence from these and other studies strongly indicates a direct correlation between the attractions of an area and the distance people are prepared to travel to reach it. Attraction in

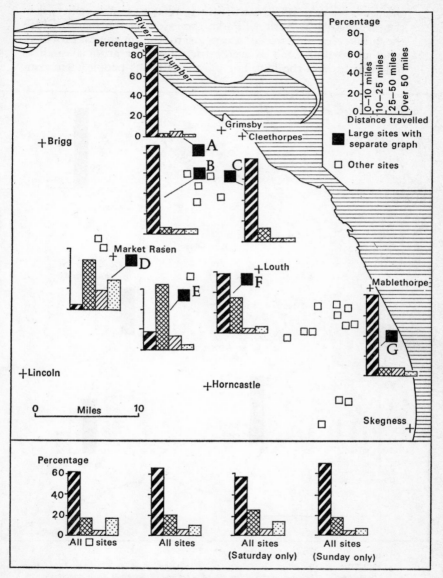

Fig 32. Distance travelled by visitors to recreational sites in Lindsey (data from
Lindsey Countryside Recreational Survey).

this sense is a very broad term: it may refer to visual quality, as in the scenery of the National Parks, the extent of the area to which the public has unfettered access or to the amenities provided, whether natural, such as water for sailing, or artificial such as toilets, cafés and the like. For most excursions people seem con-

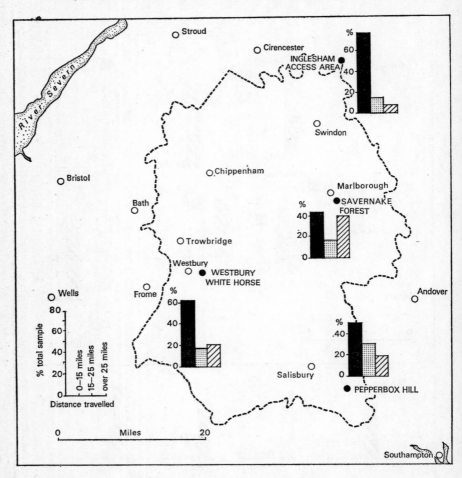

Fig 33. Distance travelled by visitors to recreational sites in Wiltshire (data from Wiltshire CC *Leisure in the countryside – survey of selected open spaces*).

tent with a modest destination close at hand, but will make occasional exertions in terms of effort, time or cost, to reach more attractive places much further afield. In Wager's study of thirty commons, the median distance travelled was only 10 miles, the majority had travelled less than 20 miles but 15 per cent had made journeys of 30 miles or more.

Sylvia Law has suggested that such considerations can be used to classify facilities into categories based on their relative powers of attraction: [24]

Zone of influence	Radius of attraction for bulk of visitors
local	
intermediate	5–10 miles
sub-regional	20–30 miles
regional	50 miles
national	unlimited

The first three are within the range of the half-day visitor, and regional facilities day-visitor range. These groupings form a hierarchy in more senses than one, for the higher their status, the fewer their numbers, though most people tend to travel to the nearest site which will satisfy the level of their needs on a particular occasion. The Peak District, for example, though of national status attracts most of its visitors from the ring of industrial cities which surround it: in 1963, 60 per cent of weekend motorists lived near the Park, 30 per cent in Manchester and Sheffield alone. Similarly for the New Forest: its marginally national importance can be seen in that it was visited on day trips from as far afield as East Anglia and the East and West Midlands, but such stalwarts numbered only 0·7 per cent of the total. All the remainder came from the South East or South West, 61·1 per cent from within the Poole-Winchester-Portsmouth area alone.[25]

The accessibility of a site and its attractiveness strongly influence the number of people who will visit it. Its capacity to accommodate those visitors at peak periods is related not only to its size and the degree of crowding visitors will tolerate, but to the time they arrive and the duration of their stay.

In places where holiday traffic does not add complications, the weekend peak reaches its height on Sunday afternoons, with a clearly defined maximum between 4 pm and 5 pm and a fairly rapid decline thereafter (Figure 34). The evidence of such sur-

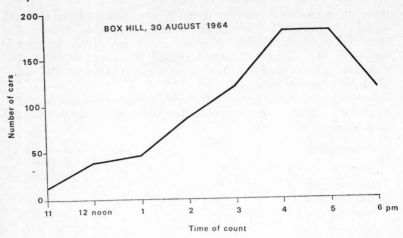

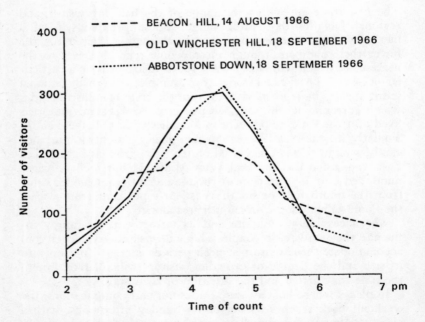

Fig 34. Numbers of visitors present on Sunday afternoons at sites in Hampshire (upper) and at Box Hill (lower) (data from Hampshire CC and T. L. Burton).

veys as those in Hampshire and at Box Hill is corroborated by analysis of traffic flows on roads which carry heavy weekend traffic.[26]

The length of time people stay at sites is far more variable, for it depends upon the purpose of their visit and the nature of the site. As has been seen, at the one extreme there are those whose pleasure is in driving to enjoy scenery and who stop, if at all, merely to savour more fully for a short while the view from a particular point: at the other, the journey itself is incidental, pleasure being principally derived from the facilities the site itself can afford and the aim of the excursion to get there as quickly as possible and to stay as long as possible. The degree of contrast is aptly illustrated in the Staffordshire and Worcestershire survey (Figure 35). Group 1 sites are essentially viewpoints, whether in the rolling country of the Lickey and Clent Hills or at the 'picture village' of Broadway. Some may wish to walk or stay longer for other purposes, but for most a short stay suffices to look at natural or created beauty. Group 2 sites have more attractions in themselves—the open heath and woodland of Cannock Chase, the woodland and glades of Kinver, the accessible hills and the town itself at Malvern. Visits are of longer duration —most stay for an hour or two and there is a greater proportion of longer stays of four hours or more. At group 3 sites, far more come for really long periods: the attraction is not the quickly absorbed view but the variety of activities related to the river and its banks at Arley, Bewdley and Stourport and to both river and town at Evesham.

The impact of outdoor recreation on the countryside is, of course, far from continuously sustained, with variation not only throughout the day but also according to the day of the week and the time of year. Away from areas with marked holiday traffic, the Sunday peak is everywhere evident. Wager in his study of commons showed that when other factors are equal, Sunday use can be as much as five times that of ordinary weekdays. The variation at one site can be seen in Figure 36. Speke Hall, on the outskirts of Liverpool, attracts visitors to its grounds and to the Elizabethan house itself: the record is based on paid admissions to the house. Although the general level of visits increases during late July, August and early September, the striking feature is the consistently high Sunday total, surpassed only by the exceptionally high level of Bank Holiday Monday (28 August). Sunday

H

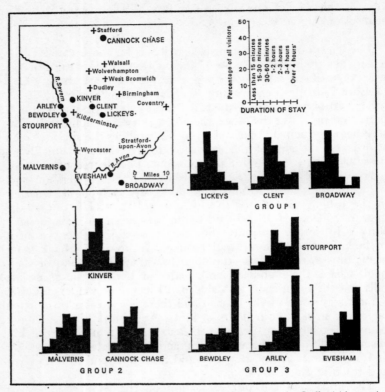

Fig 35. Length of stay of visitors to recreational sites in Staffordshire and Worcestershire (data from J. R. Duffell and G. R. Goodall).

totals of 200 or more are sustained throughout June and early July—up to six or seven times the weekday total—and only with the advent of school holidays do weekday totals improve to one-third or more those of Sunday.[27]

Rather less is known about the extent of seasonal fluctuations, for most studies have naturally concentrated on periods of peak demand. Figure 37 illustrates the monthly fluctuations in the number of visitors at a random selection of sites where charges are made and a continuous record of admissions is obtainable. Some of the sites, such as Epworth Old Rectory (John Wesley's boy-

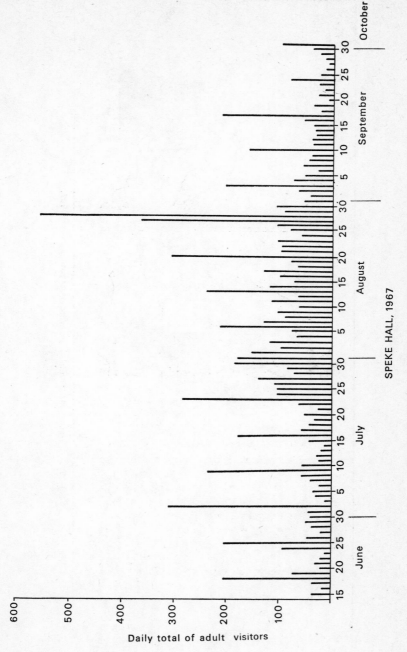

Daily total of adult visitors

600 500 400 300 200 100

SPEKE HALL, 1967

June   July   August   September   October

Fig 36.   Daily total of adult visitors to Speke Hall, summer 1967.

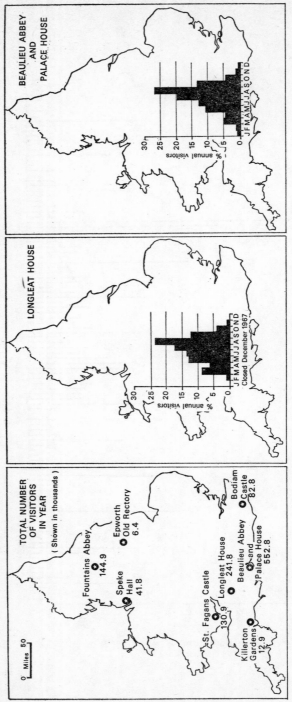

Fig 37A. Seasonal variation in visitor numbers at selected sites. 1967.

hood home) are essentially indoor attractions but together they compass a typical range of objectives for day or half-day excursions. Three broad categories may be distinguished, though the differences are of degree rather than of kind. Occasionally, the summer peak may be distorted by unusual attractions at other seasons, as is the case with the spring and early summer display at Killerton Gardens, or by visits from organised parties such as schoolchildren in term time at Speke Hall and St Fagans Castle. Spreading of the peak load in this fashion may help to ease some of the economic problems of year-round maintenance. At places where many visitors are holidaymakers, the summer peak tends to be more narrowly concentrated and extreme. At both Beaulieu and Bodiam, for example, August visitors exceed one-quarter of the annual total and are markedly above the July level. The same trend, though not in quite such an exaggerated fashion, is evident at Longleat. The seasonal characteristics of holidaymaking will be treated in more detail in the next chapter.

The third category, exemplified to some extent by Epworth (though here the total sample is small) but even more particularly by Fountains Abbey, comprises sites which lack undue distortion from holidaymakers but are typical objectives for the townsman's 'day in the country'. Fountains Abbey has many of the characteristics which will be sought in the new generation of country parks. The ruins of the Abbey are merely a focal point in the extensive landscaped grounds of Studley Park, where facilities include a café and ample open space for playing, picnicking and walking: they are easy of access from Leeds and the West Riding (25 miles) and Teesside (30-35 miles). Here the summer peak is rather less extreme—indeed July exceeds August—though this may simply reflect fewer visitors on weekdays than in holiday areas.

In every case, however, the seasonal contrasts are striking. There is negligible interest from November to February, and it is only between May and September that monthly figures exceed 10 per cent of the annual total. Apart from Killerton and Speke, where conditions are anomalous, July and August alone account for between 36 and 49 per cent of all visitors.[28] The incidence and intensity of the peak may vary a little, but its impact is unmistakable.

It is the cruel dilemma of urban activity in the countryside that so much pressure is exerted in such a short compass of time. Peak

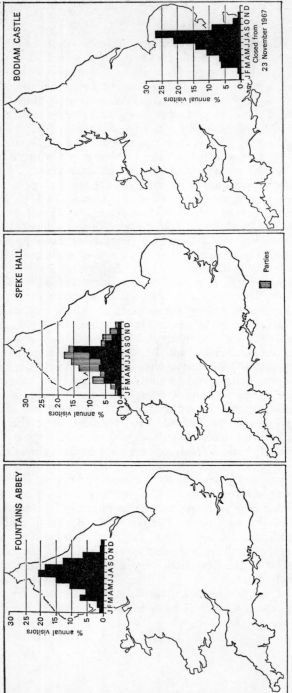

Fig 37B.   Seasonal variation in visitor numbers at selected sites, 1967.

demand is confined to a few hours on a few days each year: to cater for it 'will seldom be financially possible or environmentally desirable'[29] yet to spread it more evenly involves social, economic and physical obstacles of a formidable order.

The most immutable is climate. We claim a stoic disregard for the vagaries of weather, but observed fact is more revealing. Wager's studies of commons suggested the following adjustment factors to compare attendance at open spaces under different weather conditions: constant sun 1; intermittent sun 0·8; overcast 0·5; showers 0·6; continuous rain 0·2. A great deal of work remains to be done in assessing the effects of weather on outdoor recreation. Charles II could aver that 'the English climate is the best in the world. A man can enjoy outdoor exercise on all but five days in a year'.[30] In vigorous mood, many would echo the sentiment, but others might feel he was nearer their appreciation of the truth in his claim that 'the English summer consists of three fine days and a thunderstorm'.[31] The paradox is self-evident, but purpose conditions response. The active find little at any season to deter their outdoor pursuits, but all too rare and unpredictable are halcyon days when the lazy spirit can seek warm pleasure in unsheltered picnic or outdoor bathe. 'Astringent mildness' may, in Gordon Manley's phrase, be the dominant characteristic of our climate, where we 'enjoy, but are not subordinate to, the power of the sun' but it sets real limits on passive recreation, limits which have not yet been fully explored. In the adaptation of outdoor leisure to climate, the car has played a major part, in shelter as much as in the mobility it affords. This country may be blessed with 'days when the tears of the rain are swept away by the laughter of the breeze and the sun shines through clean and sparkling airs on the vivid colours of the countryside'[32] but for many, such vistas are more comfortably seen through windscreen glass than experienced in the real outdoors.

COUNTRY PURSUITS

The dominance of the car as an integral part of passive recreation in the countryside is emphasised in a variety of studies. Observed activities will obviously vary according to the nature of the site in question, but in so many cases the car is far more than just a means of transport and becomes the focal point of the recreation experience.

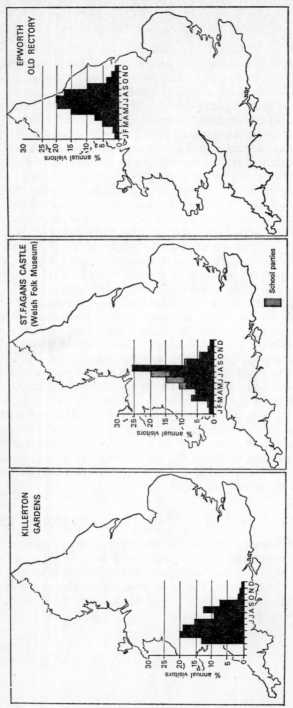

Fig 37C.   Seasonal variation in visitor numbers at selected sites. 1967.

The findings of three studies are summarised on Figure 38. Detailed comparisons have little meaning not only because of differences between sites but also because of the definitions used by individual workers. The Lindsey survey, for example, distinguishes 'strolling' only, the commons study 'walking' and 'pottering'. Site character has an obvious effect: one would expect far more people to visit the open spaces of the commons to get out of a car and stroll or walk than one would in Lindsey where many of the sites were simple parking places or viewpoints. Again, in the forest studies, Allerston's particular attraction lies in the through motor route of Dalby Forest Drive, whereas the heaths and glades of Cannock Chase and the New Forest are more inviting for picnicking and other informal activities.

These qualifications apart, the overwhelming impression which emerges from these and other studies is of informal, car-oriented activity. The inherent reluctance to move far from the car is a continuing theme. On the dunes and beaches of the Lancashire coast at Formby, where 10–15,000 visitors congregate on a fine summer Sunday afternoon, the major concentrations were at the seaward ends of the main access roads, 'with traffic chaos prevailing in the most accessible areas and halcyon quiet in the others'. The East Sussex survey, the most comprehensive study yet made in an areal sense of recreation in the countryside, emphasises the same point with picnicking or sitting near cars the primary activities. At two inland sites surveyed on the ground the following results were obtained:

Activity	Ashdown Forest (per cent)	Piltdown Pond (per cent)
Picnicking away from cars	80	50
Sitting in cars	5	24
Picnicking and playing games	6	—
Fishing	—	16
Walking	—	4
Swimming	—	4
Boating	—	2
Others (including rock climbing)	9	—

When 'picnicking away from cars' is examined in more detail, the role of the car is further underlined:

	Picnicking away from cars (per cent of total engaged in activity)	
	Ashdown Forest	Piltdown Pond
Immediately adjacent	83	30
Within 6 yards	16	—
Within 80 yards	—	57
¼ mile away	1	13

Games players at Ashdown Forest were an average of eleven yards from their car, and fishermen at Piltdown Pond 120 yards. One constraint on movement, so devastatingly parodied in Peter Nichols' television play, *The Gorge*,[33] was 'the considerable amount of equipment . . . carried on day-trips', for rural amenities seem by many to need immoderate supplement.

Observed patterns of activity point the question as to what kind of site is really wanted by most people for their 'day in the country'. The answer varies with temperament and age. The specialised needs of climber, fell-walker or fisherman are obvious, but these are in a minority: in the countryside of East Hampshire there is an extensive network of footpaths but 'to judge from their appearance, many . . . are rarely if ever used, even when signposted'. Family groups seek areas where the children can play, teenagers are more likely to want a wider range of artificial attractions. For most, the impression emerges, in Wagers' words, that 'the motor car has become an extension of the Sunday parlour; it is picnic hamper, carrycot and rucksack all in one' and many seek a visual as much as a physical contact with the countryside, 'a place to relax and a change of environment'[34].

For the commons he studied, Wager devised an 'index of popularity' for differing kinds of location, with the average number of visitors to each type of site expressed as an index of the most popular:

Type of environment[35]	Index of popularity
Car parking area (large grass car parks where people can remain in or by car)	100
Pasture	94
Open woodland (clumps of trees and scrub broken by grass or bracken)	93
Parkland (formal groupings of trees and grass areas)	68

Playing fields (mostly on urban commons and popular because of location)	58
By water	44
Moorland	29
Meadow	25
Heathland	11
Timber plantation	9
Cultivated land	4
Scrub	3

Given that most visitors to commons are seeking informal areas, the dominance in favour of areas where cars can be easily parked and with some open space closely adjacent is striking. Solitude is wanted in a relative rather than an absolute sense: 60 per cent of Wager's sample preferred to be on their own but 'wanting to be on one's own does not mean, for many people, actually getting away from others' but to be 'simply left quietly to pursue their own activities'.

This picture of passivity may not always persist. There is some evidence that with better education and greater familiarity with the rural scene more sophisticated tastes develop and that more countryside activity will be less car-oriented in pattern, though many forecasts of future trends are based on American or continental experience, where climate is frequently less of a constraint.

CAPACITY

Earlier in the chapter, the volume of recreational traffic already being absorbed by differing urban and rural areas was discussed. To be meaningful, such figures must be related to the theoretical capacity of the area for this purpose, though capacity ratings are not easy to derive in anything other than an empirical way.

For the motorist in the countryside, two differing problems are involved. In the first place, there is the volume of traffic the roads themselves can sustain, whether of motorists making for a particular destination or simply 'going for a drive'. Part of the attraction of many rural areas is the intricate network of minor roads, but these may be required to sustain a volume of traffic beyond their effective capacity and a volume certainly far in excess of that which makes driving through attractive scenery

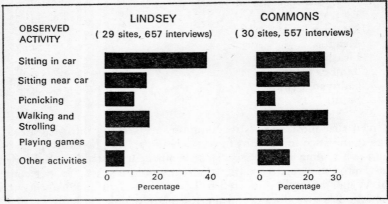

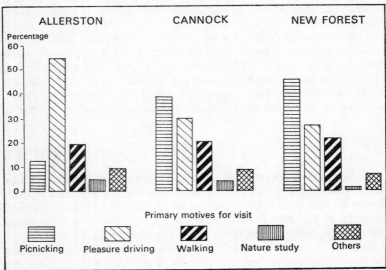

Fig 38.   Observed activities of visitors to open spaces. References to the various surveys summarised on this diagram will be found in the text.

itself a pleasure. In the Forest of Bowland, the main route through the Trough of Bowland is barely sufficient for two-way traffic in parts, but is adequate for the everyday needs of residents and through traffic. However, on an August Sunday afternoon in 1966 it had to cope with a two-way peak flow of up to 500 vehicles an hour, and an average flow during the weekend of some 250 vehicles an hour.[36] In Borrowdale in the Lake District, maximum hourly flows in an inbound direction at Great Wood on August weekends varied from 196 to 246 vehicles, and maximum outbound flows from 123 to 250. On one Sunday a raft race and barbecue more than doubled this 'normal' maximum, and flows exceeded 550 vehicles in one direction with resulting congestion between Keswick and Shepherd's Crag. In Langdale in the same period, vehicle flows at Skelwith Bridge reached maximum hourly flows of 142 vehicles inbound, and 191 vehicles outbound.[37]

Such demands on relatively minor roads must be measured against standards of 'absolute' and 'acceptable' capacity. For the former, Ministry of Transport estimates can be applied. A well-designed two-lane, single carriageway road 18ft wide, but with obstructions two feet from each side of the carriageway (such as dry stone walls) has a maximum hourly two-way capacity of 513 passenger car units, assuming uninterrupted vision for overtaking and no hills. If 60 per cent of the road has substandard visibility for overtaking (less than 950 feet at 40 mph), hourly capacity is reduced to 333 passenger car units.[38] Many minor roads, of course, fall well below these standards and the effective capacity of a road is conditioned by its most restricted sections.[39] As for 'acceptable' capacity, 250 vehicles an hour is more than four vehicles a minute, sufficient to demand very considerable driving concentration and effectively shattering rural solitude and calm enjoyment of the rural scene.

One interesting application of the concept of capacity applied to recreational traffic on rural roads has been developed by Basil Cracknell.[40] As seen already, most pleasure journeys into the countryside cover comparatively short distances, with the result that the area immediately surrounding the cities has become, in Cracknell's words, 'an extension of life in the city—it is the garden for children to play in—a vista people can enjoy from their mobile room—their car'. He calculated how much of the surrounding area would be needed to absorb this demand as far as the rural road network was concerned, a belt of countryside giving adequate 'living space', with the following result: [41]

Population of town	Radius of required 'living space' in miles
10,000	2
100,000	6
1,000,000	20

Figure 39 illustrates the application of this concept on a national scale.

Living space in this context is related only to the road network as such. Different problems are encountered once recreation sites

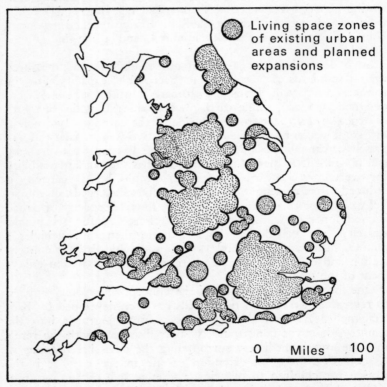

Living space zones of existing urban areas and planned expansions

0   Miles   100

Fig 39.   B. Cracknell's concept of the 'living space' of urban areas. Only towns exceeding 30,000 in population are included.

themselves are considered. To the planner's tidy mind much of the demand should be catered for by areas specifically managed for recreation to 'reduce the risk of damage to the countryside —aesthetic as well as physical—which often comes about when people simply settle down for an hour or a day where it suits them . . . to the inconvenience and indeed expense of the countryman who lives and works there'[42]. In this sense, demand is already well in excess of supply so far as formal provision is concerned, and dangerously close to it in others. In many areas of the Lake District, cars are parked in numbers greatly in excess of the capacity of recognised parking areas and laybys (Figure 40), while in the East Sussex survey it was calculated that the Sussex Downs were being used to 46 per cent of their maximum capacity at picnicking locations, and Ashdown Forest to 62 per cent.

In the latter study, an attempt was made to define 'capacity' on the basis of the following observations:

Activity	Average area occupied by activity (sq yds per group)		
	Ashdown Forest	Piltdown Pond	Rye Bay (coast)
Picnicking away from cars	36·0	9·0	9·4
Playing games	195·0	—	—
Beach: picnicking, etc	—	—	12·6

A set of minimum standards was evolved from this data by coupling the 'activity area' to the space needed for parking and manœuvring the attendant car. For car park, roadside verge or layby little more than the car space itself is needed (200–270sq ft). For forest or downland car parks used also for picnicking or other activities but with limited space, 620sq ft will suffice, including 81sq ft of 'activity area'. For similar areas but where space is not at such a premium, 1,000sq ft is suggested with 323sq ft of activity area. Such standards are based purely on maximum physical capacity with no regard to visual effect and could not be sustained continuously over a large area even in their most spacious form without a major deterioration in the appearance of that area. They mean, with an average of four persons per group, densities of 172–272 persons per acre, but are feasible for intensively used areas set within wider expanses of grassland, heath or woodland. They compare with Wager's suggestion of a density of thirty cars (120 persons) per acre as allowing sufficient space for picnicking and family play close to the car.

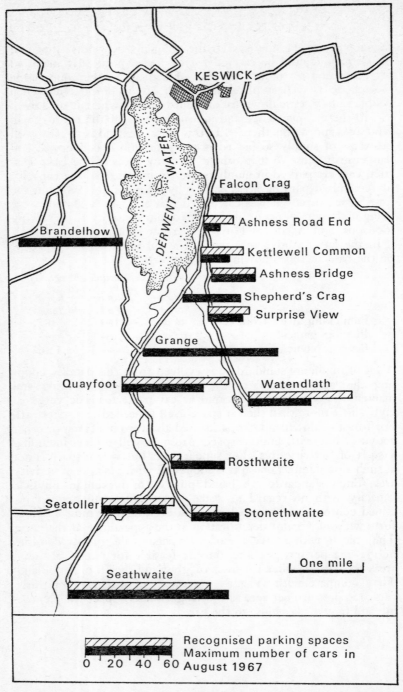

KESWICK

DERWENT WATER

Falcon Crag

Ashness Road End

Kettlewell Common

Ashness Bridge

Shepherd's Crag

Surprise View

Brandelhow

Grange

Quayfoot

Watendlath

Rosthwaite

Seatoller

Stonethwaite

One mile

Seathwaite

Recognised parking spaces
Maximum number of cars in
August 1967

0 20 40 60

Fig 40. Car parking in Borrowdale, August 1967 (data from Lake District Planning Board).

Throughout this discussion of the demands made by the car and its occupants on the countryside has run the thread of intensive use of limited areas, whether related to the roads themselves or to places to picnic and play. It cannot be too strongly stressed that the actual areal demands (made by the town on the country), in the sense of land largely or exclusively devoted to recreation, are comparatively small. The demands focus on a network of *lines*, roads, tracks and footpaths, with *nodes* of intensive activity at parking and picnic areas. Within the network are the large areas of rural landscape serving simply as a backcloth, but whose existing visual form is an inherent part of the whole recreational experience. The protection of that visual form is as much a part of the effective use of rural areas for outdoor recreation as the creation of laybys and picnic areas, and protection can mean most often the continuation of existing agricultural use.

One example must serve of what this could mean in areal terms. It has been suggested that the East Hampshire Area of Outstanding Natural Beauty will receive a peak hour total of perhaps 6,400 car-borne visitors in the early 1980s requiring space for picnicking and other pursuits.[43] Assuming an average occupancy of six persons to the acre, far below the maximum capacity possible, something of the order of 1,000 acres of land would be needed, paying no regard whatsoever to existing provision. This in itself represents almost exactly 1 per cent of the total area. In practice the impact would be far less in real terms, for many areas could serve other purposes in addition to that of recreation, while a few would be more specifically developed for intensive use. Even when road space is added—and Cracknell suggests this represents perhaps 0·7 per cent of the total area in rural Britain—the demands of urban dwellers for rural playgrounds are not as space-consuming as is sometimes believed, nor as incompatible with existing uses of the land.

BEYOND THE CAR

The family motorist seeking passive enjoyment in the country-side is far from the only urban denizen of the rural scene, albeit the most numerous and the one about which most is known. Participation and growth rates in the varied forms of countryside activity were discussed in Chapter 2, but brief mention must be made of the type of demand these other forms make on countryside and coast.

I

In this sense, five groups of activity may be distinguished, though the margins between them are not always clearly defined. The first is the passive contemplation of the rural scene, the visual appreciation of the harmony of nature and of man. Contemplation may require no actual contact, for to most, as has already been emphasised, the rural scene is framed in the windscreen of a moving car. Yet though the direct demands of such appreciation on the land itself are minimal, the indirect demands lie at the roots of conservation and of rural planning if the scene itself is to be retained. Despite Cowper's aphorism, much of rural beauty is man-made. In a perceptive essay on English Landscape David Lowenthal and Hugh Prince aver that

> England has its nature lovers who disdain the domesticated and swear by the wild fells of Westmorland . . . but the countryside beloved by the great majority is tamed and in-habited, warm, comfortable, humanized . . . The English like landscapes compartmented into small scenes furnished with belfried church towers, half-timbered thatched cottages, rutted lanes, rookeried elms, lich gates, and stiles—in short 'the intimate and appealing beauty which our forbears impressed upon it'.[44]

Intimacy and appeal may be inefficient for the resident, they may deprive towns, transport and industry of land and resources: it is a delicate task to balance all demands, to rate visual amenity against efficiency and national prosperity. The measures taken and the success achieved in attempting to resolve the conflicts are the theme of ensuing chapters.

For other activities, distant perception will not suffice. Active pursuits demand access, actual physical contact with the rural scene. Contact is sought in many ways, and the variations are the framework of the remaining four groups of activity. Of these, the first is an extension of roadside contemplation, with penetration on foot or on horseback into the countryside. Again, such penetration is aimed at visual pleasure while enjoying physical exercise. It is concerned with the preservation of visual amenity but also with the establishment and maintenance of adequate access. Access is rarely needed (though sometimes demanded) to the whole of an area, whatever may be the appeal of trackless upland, but again focuses on a network of routes, tracks and paths of varying degrees of formality. It is a linear demand, with satisfaction from movement and vista. By its very informal nature, its scale is difficult to assess except in relation to particular areas. The British Horse Society claims that 100,000 people ride in Britain each week, and that there are 1,900 riding establishments licensed by local authorities. The British Horse Society itself has a membership of 12,000, together with an additional 12,000 members of affiliated riding clubs. The Pony Club has over 30,000 members, the British Show Jumping Association some 6,000.[45] Walkers and hikers are even more difficult to enumerate adequately in a meaningful way. The hard core of earnest enthusiasts is represented by such bodies as the Ramblers Association and the Youth Hostels Association, the former having almost 400 affiliated groups, the later 219,000 members and 261 hostels. Interest expressed in this way is relatively static (Figure 41) but the role of these bodies in effectively underlining the needs of those who only ramble or hike in an informal way needs much emphasis.

The second group has needs which are satisfied at particular sites, a nodal rather than a linear demand. In the first place, there are those who enjoy some particular, but limited, aspect of the countryside. The study of natural history has become increasingly important, with a consequent concern for both access and conservation. Caving and climbing are restricted to suitable limestone areas for the former (principally the Mendips, parts of South Wales, the Peak and Craven) and to rocky outcrops for the latter, found in profusion only in the more rugged areas of North Wales and the Lakes. Most enthusiasts are prepared to travel some way to satisfy their needs, but accessibility means that relatively modest climbs in such areas as the Peak, the coastal cliffs of southern England or at Harrison Rocks in Sussex have a popularity which belies their challenge. Real congestion can then occur: Stanage Edge in the Peak, for example, perhaps the best gritstone face within easy access of Sheffield, may have up to 600 climbers around it at one time, with erosion of holds a major problem. In these circumstances, climbing belies its more usual air and becomes gregarious in the extreme. Another sport where the requirements are related to the season as much as the nature of the site is ski-ing. The real explosion of interest has been in Scotland, but though opportunities are chancy and unpredictable they are avidly seized in the Lakes and the northern Pennines. Climate would seem to ensure that ski-ing south of the border is 'really a welcome bonus rather than an end in itself'.[46]

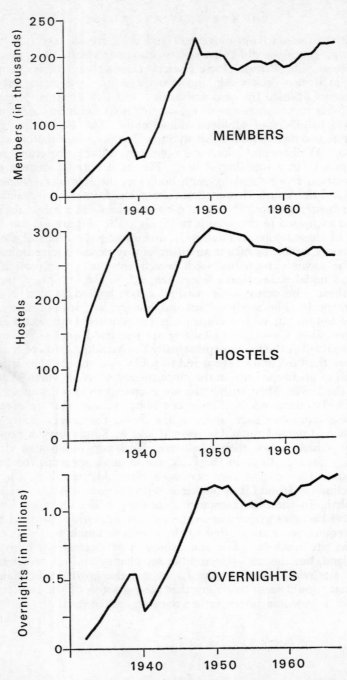

Fig 41.   Membership, hostels, and hostel use of the Youth Hostels
Association, 1931–67 (data from Youth Hostels Association).

Other sports where interest focuses on particular sites are of a more organised nature, and their requirement is more often land as such, rather than an inherently rural setting. Race courses, motor and motor-cycle race tracks, airfields for gliding and private flying come into this category: although the land is required almost exclusively for the purpose, the actual areas involved are comparatively small and the satisfaction of demand raises few problems.

The third group has needs which are not restricted to a route network or to specific sites, but range uninterrupted over a considerable area. It is rare that these needs demand the exclusive use of land, however, and by and large they are compatible with agricultural and other uses. Field sports of various kinds are by far the most important such category, though information about the scale and range of activities is relatively scanty. J. T. Coppock has estimated that some 50,000 people weekly attend meetings of foxhounds, and there are two hundred packs of foxhounds in England and Wales.[47] Stag, otter and hare are also hunted. Stag-hunting is restricted to Exmoor, the Quantocks, Savernake Forest and the New Forest. There are nineteen packs of otter-hounds and 127 packs of beagles, basset-hounds and harriers. Hunting involves no direct reservation or management of land, and many of those who take part themselves belong to the rural community.

Many forms of shooting demand active management of land or livestock, but being an informal activity and ranging over private land, little is known in quantitative terms. The most widespread is the shooting of game birds, an autumn and winter sport. In Britain as a whole, there is a shootable surplus on perhaps 15–20 million acres and a potential area roughly double. Estimates of the annual kill vary from three to six million for pheasants, perhaps two million for grouse and half a million for partridge.[48] There are more than 60,000 holders of game licences.[49] Shooting does not demand the exclusive use of land, but certainly conditions attitudes of landowners to questions of access. The shooting of wildfowl is less organised, though thought to attract up to 500,000 participants each year. The major areas concerned are stretches of coastal marsh in such areas as the estuaries of the Dee and Ribble, Morecambe Bay, Solway Firth and the Wash. Increasingly shooting rights are rented: in 1963, organisations affiliated to the Wildfowlers Association of Great Britain and Ireland held sporting rights over some 300,000 acres.[50] It must be stressed that though field sports of some kind or another take place over much of rural Britain they only rarely give rise to serious conflicts of interest and make little exclusive demand on land.

Before considering the final group, of water-based activities, the extent to which a given area can sustain the demands made by the varied forms of recreation may be examined. Capacity in relation to car-borne use has already been discussed, but objective criteria for other activities are much harder to derive. Many of the informal pursuits are of a relatively solitary nature, but the degree of crowding an individual will accept in walking or climbing is a very personal matter. One acquaintance, living in the heart of the Yorkshire Dales National Park, declared with disgust that meeting no less than seventy-three people during a Bank Holiday walk over twelve miles of upland in the vicinity of Great Whernside was more than sufficient to deter him from similar expeditions on such a day. Others would feel rambling with a group that size was part of the pleasure of the excursion.

Most standards of capacity have been based on American experience and are particularly related to the intensive use of land and water in managed recreation areas, that is suitable values for nodes of attraction. In California, for example, design standards range from 580 persons per acre of bathing beach to 40 persons per mile of hiking and riding trail,[51] while the design of parks around the fringes of Detroit is based on a density of use of ten persons per acre, allowing both intensively and extensively exploited areas.[52]

In Donegal, Michael Dower derived empirical formulae for conditions existing there, though he rightly emphasised that these were estimates only and needed refining by further research.[53] They were designed to suggest how many people could be served by each resource without crowding or congestion and without physical or ecological damage, and some of the more important are listed below:

Resource	Capacity (persons per sq ml)	Notes
Rough hill land	1	These are *basic* estimates for number of people who can be entertained sight-seeing or walking in ordinary countryside
Enclosed land with few roads or paths	5	
Enclosed land well served by roads and paths	50	

Woodland	6–128	Additional to 'basic' capacity
Grouse-shooting	5	Additional to 'basic' capacity
Hill-walking (more attractive hill areas)	12	Additional to 'basic' capacity
Pony-trekking	6	Additional to 'basic' capacity
Rock climbing	One rope of 4 climbers for each 500 vertical feet of climb	
Coast	40 per mile	'basic' standard
Coast (attractive and accessible)	240 per mile	
Beach	440 per mile	
Scenic driving		
Major road	1 car every 400 yards	
Minor road (surfaced)	1 car every 800 yards	

Some of these standards may seem a counsel of perfection under English conditions, but there is need for much more work to establish realistic estimates for both visually and physically acceptable densities.

THE LURE OF WATER

The explosive growth of water-based activities has already been outlined in relative terms (Chapter 2). For sheer numbers, swimming and angling are by far the most important. In the British climate, outdoor swimming is really attractive for comparatively brief periods, but is a traditional part of the seaside scene however spartan the conditions.

Angling numbers close to 1½ million adherents.[54] One indication of the intensity of activity is the annual count made of all anglers fishing on a particular day on the canals and reservoirs of the British Waterways Board, a total of 27,126 on Sunday 22 June 1968.[55] The average density over the whole system was almost sixteen anglers to the mile, and in 1967 reached sixty-two to the mile on the Lee Navigation.[56] With numbers on this scale, pressure on available water becomes extreme, and like other sports with comparable pressures, has become largely organised on a club basis, with fishing rights made available in this way. The

London Anglers Association, for example, recently paid £37,000 for fishing rights on an 8,200 yard length of the Wiltshire Avon.[57]

Other water activities do not permit of easy enumeration, for club memberships do not represent the sum of those engaged in what are essentially informal activities. Some recent estimates are suggested in the following table:[58]

Activity	Club membership 1966	Estimate of other participants	Total
Sailing	465,000	not available but comparatively small number	c 500,000
Canoeing	13,000	37,000	50,000
Water ski-ing	not known		60–70,000
Sub-aqua	8,000	5,000	13,000

No estimate is available of the number of motor boats of varying types, for the majority of owners belong to no club of any kind. In all these instances, however, growth must be related to the rapid rise in car ownership, and the consequent ability to transport equipment easily. Most power boats, for example, are usually kept at home and trailed to water, while much of the popularity of sailing stems from the small dinghy which is hauled ashore when sailing is finished, and kept in a park at the sailing club or, for casual users, hauled home.

The evident volume of demand must be related to the resources available. In this context, the proximity of the coast to virtually all parts of the country is of supreme importance, for inland resources are comparatively meagre. The question, moreover, is not a simple one of matching available water to demand, for not only are problems of location and accessibility important, but also compatibility. Not all water users can co-exist, and this exacerbates the inherent problems (Figure 42). Differing activities have differing water requirements. Angling and wild-life studies can use most types of unpolluted water, canoeing and rowing are satisfied by the sea and canals and rivers. The most formidable problems are in the demands of sailing and power-boating, particularly for accessible inland water. Power-boating is especially 'unsociable', bringing problems of noise, pollution and wash, and for racing and water ski-ing the sole use of large, uninterrupted stretches with a minimum area of 16 acres for the former and 25

acres for the latter.[59] While boat-owners have not yet been sub-
jected to the close scrutiny of range and habit meted out to the
weekend motorist, the scale of demand on a meagre resource is
obvious enough.

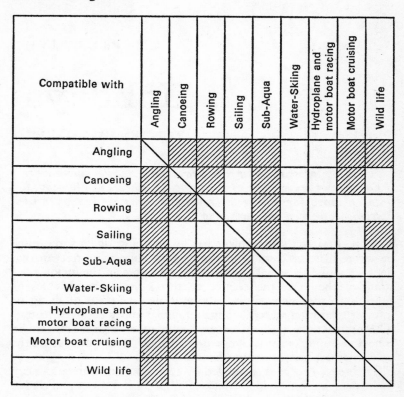

WATER SPORTS : COMPATIBILITY OF USE OF WATER

Fig 42. The compatibility of the use of water by various water sports (data from
Gloucestershire CC, *Outdoor Water Recreation, Table 1*). Compatible activities are
shown by the shaded squares: thus sailing is compatible with the study of wild life
but not with water ski-ing. The diagram is necessarily generalised: angling, for
example, is not compatible with such activities as rowing in narrow rivers, but can
take place from the banks of lakes where there is hydroplane racing, provided a
restricted area some 100 ft wide can be maintained.

CHAPTER FIVE

Holidays

THE HOLIDAYMAKER

. . . in the present century holidays have . . . become a cult. For many they are one of the principal objects of life—saved and planned for during the rest of the year, and enjoyed in retrospect when they are over.

J. A. R. PIMLOTT's assessment has lost nothing of its force since he wrote his classic study of the English holiday more than two decades ago. As a social phenomenon they remain the major milestone of the year, the chance to throw aside the shackles of routine, to seek new vistas, to sample new patterns of living or in utter relaxation search out again familiar and well-loved haunts. They remain the peak of leisure experience, with a freedom in time and opportunity to range more widely than can ever be the case in other, briefer, leisure hours.

Their social force is shadowed by their economic impact. They make demands on a wide variety of different industries and trades. Exact estimates of expenditure, and its direction, are almost impossible to derive, for internal movement is unhindered and largely uncharted and the purchase of goods and services hard to isolate and categorise. On a broader scale, they are intimately involved with national economic health and the balance of payments. Between November 1966 and January 1970 currency restrictions limited the scale of expenditure abroad. In 1968, British travellers spent £271 million in foreign currency while incoming visitors spent £282 million here, a net gain of £11 million.[1]

At home, the main basis for gauging the economic impact is the annual British National Travel Survey of the British Travel Association.[2] This estimated that in 1968 British holidaymakers spent some £890 million, £570 million in Britain itself. The figures refer only to direct expenditure on holidays of four nights or more away from home and are, of course, far from the total of leisure, or even holiday, spending. The wider impact is seen in the development of the holiday industry as such and not least in the creation of inland and coastal resorts, that 'peculiarly English contribution to urban life',[3] whose rise was briefly traced in Chapter 1.

The present chapter is concerned only incidentally with holidaymaking as a social and economic phenomenon, for this has been ably chronicled elsewhere. Rather, it seeks to trace the demands made by holidaymakers on resources of land and water. Many of the activities discussed in the last chapter are not only a part of general leisure habits, but belong especially to holidays. This applies particularly to activities which are most fully satisfied by the highest standards of resources—the finest scenery, the most attractive beaches, the widest expanses of water—for the holidaymaker need not be content in terms of time and opportunity with local or regional standards of provision, but can seek the outstanding examples at national or, on occasion, international levels. In an area the size of England and Wales, this holiday demand frequently overlaps in both location and time the demands of weekend leisure and exacerbates existing pressures. If these pressures are to be fully understood, the volume of holidaymaking and its range, season and form must be outlined.

Holidays with pay brought almost universal opportunity for holidays, but holidays themselves, in the sense of a continuous period away from home, are far from universal. It would seem, indeed, that demand has largely levelled off, with some six people out of every ten taking an annual holiday and the proportion scarcely varying since the early 1960s (Figure 43). This does not, of course, mean that the same people go away each year. In the period 1966–8, 75 per cent of the total population took one or more holidays, but only 43 per cent in each of the three years. The remaining 25 per cent represent a hard core of those who rarely if ever take a holiday, a lack, not surprisingly, most prevalent among the elderly and the lowest income groups.

The number travelling abroad has also remained surprisingly

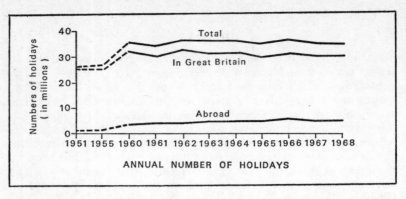

ANNUAL NUMBER OF HOLIDAYS

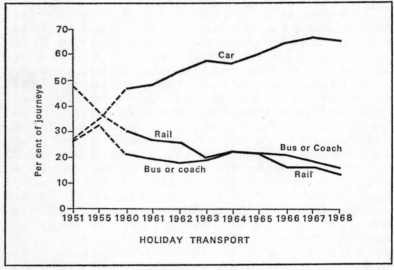

HOLIDAY TRANSPORT

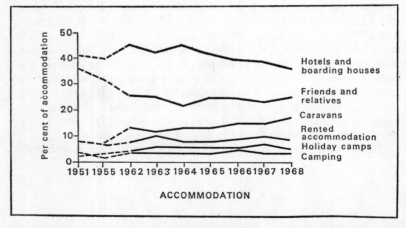

ACCOMMODATION

Fig 43. Holidays, holiday transport and accommodation used in Britain, 1951–68
(data from British Travel Association).

constant, though here apparent stability has come more recently, remaining at a total of about five million since 1965 after rising continuously from some 1·5 million in 1951. It remains to be seen whether this stability is real or illusory, induced by the currency restrictions in force from 1966 to the beginning of 1970. There have already been substantial changes in the pattern of destinations for holidays abroad, with favourable rates of exchange as well as the lure of the sun having a marked effect. Spain has shown a dramatic rise as have more distant destinations such as Austria and Yugoslavia. France, Switzerland and Ireland have experienced a relative fall in favour.

Holidaymakers going abroad are characterised by both higher incomes and freedom from family ties. In 1968 33 per cent of those who went abroad had family incomes exceeding £1,950 a year, but only 14 per cent of those who stayed in Britain. Similarly, of those who went abroad 31 per cent were single and only 17 per cent had children, compared with proportions of 20 per cent and 34 per cent respectively of those who took their holiday in Britain. Future trends are perhaps best indicated by the fact that by far the most important reason given for going abroad was the weather (36 per cent): of those who stayed at home, almost half had never even considered going abroad, 18 per cent thought Britain was cheaper and only 1 per cent averred they had been deterred by currency regulations. The future extent of foreign holidaymaking would seem to be very much a case of climatic attraction being weighted against family commitment and comparative costs.

At home, holiday patterns have been more static both in terms of numbers and of destinations. In 1968, there were twenty-six million 'main' holidays and four million additional holidays. However, while 'main' holidays have remained for some time little changed in number or incidence, the growth of second holidays is an important phenomenon and one greatly understated by these figures which refer only to holidays of four consecutive nights or more away from home. A small-scale pilot survey carried out by the BTA in 1968 suggested that ten million adults take short holidays of up to three nights away from home each year, though on 61 per cent of such holidays, accommodation was provided by relatives or friends.[4]

One particular aspect of this short holiday increase deserves emphasis, and that is the rapid rise in the ownership of second homes, and their use for weekends as well as holidays as such. As yet, very little is known in quantitative terms about the extent of this movement or the areas most affected,[5] but indications are the numbers of caravans on permanent coastal sites, and the rapidly escalating price of suitable properties in many rural areas.

> Snapping up a primitive country cottage for a song and doing it up as a charming weekend retreat is an English middle-class sport that is in its desperate phase . . . The bargains can still be found, but the urban refugee needs to be very lucky, determined, or skilful.[6]

The impact this has already made on some areas is seen in Lleyn (Figure 44). In specific terms, the map must be regarded as tentative only for it is based on the evidence of rate books alone,[7] but the marked concentrations around the coast and adjacent to the National Park are clearly evident. In the parish of Llanengan, which contains the yachting centre and resort of Abersoch, the proportion of properties where the ratepayer has an address different from the dwelling itself rises as high as 36 per cent; even

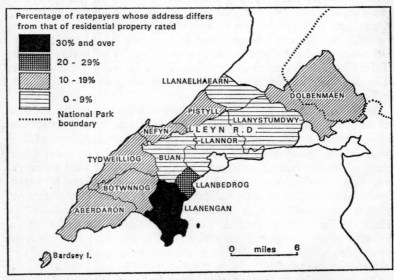

Fig 44.   Second homes in the Lleyn Peninsula (data from Caernarvonshire County Planning Officer).

though many of these properties are undoubtedly 'holiday' rather than 'weekend' in function.

Two comments arise from this trend. In the first place, the acquisition of a second home not only provides increased incentive to spend more time in countryside or coast, but it tends to emphasise longer journeys at weekends. Lleyn, for example, is seventy-five miles or more from Merseyside, the nearest conurbation: a journey of 150 miles may be an effective deterrent to a Saturday or Sunday excursion, but is well worth-while if it can compass the whole weekend from Friday evening and allow a full day and a half in the chosen area. Secondly, the stock of suitable properties, being comparatively small, will soon be exhausted in practical terms, and the question then arises as to whether the movement itself ought to be encouraged by permitting new construction in selected areas. The same problem is evident in connection with the permitted capacity of caravan sites. This potential could have important implications for the location and design of country parks, a theme which will be further considered in Chapter 8. It is interesting to compare practice and prospects in other European countries. In Sweden, with much lower densities of population and thus far less intense demands on the land, possession of a country cottage is widespread. In 1965, 300,000 families already owned one (about one in eight of all families) and the number was increasing by 5 per cent each year.[8] In 1966, there were $1\frac{1}{4}$ million second homes in France or one in every fourteen households.[9] In Denmark, the national plan envisaged a demand as great as one for every three families, on sites averaging half an acre.[10] It is a moot point whether the design of cities should be such that the drive to escape to a country home should be so deep-rooted as to require satisfaction in this way.

BESIDE THE SEASIDE

In terms of land, it is not so much the sheer volume of holiday-making in its varied guises which is so important as the location of its impact and its extent in time. In this respect, little has changed since Cowper wrote in 1782 of those who,

> *Ingenious to diversify dull life . . .*
> *Fly to the coast for daily, nightly joys,*
> *And all, impatient of dry land, agree*
> *With one consent to rush into the sea.*[11]

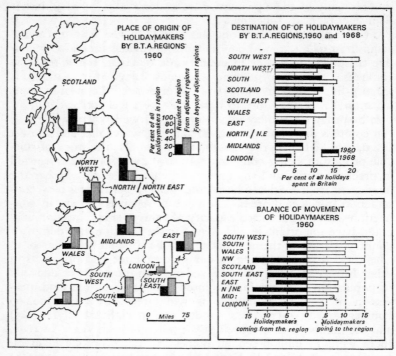

Fig 45. Origins and destinations of holidaymakers in Britain (data from British Travel Association).

For the Briton on holiday, the coast is still the major magnet to which his annual treks 'occur with a majestic rhythm'.[12] In more prosaic terms, 75 per cent of all main holidays in Britain included a stay by the seaside, compared with 16 per cent in other towns and cities, 11 per cent amid mountains and moors, 7 per cent by lake and riverside and 9 per cent in other inland destinations.[13] The proportions fluctuate between differing social categories: of those branded middle- and upper middle-class, only 69 per cent stayed by the sea, but 78 per cent of all manual workers. In contrast, 21 per cent of the former but only 8 per cent of the latter recorded holidays in mountain and upland areas.

The impact is not equally felt around all coasts. Apart from

questions of amount and type of accommodation available, the
twin magnets (which may pull in opposing directions) appear to
be climate and accessibility (Figure 45). The South West is by
far the most important single region, and has increased its share to
a significant degree during the 1960s from 16 per cent in 1960 to
22 per cent in 1968. Devon and Cornwall alone now absorb 18
per cent of all British holidaymakers.[14] The BTA figures in themselves do not allow any differentiation between varied destinations within the region, but the lure of the coast is made quite
clear when individual counties are examined in detail. In Devon
(Figure 46), over 93 per cent of all visitors in early August 1967
were staying in the four coastal zones and 40 per cent in the Torbay area alone.[15]

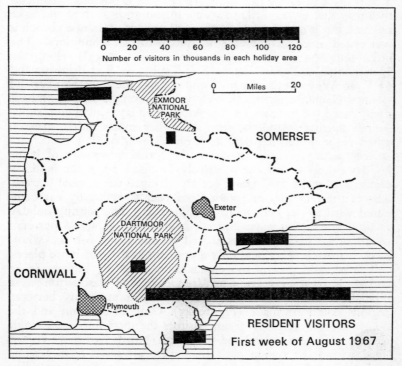

Fig 46.   Destination of holidaymakers in Devon, August 1967 (data from Devon
County Planning Officer).

K

The South also continued to increase its share throughout the 1960s and, although the South East appears to have declined marginally, the three southern regions between them accounted for 48 per cent of all holiday traffic in 1968. Apart from the slight increase in Wales, the relative popularity of other regions has not changed to any significant degree: the apparent decline of the North West is largely due to the exclusion of Northern Ireland from this total in 1968.

The pull of the South and West is emphasised by the diagram showing the balance of movement of holidaymakers in 1960.[16] Relative movement has changed only a little since that date: the South West, South and Wales emerge as major net importers, and the North/North East, Midlands and London as major exporters. The relative attraction of the warmer areas is obvious: temperature may matter but little in scenic inland areas such as the Lake District, but it certainly does when enjoyment of an open beach is concerned under somewhat marginal British conditions. The mean temperature for August, for example, is 57°F along the Northumberland coast, but 61°F at Tenby, 63°F at Brighton and 63°F at Weymouth. Small wonder that the Northumberland County Council suggests that along the county's coast 'emphasis might well be placed on "activity" holidays involving sightseeing, touring inland, boating and other sports rather than on what might be termed the "deck chair" holiday'.[17]

Despite these trends, however, the actual movement of home holidaymakers is still comparatively localised. Even the mobility conferred by the car has not greatly changed the general pattern, despite the fact that in 1968 66 per cent travelled by car compared with 27 per cent in 1951 (Figure 43). The touring holiday as such has shown some increase in popularity, but 86 per cent of all home holidaymakers stayed in one place for the whole of their main holiday, and only 8 per cent in three or more places.

The actual degree of movement is illustrated by Figures 45, 47 and 48. For earlier years, when 'residence' and 'destination' were tabulated for the same regions, direct comparisons between regions could be made (Figure 45). Only in London and the South West were more distant visitors the most important single source, while in Scotland and the North/North East more visitors lived within the region itself than were attracted from beyond its borders.[18] Elsewhere, the adjacent areas were the outstanding contributors, though in some cases the actual movement involved

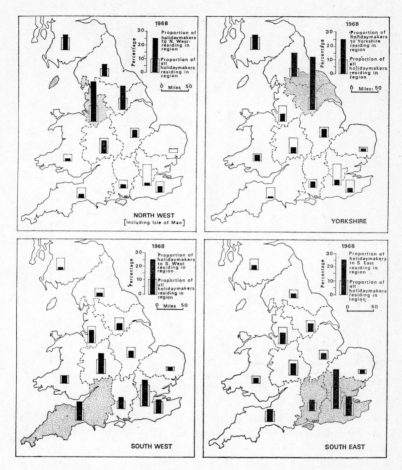

Fig 47. Origins of holidaymakers in selected areas of England, 1968 (data from British Travel Association).

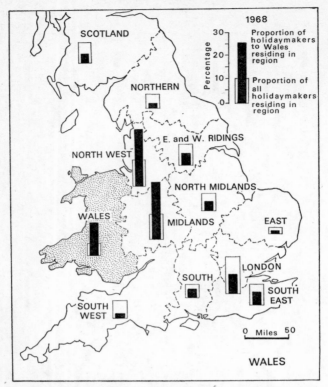

Fig 48. Origins of holidaymakers in Wales, 1968 (data from British Travel Association).

(eg from Merseyside to North Wales) might be no greater than some internal movements (eg from the West Riding to the Yorkshire coast).

The dominance of short- and intermediate-range journeys persists in more recent times (Figures 47 and 48). These maps have been compiled for the five most popular holiday regions though these do not always wholly coincide with the regions of residence now used by the BTA. In each case, the region of destination is stippled and the boundaries of the regions used in defining area of residence are shown by pecked lines. The open symbols are proportional to the total number of those who go on holiday from the region, the solid symbol proportional to those who go to the particular destination concerned. To give an example from the Yorkshire map, people living in the East and West Ridings and Humberside comprise 9 per cent of all holidaymakers in Britain, but no less than 39 per cent of those who make Yorkshire their holiday destination. The local pull is greatest for Yorkshire and the North West and a little less for southern areas. There seems indeed a greater reluctance for denizens of the South to journey northwards than for movement in the reverse direction. Throughout, however, there is the obvious tendency for an area to be most attractive to those who live nearest to it, easy accessibility in terms of time and distance remaining of paramount importance. In this sense, with no part of England and Wales more than seventy-five miles from the coast and three-quarters of holidaymakers seeking a coastal destination, most needs can be satisfied at relatively short range. Only a few areas, such as the South West, offer sufficient in terms of climate and amenity to exert a disproportionate attraction in terms of the country as a whole.

THE HOLIDAY RUSH

By any standards, the holiday season is crowded into very brief compass. When main holidays alone are considered, 62 per cent of all holidays in 1968 began in July and August, 91 per cent between June and September (Figure 49). The pattern has not varied to any significant degree over the years: in 1951, 64 per per cent began in July and August, 92 per cent between June and September, while in 1967 the proportions were 64 per cent and 91 per cent respectively. Even when all holidays are considered, and a mild area favoured for out of season holidays is taken as an example, the basic problem is but little alleviated. In Devon 52·4 per cent of all visitors came during July and August in 1968, 86 per cent between June and September. The basic constraints are obvious enough. Works closures and the limited extent of summer itself play their part, but the incidence of school holidays is most important of all. Of those with children, 73 per cent went on holiday in July and August 1968, compared with 58 per cent of those without. There is little prospect of real change: 'until school holidays are really radically staggered throughout the summer months, shutdowns, holiday-camp offers, rail rates and the rest will be at the mercy of the headmasters'.[19]

In economic terms, the problem is the profitable operation of facilities which for a short spell are intensively used to the point of overcrowding and for much of the remainder of the year are grossly underused. The extent of the variation in demand is illustrated in Figures 50 and 51. The Isle of Wight and Cornwall are areas which by reason of isolation or distance are relatively unattractive to the weekend and day visitor: apart from the brief influx at Christmas and Easter, a quiescent seven months is followed by the turbulence of the season as such, reaching a clear peak in late July and early August rather than a sustained plateau over a longer period. At Beaulieu, demand is overlain to some

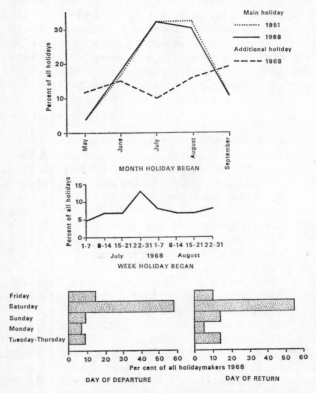

Fig 49. The timing of holidays (data from British Travel Association).

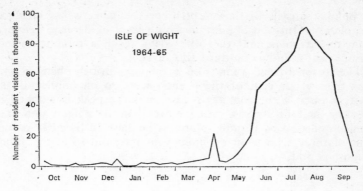

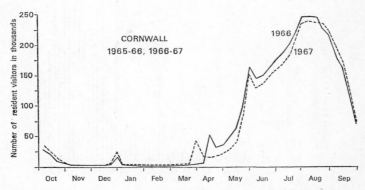

Fig 50. The holiday season, the Isle of Wight and Cornwall (data from *The coasts of Hampshire and the Isle of Wight* and Cornwall County Planning Officer).

extent by the additional pressure of day visitors. Easter and Spring Bank Holiday peaks are more marked and interest is sustained at relatively higher levels in April-May and September-October. The differing sources of visitors are suggested by the daily totals for weeks in July, August and September. Late July and August show a sustained demand throughout the week, even though totals on individual days may fluctuate for climatic or other reasons. Sunday is no different from any other day and totals only fall consistently on Saturday, the traditional 'changeover' day (a habit which itself exacerbates traffic problems on major access routes to holiday areas). By late September the pattern has changed completely. Only on Sunday is a high level of demand retained from day-trippers, and the other days reach a total from late season visitors only one-third this level.

The seasonal peak is far from a uniquely British phenomenon. Less than 5 per cent of the French who go on holiday do so entirely outside the summer season, and the peak is reached in the first half of August when more than 10 million out of a total population of 50 million are on holiday. In Sweden, 90 per cent of those who went on holiday in 1963 did so in the June–August period.

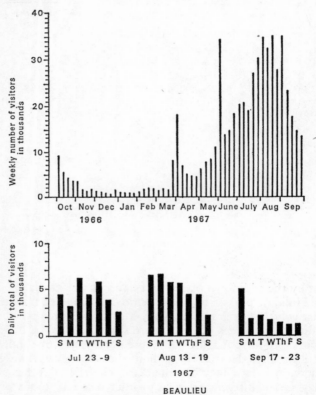

Fig 51. The holiday season, Beaulieu Abbey and Palace House (data from Montagu Ventures Ltd).

BOARD AND LODGING

Accommodation for the annual rush presents its own problems of both demand and supply. Many of these are purely economic, and not related directly to the present study, but the location of differing types of accommodation and the demands they make on land are highly pertinent.

The pattern of demand on a national scale is illustrated on Figure 43. The changes over the last two decades have been striking. The larger hotels have just about retained their share, but there has been a relative decline in holidays spent in boarding houses and unlicensed hotels. A much sharper decline, perhaps most closely reflecting the rise in real incomes, has been that in the proportion of holidays spent with relations or friends—from 36 per cent of the total in 1951 to 26 per cent in 1962 and since remaining more stable at about a quarter of the whole.

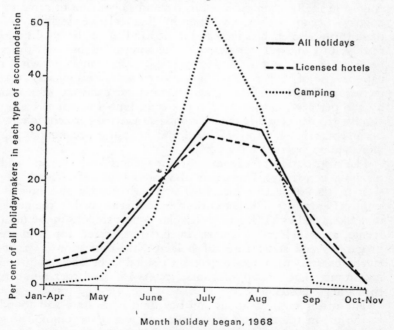

Fig 52. Types of holiday accommodation used throughout the year (data from British Travel Association).

The major increases have come in the more informal kinds of accommodation; in rented flats, houses and cottages which give a greater measure of freedom to the holidaymaker and far fewer problems of labour and personal involvement to the owner of the property than if it were exploited on bed and breakfast or boarding house lines; in camping, with its possibility of cutting total holiday costs to a minimum; and above all in caravans. Of the last named, numbers were insufficient to merit separate attention in 1951. By 1955 about two million were taking holidays in caravans and by 1968 the total had risen to some four and a half million— 16 per cent of all main holidays and 12 per cent of additional holidays. The importance of caravans for casual weekend use has already been underlined.

These varied types of accommodation have a differing seasonal impact. Informal kinds absorb the excess at peak periods (Figure 52). Whereas 62 per cent of all main holidays began in July and August in 1968, 71 per cent of caravan and 86 per cent of camping holidays began in these two months. The relative flexibility of these forms also enables increases in demand to be absorbed more readily. In Cornwall, for example, the annual number of visitors rose by 48 per cent between 1954 and 1964 compared with a national rise of 11 per cent. The greater part of this increase was in informal types of accommodation—static caravans increased by 240 per cent, chalets by 310 per cent, rented accommodation also by 310 per cent and tents by no less than 370 per cent whereas, in contrast, all types of hotel and boarding accommodation increased by less than 9 per cent.[20]

The distribution of accommodation reflects both demand and planning constraint. The needs of various types of clientele are seen in the respective locations of youth hostels and holiday camps (Figure 53). The network of hostels is attuned to the needs of walkers and cyclists, with particular concentrations in the most scenic areas. Holiday camps, in contrast, cater for a more gregarious and static form of holiday: their location is exclusively coastal, with ready access to suitable beaches of prime importance. Each camp, of course, caters for far larger numbers than a single hostel.

The major mass of hotels and boarding houses are still found in the urban resorts, and the whole problem of accommodating holidaymakers would be immeasurably greater without the capacity of the resorts to absorb large numbers. Many may

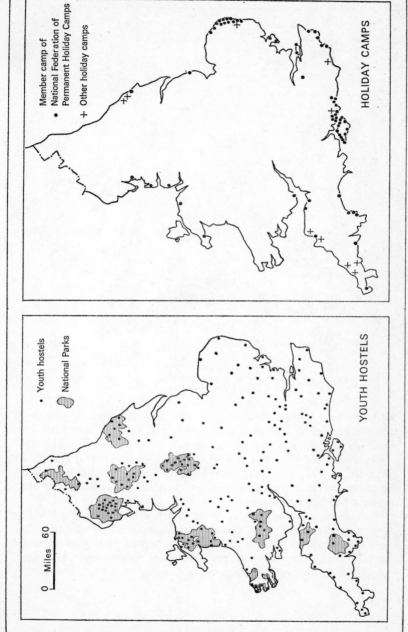

Fig 53. Distribution of youth hostels and holiday camps (data from *YHA handbook, Holiday camps guide, 1968* and *Holiday camps directory and magazine, 1968.*

YOUTH HOSTELS

- Youth hostels
- National Parks

HOLIDAY CAMPS

- Member camp of National Federation of Permanent Holiday Camps
+ Other holiday camps

0 Miles 60

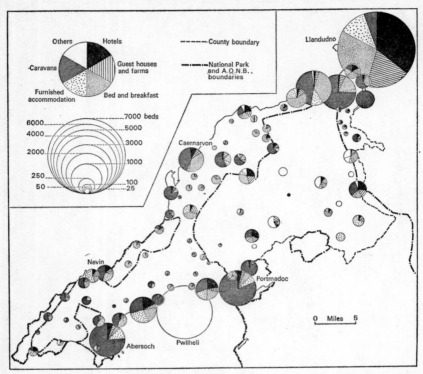

Fig 54.   Holiday accommodation in Caernarvonshire (data from Snowdonia National Park Survey).

deplore their gregarious compatriots, but they alone make it possible for others still to find quietude and relative isolation. The situation within one county is illustrated in Figure 54: the role of the hotels of Llandudno and the holiday camp at Pwllheli in catering for Caernarvonshire's influx of visitors is evident enough, for these two centres between them provide virtually 45 per cent of the total accommodation.

Outside the towns, the keynote has been increasing planning constraint. Prior to 1939, sporadic uncontrolled development of both dwellings and holiday cabins had begun to disfigure many coastal areas, but the real pressures developed after the war, especially in the case of caravans. In Conrad Rawnsley's words,

It began with the idea of a holiday home on wheels, admirable in itself, but the rating laws for many years exempted this form of dwelling and so it put down its roots by the thousand, its obtrusive colours and uncompromising shape dominating the shores and cliffs.[21]

Not unexpectedly, the major concentrations were in coastal areas: in 1965, although only just over half of all caravan sites in Britain were located within about three miles of the sea, they included over four-fifths of the total capacity for holiday caravans.[22] In some parts, the sites have developed an urban intensity —if one assumes an average of four berths per caravan, over 25,000 can be accommodated in this way around Abergele in North Wales, 20,400 at Porthcawl, the 'caravan capital' of South Wales, and 17,500 at Ingoldmells on the Lincolnshire coast. In some areas of the country, caravans and tents form a disproportionate share of accommodation, as the following table shows:

Per cent of all main holidays spent	Great Britain	Cumberland and Westmorland	E. Anglia	Wales	South West
Caravaning	16	18	25	34	15
Camping	4	13	3	4	10

For caravans, the case of Wales is especially striking.[23] When accommodation is mapped for the counties of Wales (Figure 55), not only is its mainly coastal location clearly evident, but also the fact that in many areas caravans alone account for over half the total available.

Control over caravans is exercised under the powers of the Caravan Sites and Control of Development Act of 1960. This requires operators to obtain planning permission to establish a site and then secure a site licence from the licensing authority. There are exemptions, but they relate largely to sites occupied for very restricted periods of time, or by very limited numbers of caravans, or both. Any constraint of this kind will bring conflicting pressures of demand but it has effectively limited and channelled growth in many areas. County planning authorities differ in their detailed approach, declaring 'saturation areas' like Cornwall where no new sites or extensions to existing sites are permitted,[24] or 'concentration areas' like Anglesey within which development is concentrated and expansion allowed up to a specific ceiling, but they endeavour to balance in as equitable a

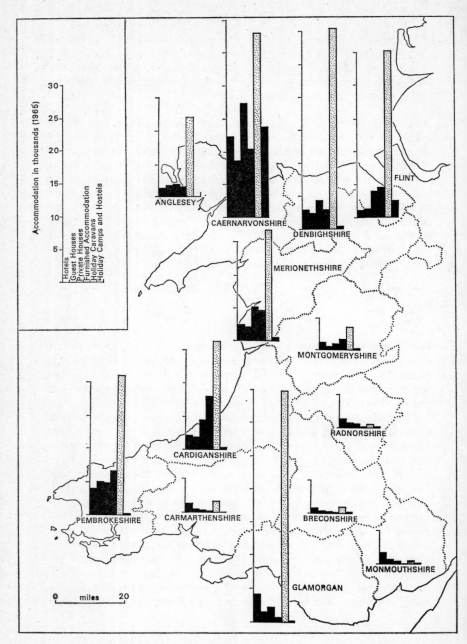

Fig 55.   Holiday accommodation in Wales (data from *Tourism in Wales*).

way as possible the opposing claims of continued demand and the preservation of visual amenity. The net result is to create nodes of development with protected interstices, though such nodes do not necessarily coincide with existing urban areas.

HOLIDAY HABITS

Although the British holidaymaker seeks out the coast in an overwhelming majority of cases, his impact is not confined there. Once resident by the sea, he can then range widely on day excursions. In this sense, the mobility created by the car has been far more important: it may have changed but little his general destination, but it has profoundly influenced his habits once there. He need not necessarily be content with the beach at his chosen resort, but can search out hitherto isolated coves, devoid of adjacent settlement. Excursions inland into scenic areas become an inherent part of the holiday experience. In Devon, for example, the Dartmoor area may accommodate only a little over 3 per cent of all visitors to the county (Figure 46) but the National Park is visited by up to 55,000 people in a single day, equivalent to 23 per cent of those staying in the county at the time (though not all visitors to the Park, of course, come from within Devon).[25]

With the exception of the Peak District and, to a lesser extent, the Yorkshire Dales and the Brecon Beacons, all the National Parks are not far removed from the coast and can be visited easily on day excursions as well as being holiday areas in their own right. In a wider sense, the coastal hinterland is frequently part of the attraction of a particular resort area.

It is difficult to assess in any meaningful way the range of the holidaymaker from where he is staying, for too many variables of place and time are involved. A 1961 survey suggested that, of holidaymakers in Wales, 50 per cent spent their entire holiday within about 10 miles of their holiday accommodation and a further 42 per cent stayed at one place only but made day excursions further than ten miles from their holiday address. The proportions for those staying in the rest of Britain were 54 and 39 per cent respectively.[26] Such evidence can be no more than the most general of indications, but it does emphasise the degree of mobility involved.

The demands exerted by holidaymakers are most acute when they are superimposed on areas also frequented by weekend, day and half-day trippers. All these demands collectively may be limited in both time and place in the ways described, but they are no less severe when they do occur. They are exacerbated by the relatively short distances involved in England and Wales as a whole. No part of the country is so remote from the coast as to be more than a comfortable three hours drive away under normal circumstances: $21\frac{1}{2}$ million people will live within a three-hour drive of the Lake District by 1974.[27] Few parts of England and Wales are beyond weekend range of any other part. Demand may still be relatively localised, but potential mobility continues to increase. Congestion may stifle movement, but burgeoning demand will seek increased quality in satisfaction. It remains to examine the resources both actual and potential this country possesses to give that satisfaction.

CHAPTER SIX

Conserving the Heritage

PARADOX AND CONFLICT

*The most striking aspect of the supply of outdoor recreation
resources . . . is one of paradox . . . apparent abundance in
many ways fails to provide an adequate supply of outdoor
recreation opportunities for the public.*[1]

THIS assessment of the American situation gains added weight in
a British context. Two-fifths of England and Wales is subject to
some degree of active conservation, and the 1968 Countryside Act
further enjoined that 'In the exercise of their functions relating
to land under any enactment every Minister, government Department and public body shall *have regard to the desirability of conserving the natural beauty and amenity of the countryside*'. The
italics are the author's, but the intention is clear: conservation
and the preservation of amenity are not only a national concern,
but applicable on a national scale.

Even when more restricted categories of land are considered,
abundance appears more characteristic than scarcity in any reasonable assessment. It has been estimated that some 3 million acres
of land in England and Wales are in effective recreational use,[2]
and this in itself represents 8 per cent of the total area, little less
than the 11 per cent devoted to urban use and some 65
acres for every thousand persons. This level of provision may be

compared with the National Playing Fields Association recommended standard for urban areas of 6 acres per thousand persons
of permanently preserved playing space, together with 1 acre of
ornamental public open space and 3 acres of school playing fields
(Chapter 3).

But this abundance is illusory. The matching of supply and
demand is no simple equation. The problem lies not in the number
of acres which have been conserved or in the total area nominally
available for public access, but in the effectiveness of both conservation and access and in the location of the land concerned.

In the nature of the land lies the heart of the paradox. Demand
is characterised by diversity: 'a variety of tastes must be satisfied,
from the love of solitude and of wild and beautiful scenery to the
desire to share interests, activities and facilities with others,
whether for active sports or passive recreation'.[3] Some tastes raise
few problems, others impose acute pressures in time and place on
areas ill-suited or ill-equipped to satisfy them. It is on these quite
limited areas that concern is focused: emotive charge and counter
charge all too often obscure the realities of the issues involved
but serious imbalance between demand and supply does exist,
leading ultimately to the aesthetic and even physical erosion of
resources.

Pressures are increased by conflicts of use. Land to which there
is access for recreation is rarely reserved for this purpose alone:
while much of its attraction may lie in the beauty of an agricultural or woodland setting, the enjoyment of that beauty may
be at 'the inconvenience and indeed expense of the countryman
who lives and works there'.[4] Multiple use of a scarce resource is
to be encouraged, more especially as the recreational use is rarely
sustained for long, continuous periods, but conflicts are all too
frequent between the interests involved. Seemingly compatible
uses may be jeopardised by the careless or ignorant behaviour
of those seeking relaxation, or hostility be aroused by the actions
of those wishing to preserve exclusive rights over the land, or
water, concerned. Conflicting demands inevitably mean that the
freedom of the countryside can be but relative at best: wise
management and a clear understanding of the issues involved not
only reduce conflict but ensure the fullest use of scarce resources
in economic, social and aesthetic terms.

Previous chapters have traced the pattern of demand and have
emphasised both its varied nature and its frequent restriction in

time or place. It remains to examine the existing supply of land and water available to match that demand, a supply which has hitherto been reviewed only in an urban context. Resources are as diverse as demand, but many of the problems concerned in their utilisation are common to widely differing categories. Such problems and the further opportunities which exist for developing land for recreational use will be examined in the final chapter, but the characteristics, extent and distribution of each type of existing resource must first be outlined and the problems peculiar to each considered.

RESOURCES AND CONSERVATION

Land devoted to recreation falls into two broad categories, resource-based and user-oriented, though these are not mutually exclusive. In the former case it is the quality of the resource irrespective of its location which is important. It may be a unique landscape, as in the National Parks, or a scarce resource of a very different kind—for example crags of high quality for the climber, or the habitat of a rare species of animal or wild flower. Adequate quality is attraction enough: those who wish to exploit the resource will not be deterred unduly by distance and its appeal may well be national rather than regional or local.

In contrast, user-oriented facilities are important more for their location than their inherent quality. That quality must be adequate for the intended purpose, but the facility must above all be accessible to the potential user. The angler may know of far more productive waters in a far grander setting than the local canal, but when his concern is simply an evening's fishing, the towpath close to home will be satisfaction enough. Equally, the ardent walker may prefer Striding Edge or the Snowdon Horseshoe, but when time forbids seeking opportunity far afield, a ramble through fields half an hour from where he lives may be better than an armchair. Such facilities cater primarily for local or regional needs, their prime market adjacent urban areas.

The present chapter is concerned with resource-based land. It is here that the most serious conflicts arise between those who seek to enjoy the resource and those concerned, with varying motives, for its preservation. Their aims, though often seemingly opposed, are far from being incompatible, though it would be facile to suppose that all problems permit easy solution or that all claimants can be wholly satisfied.

The inevitable paradox was enshrined within the very legislation which created the National Parks in 1949, charging the nascent Commission with not only preserving and enhancing the natural beauty of the Park landscapes, but also providing opportunities for outdoor recreation within them. In so far as the quality of the recreational experience stems directly from the quality of the environment, the prime task is obviously one of conservation. President Kennedy, in a message to Congress in 1962, defined conservation as 'the wise use of our natural environment: it is, in the final analysis, the highest form of national thrift—the prevention of waste and despoilment while preserving, improving and renewing the quality and usefulness of all our resources'. These words have added weight in a British context, where population densities are so much higher and pressure on limited land resources correspondingly enhanced. They stress not only preservation but usefulness, quality through wise utilisation rather than sterile fossilisation.

Conservation can take many forms, each appropriate to particular circumstances. At one extreme, conservation may well mean the absolute preservation of a resource by the rigorous denial of any access or development. This can only rarely be justified on scientific or economic grounds, but when it is shown to be appropriate it must be complete to be effective. More typically in Britain in the last two decades, conservation has been pursued through development control in the planning process, control being exercised with varying rigour according to the status and the quality of the areas concerned. This approach is inevitably negative in concept: it can effectively prevent despoliation, but has only limited powers to stimulate more positive utilisation.

So far as outdoor recreation is concerned, it was the recognition of this inadequacy and the need for more creative measures which lay behind the Countryside Act of 1968. The Countryside Commission has a much wider area of responsibility than its precursor, the National Parks Commission, for no longer are its activities confined to the designated Parks alone but it is charged in the Act with keeping under review all matters relating to:

(a) the provision and improvement of facilities for the enjoyment of the countryside,
(b) the conservation and enhancement of the natural beauty and amenity of the countryside, and

(c) the need to secure public access to the countryside for the purposes of open-air recreation, and shall . . . encourage, assist, concert or promote the implementation of any proposals with respect to those matters made by any person or body, being proposals which the Commission consider to be suitable.

The Act also conferred new powers on local authorities 'for the purpose of providing, or improving, opportunities for the enjoyment of the countryside by the public'. The full exercise of these powers lies in the future, but their existence implies a view of the whole countryside as a resource for conservation in the fullest sense of the term. Increasing pressures and increasing mobility have tended to blur the distinction between resource-based and user-oriented facilities, but it is these same pressures which make the recognition of that distinction even more imperative and the task of conservation both more complex and more necessary.

In the following discussion of resource-based facilities, two main themes will be pursued. Firstly, the degree of protection accorded to the resource itself must be considered, the ownership and administrative mechanisms involved. Secondly, there is the extent to which the area concerned satisfies recreation demands and in particular the degree of access which is afforded.

NATURE RESERVES

At one extreme lies land which is managed as a living museum of natural history and where the key to successful conservation may be the almost total exclusion of human access for other than strictly scientific purposes or under very carefully controlled conditions.

The creation of nature reserves mirrors the pattern of the whole concern for conservation in this country. Victorian industrialisation and its concomitant urbanisation, limited though they were in areal extent, alerted the attention of pioneers. The first formal move towards active conservation was the founding of the Society for the Protection of Birds in 1889, a body which received its Royal Charter in 1904.[5] In 1895, the National Trust was created: though a concern with conservation was incidental to its prime purpose, among its early properties were the nature reserves of Wicken Fen (1899) and Blakeney Point (1912). In Edwardian times came a quickening interest in ecology, the study of plants and subsequently animals in their habitat as such, rather than as isolated specimens. In 1912, the Society for the Promotion of Nature Reserves was established. In 1915 it submitted a schedule to the Board of Agriculture of areas thought worthy of designation as nature reserves, and in 1919 itself acquired Woodwalton Fen in Huntingdonshire.

Between the wars concern and voluntary action gained impetus, spurred by the rapid extension of the urban area, by increased afforestation and by agricultural change. In 1926, the Norfolk Naturalists Trust was created. This was the first of the County Trusts whose full flowering was to come thirty years later, and which are not simply local natural history societies, but have as a primary object the acquisition and management of local nature reserves. But this was still a minority concern, thought of by many as 'the attempt by a few rather eccentric sentimentalists to safeguard a hobby'.[6]

Official recognition and action belong to the post-war period, prompted by the stimulus for thinking which the war itself provided. In 1941, a conference convened by the Society for the Promotion of Nature Reserves established a Nature Reserves Investigation Committee which published reports recommending specific areas as National Nature Reserves. The Scott Report of 1942[7] advised the creation of nature reserves for which 'prohibition of access shall be a first consideration'. In 1945, the Government appointed the Wild Life Conservation Special Committee, whose report published in 1947 (Cmnd 7122) contained a list of proposed National Nature Reserves in England and Wales.

The result of this prompting and thinking was the foundation of the Nature Conservancy in 1949 with one of its functions 'to establish, maintain and manage nature reserves in Great Britain, including the maintenance of physical features of scientific interest'.[8] In November 1951, the first National Nature Reserve was declared, Beinn Eighe in the Highlands of Scotland, and in March 1954, the first in England at Scolt Head on the Norfolk Coast. The Conservancy pursued its tasks with great energy and devotion. By September 1958 there were seventy National Nature Reserves, covering 133,081 acres. Despite some management problems, acquisition was pursued with vigour, for the threat to many habitats was increasingly plain. Agricultural mechanisation and the widespread use of pesticides and herbicides was having widespread repercussions on the whole rural scene, and evoked the Commission's timely statement to the Royal Commission on Common Land in 1956 that

the widely fashionable idea that it is a sign of progress to destroy and remould every reminder of the origins of our landscape and our rural economy may need to be reconsidered if posterity is not to view this generation's treatment of the countryside as harshly as we view the towns of the industrial revolution, about which the nineteenth century felt equally complacent.

By 1968, the Nature Conservancy (a component part of the Natural Environment Research Council since 1965) was responsible for 124 National Nature Reserves in Great Britain, covering 257,239 acres: of these, eighty-seven, covering 74,704 acres, were in England and Wales (Figure 56). Size alone is, of course, no indication of relative importance: it is easier to acquire extensive tracts in upland areas but many smaller lowland areas are at least equally significant.[9] The Reserves have been chosen

to protect landforms, habitats and associations of plants and animals rather than individual species. The aim is to maintain samples of the most important kinds of vegetation in Britain, with their associated animals.

Not all the land on which Reserves are sited is in the ownership of the Conservancy. Initially, the purchase or leasing of land was the quickest way to establish Reserves, but the Conservancy also had powers to make agreements with landowners to manage areas not actually held by the Conservancy. The first Reserve established by agreement dates from 1954: by 1968 over half the total acreage involved was managed under such agreements— 159,744 acres in Great Britain as a whole, and 31,323 acres in England and Wales.

In all the Reserves the prime emphasis is on conservation, and recreational use is incidental. Nevertheless, it is the Conservancy's policy to make their land accessible for the use and enjoyment of visitors whenever possible. Obviously this cannot be the case when visitors would themselves seriously disturb the ecological balance, or when the land belongs to a private owner whose rights, or those of his tenants, must be considered. Reserves are of widely

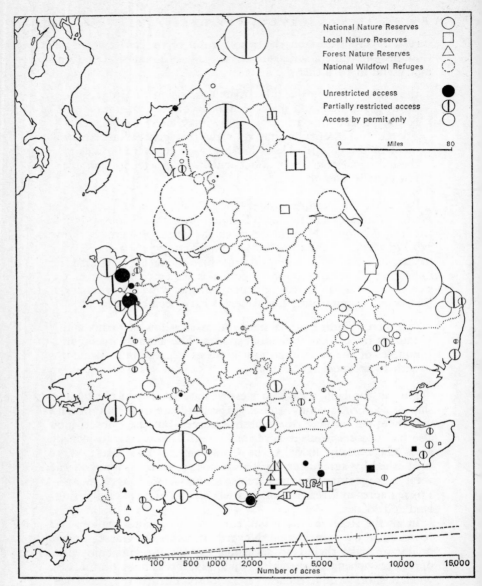

Fig 56. National, Local and Forest Nature Reserves and National Wildfowl Refuges (data from *The Nature Conservancy Handbook*. The categories of access shown have been derived from the details given in the Handbook, which are more varied than this simplified classification suggests. 'Partially restricted access' means in general access only along existing rights of way or marked paths. Categories of access have not been distinguished for the National Wildfowl Refuges).

differing types, and conditions of access vary equally, but a broad distinction can be drawn between those where access is unrestricted, those where access is normally restricted to existing rights of way or marked trails, and those where a permit is required before visiting.

Much of the recreational use is directly concerned with nature study, and the Nature Conservancy has shown an increasing awareness of its educational role. This interest is not entirely selfless: it enables the public to see what they are paying to conserve and the necessity for this; it tends, by providing facilities and increasing understanding, to enlarge public respect and reduce damage; it also provides information on the impact of people themselves on rural areas. Nature trails are particularly useful: the Conservancy has actively developed them since 1963 and by 1967 had thirteen on Reserves in England and Wales. At Old Winchester Hill in Hampshire, 10,000 copies of the trail leaflet were distributed in ten weeks in 1967.[10]

As many Reserves are in coastal or mountain areas, they are frequently attractive for more general recreational purposes. Problems can arise where conservation and recreation co-exist. The use of Great Dun Fell, in the northern Pennines and a part of the Moor House Reserve, is a case in point: as the second highest Pennine fell, its snow-fields have attracted increasing attention from skiers who have become a potential hazard to existing experimental work. Compromise agreements have been reached to limit the area used for ski-ing for a trial period.

In some cases, the Reserve itself has been created to conserve an area in danger of physical deterioration through over-intensive recreational use. The sand dunes at Ainsdale on the Lancashire coast had suffered much erosion in this way and wild life, including Sand Lizards and Natterjack Toads, had been seriously disturbed. A 1,216 acre Reserve was declared in 1965: the foreshore has remained freely accessible to visitors, but within the Reserve they are now restricted to the one public footpath and other designated walks.

The National Nature Reserves are not the only reserves, albeit the most important. Forest Nature Reserves are afforested areas already in public ownership and with a high scientific value: they are managed by informal agreements between their owners and the Natural Environment Research Council. Wildfowl Refuges are sanctuaries for the protection of wild geese and duck, the result of agreements reached between organised wildfowlers on the one hand and bird-protectionists on the other, recognising a common interest in the conservation of stocks of wildfowl. Local Nature Reserves are those established by county or county borough councils, and managed either by the councils themselves or by such nominees as county naturalists trusts. The county trusts have themselves also created their own reserves. Sites of Special Scientific Interest are areas which 'not being land for the time being managed as a nature reserve, is of special interest by reason of its flora, fauna or geological or physiographical features': these must be notified by the NERC to the local planning authority, who in turn must inform the Council if any development is proposed. There are some 2,000 such sites in Great Britain, including even roadside verges with uncommon species or unusually attractive communities of more familiar flowers. The protection afforded is not always as rigorous as might be desired, but preserves interesting sites from the grosser forms of despolia- tion.

THE NATIONAL TRUST

Conservation of a very different kind is the concern of the National Trust. The events which led to its creation in 1895 were traced in Chapter 1. It sprang from an enlightened enthusiasm and an attitude which were typical of their era. Victorian materialism posed many challenges to the scenic and architectural heritage of the country but, though opposition to desecration was frequent and intense, there was no mechanism for positive pre- servation. The solution sought by Hunter, Rawnsley and Octavia Hill did not envisage paternal intervention by a govern- ment agency, but the creation of 'a corporate body, capable of holding land, and representative of national institutions and interests'. Accordingly, 'The National Trust for Places of Historic Interest and Natural Beauty' was registered under the Companies Act on 12 January 1895, its Articles of Association approved by the Board of Trade, with licence as a non-profit making body to omit 'Limited' from its title.[11]

The aims of the infant Trust appealed to a small but dedicated group. By 1923, when the Trust owned 102 properties, it still had only 825 members. Its importance was growing however, and one symbol of this was increasingly strict standards in the selection of properties. By 1939, the Trust controlled 410 properties and

58,900 acres and more significant than this measure of the scale of its activities was its concern with a widening range of activities. Of these, the most important was to be the Country House Scheme made feasible by the 1937 Act. It had been evident from the 1920s that many country houses would soon be in jeopardy, the finances of their owners crippled by taxation and estate duty. The new scheme allowed the owners of houses of outstanding or architectural interest to transfer the freehold to the Trust, together with an endowment for upkeep in the form of a capital sum or rent-producing land. Under the special legislation, both property and endowment are exempt from death duty, and the income derived by the Trust from the endowment is tax-free. The donor, and his heirs or assigns, can continue to occupy the property, subject to public access on specified days. The scheme ensures the preservation of important properties, and as homes not museums, while allowing visitors to see the gardens and interiors. The first property acquired under the scheme was Blickling Hall in Norfolk in 1940, together with the 4,500 acre estate. Subsequently, the pace of acquisition rapidly quickened as owners grasped this lifebelt proffered, in Robin Fedden's words, 'when problems of money and management become insuperable'. It must, of course, be emphasised that the Trust is under no obligation to accept properties offered this way: only when the building concerned is deemed of sufficient importance and the endowment adequate is the offer taken up. The net result, however, was that the Trust was no longer associated primarily with open spaces but the dual purposes enshrined in its original title became of equal importance.

Since 1945, scope and activities have multiplied tremendously, a reminder of G. M. Trevelyan's words that 'the importance of the Trust is a measure of the constant diminution of all that is lovely and solitary in Britain'. In 1945 the Trust owned 112,000 acres and 93 historic buildings: by 1969 these totals had risen to 356,000 and over 200 respectively.[12] The Gardens Scheme of 1948 enabled gardens such as those at Bodnant in the Conway valley, or Sheffield Park in Sussex to be incorporated in a way similar to country houses. In the late 1950s, concern for vanishing industrial monuments led to a new type of acquisition of which the first, in 1959, was the southern section of the Stratford-upon-Avon Canal. Another concern was the rapid encroachment of development on the coast: following a survey in 1962–3, Enterprise Nep-

tune was launched on its stormy way in 1965. In many ways, the
most important change of all has been the more than twenty-fold
increase in membership—from 7,850 in 1945 to the present total
of over 160,000. This increase seems to reflect a more widespread
concern with the basic objectives of the Trust, the Trust's his-
torian considering that 'the most active support comes from
suburbia, from modest people who since the last war have discovered in motor cars the pleasures and beauties of the coast and
countryside'. Popularity is seen to have its dangers:

> The tail has been known to wag the dog. The Trust did great
> things with less than a thousand members, and set high
> standards. Any lowering of these standards, any compromise
> in deference to a vast membership and the irrelevant pres-
> sures that such a membership might exert, would in the long
> run undermine its authority and hazard its future.[13]

This comment emphasises the curious nature of the Trust as a
'peculiarly English institution in that it fulfils a national need without being in any way part of the State'.[14] The internal strains of
that institution are no part of the present study, but the consequent reassertion of its aims in the Benson Report of 1968 is of
prime importance in considering its contribution to recreation.

The present distribution of land and properties is shown on
Figures 57 and 58. In areal terms, the Trust now has a share of
about 1 per cent of the total area of England and Wales and is
the largest single landowner after the Crown and the State.
Ownership is far from being evenly dispersed over the country
as a whole, but reflects both opportunity and the nature and extent of existing pressure.

Many of the early acquisitions were in Kent, Surrey and the
Lake District where the founding trinity lived. Interest has now
moved away from the Home Counties where few areas of adequate quality remain, though the value of what was achieved at
places like Hindhead and Box Hill continues. In the Lake District early enthusiasm—and early need—has been maintained. At
present, the Trust owns or controls some 90,000 acres, one-sixth
of the National Park (Figure 59). Much of that ownership is
exercised at the very heart of the area and its influence is therefore more marked than the statistics alone would suggest.
Emphasis in ownership has varied with need. Early pressures were
concentrated on the lakesides. Rail access not only focused tourist

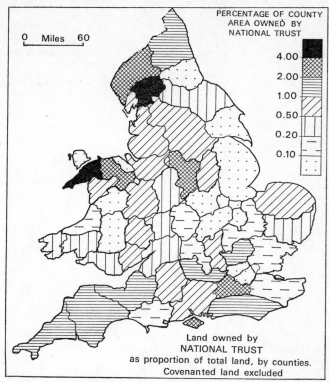

Fig 57. Land owned by the National Trust (data from *The properties of the National Trust*).

attention here, but brought wealthy businessmen to live and commute in 'club' trains between Windermere and Manchester. Hotels and villas began to dot the shores, and Trust purchases sought to forestall undue encroachment. From 1929, emphasis shifted to the upper reaches of the dales, as the motor car enhanced accessibility and brought new pressures. The most recent phase seeks to spread and manage continuing pressure. Further areas of lake shore and of the lower dales can draw the public from over-crowded areas: at Fell Foot, for example, at the south-east corner of Windermere, carefully-sited camping sites for both tents and caravans, canoe and sailing clubs and a café cater for some aspects

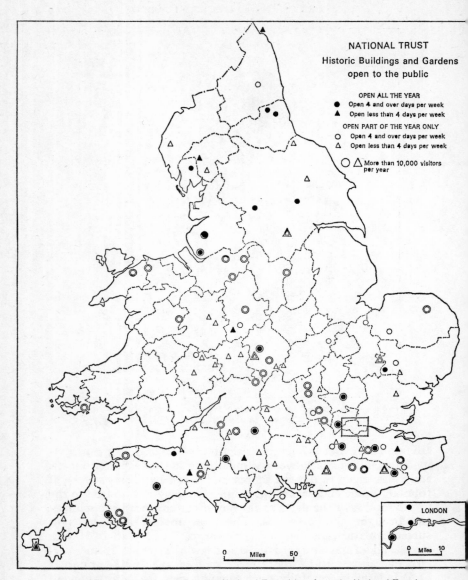

NATIONAL TRUST
Historic Buildings and Gardens
open to the public

OPEN ALL THE YEAR
● Open 4 and over days per week
▲ Open less than 4 days per week

OPEN PART OF THE YEAR ONLY
○ Open 4 and over days per week
△ Open less than 4 days per week

◯ △ More than 10,000 visitors per year

● LONDON

Fig 58. Properties owned by the National Trust (data from the National Trust).

of active and gregarious recreation. The corollary is the acquisition of more remote areas for those who still seek solitude: the 874 acres of The Side, fronting the south shore of Ennerdale Water and bought in 1949, are a case in point.

The nature of existing land ownership has conditioned attitudes to acquisition. The Trust's experience suggests that where great landlords still hold sway the danger to the existing landscape is least and little purpose would be served by Trust intervention. This is the case for example in the East Riding, where the only Trust property is the Georgian Maister House within Hull itself. In Dorset much of the coast and hinterland are still part of large estates, and most of the 3,800 acres under Trust control in the county is concentrated on the western part of the coast where ownership is fragmented.

The great reservoir of land and property in the hands of the National Trust is of incalculable value for recreation. It must be emphasised, however, that this use is, in a sense, incidental: in the words of John Bailey, Chairman 1923–31, 'preservation may always permit of access, while without preservation access becomes forever impossible'. The extent, and nature, of access has long been a vexed question. The present Chairman, the Earl of Antrim, reiterated the theme at the annual meeting in 1967:

> Our primary responsibility is the preservation of places of historic interest or natural beauty. It is also our duty to give public access to these places, but we are not designed as a money-making concern which wishes, at the expense of preservation, to have the maximum number of visitors to our properties. We are not part of the tourist industry. In a way, this makes our job, which is essentially conservation, all the more difficult.

Nonetheless, there is uninterrupted access to some 200,000 acres of Trust land, and 156 of its historic buildings are open to the public. Much of the remaining land is tenanted farmland where access would obviously provoke crop damage and its visual preservation may indeed be the prime requirement from a recreational point of view.

No tally can be kept of the number of visitors to the open spaces, but a few suffer from acute pressure. The problem is limited in extent, but severe where it does occur at places like Clumber Park or Runnymede.[15] Indeed, the Benson Report

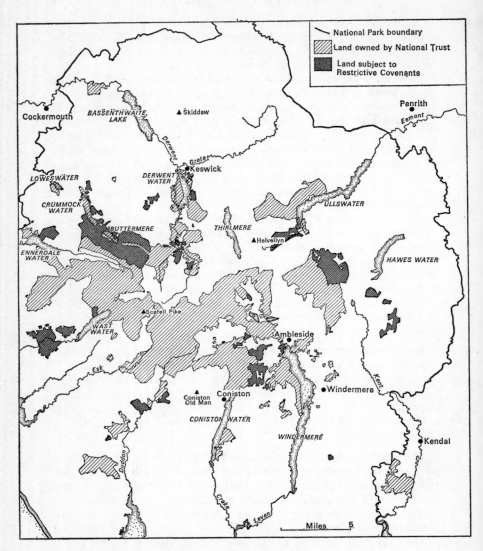

Cockermouth

Penrith

BASSENTHWAITE LAKE

▲ Skiddaw

Eamont

Derwent

LOWESWATER

Greta

● Keswick

DERWENT WATER

ULLSWATER

CRUMMOCK WATER

THIRLMERE

BUTTERMERE

▲ Helvellyn

ENNERDALE WATER

HAWES WATER

▲ Scafell Pike

WAST WATER

● Ambleside

Esk

Kent

▲ Coniston Old Man

● Coniston

● Windermere

CONISTON WATER

● Kendal

WINDERMERE

Dudon

Crake

Leven

Miles   5

Fig 59.   Land owned by the National Trust in the Lake District, 1968 (data from North-Western Area Agent of the National Trust).

stressed that 'the Trust may in extremity be forced to control access by rationing at certain properties if the number of visitors continues to increase as it has in the last decade',[16] though this would only be necessary at peak periods.

Access to historic buildings presents parallel problems. Pressure is extremely uneven in time and place. In 1967, the visitors to National Trust properties at which admission records are kept numbered 2,418,706, in addition to 150,999 visits by members of the Trust themselves. The totals at individual places (paying members and visitors) varied from 180,485 at Chartwell, and 138,518 to the grounds at Tatton House and 124,879 to the House itself, to less than 500 at eleven properties.[17] Obviously, individual places have a varied (and not always predictable) public appeal, but to some degree the problem stems from the limited access permitted at many properties (Figure 60). It is the Trust's policy that its houses should, as far as possible, be lived in and cared for as a family home and that a reasonable degree of privacy should be available for the residents. Many early agreements with donors called for very limited access: prior to the mid-1950s, the Trust 'was generally well satisfied if donor-occupied or tenanted houses, or their gardens, were opened on two afternoons a week . . . from 1st April to the end of September'.[18] In changed conditions, this is no longer considered adequate, but existing agreements must be honoured. The Trust now tries to ensure opening on four days a week as a minimum, one of the days being a Saturday or Sunday.

The National Trust has been examined in some detail, not only because of the inherent importance the extent and character of its properties command, but because it illustrates so clearly many of the problems in trying to reconcile conservation and access for recreation. It also emphasises the inherently unequal impact of demand. Many of its resources are under-used while a very few are subject to serious extremes of pressure. The need for dispersal is self-evident, if the means of achieving it are not easy to find. In Robin Fedden's words:

The putative airman and buzzard . . . look down indifferently on properties that seem to stir like anthills or that preserve an almost Saxon solitude. The Trust's aim must be to spread the load . . . There is little danger in this. Solitude will always remain for those who wish to find it.[19]

M

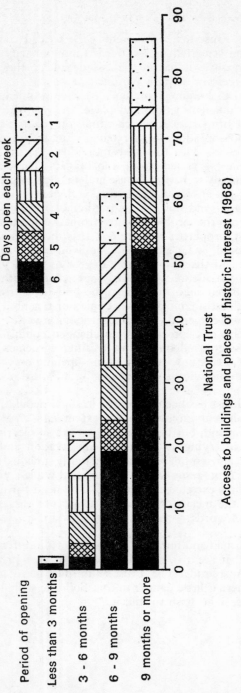

Fig 60. Access to National Trust properties (data from *The Benson Report on the National Trust*).

ANCIENT MONUMENTS AND HISTORIC BUILDINGS

Similar problems of varied pressure confront the Ministry of Public Buildings and Works in the monuments and historic buildings in its care. These monuments are of very varying character[20] and are widely distributed throughout the country (Figure 61). The basic aim of the Ministry in this respect is again to preserve a heritage rather than provide facilities for recreation, but many of the monuments are the object, or an incidental part, of a day's outing. In 1967, over eight and a half million visits were made to monuments in England and Wales where there was a charge for admission, compared with just under six and a half million in 1963. For many monuments of a comparatively minor nature there is no admission charge and there is therefore no record of the total number of visits to sites.

Access as such does not present the same problems as confront the National Trust, for apart from a few historic buildings and the three Royal Palaces,[21] the monuments are basically unoccupied and can be open every day throughout the year. Variations in attendance, however, are equally marked. In 1967, of the 177 monuments at which a charge was levied, forty-four had less than 5,000 visitors in the year while thirty-four exceeded 50,000. The former total would, of course, have been much greater if sites where access is free had been included. The variations are not always in accord with the quality of the monument. Setting and accessibility obviously have a part to play, and monuments in or near holiday areas benefit accordingly. In Wales, Caernarvon, Conway and Harlech Castles, and Tintern Abbey, all exceed 100,000 visitors annually, as do Carisbrooke, Dover, Scarborough and Tintagel Castles, Fountains Abbey and Stonehenge, in England.[22] Association is also a stimulus, as the crowds who flocked to Caernarvon Castle in the summer of 1969 after the Investiture bear witness. It is not purely a distinction in scale or inherent interest which brings Caernarvon Castle over 250,000 visitors in a normal year, while the Roman remains at nearby Segontium were viewed only by 5,000. Criccieth can scarcely compare with Caerphilly in grandeur as a ruin, but set in a holiday resort can receive nearly double the number of visitors. Many equally pointed contrasts could be made, but in this context at least the extent of use does not match the degree of conservation.

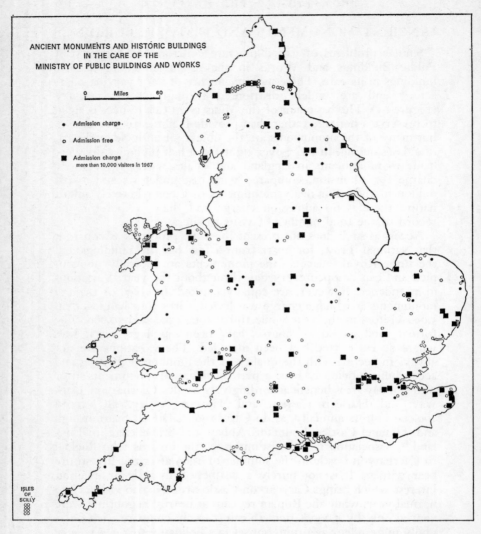

ANCIENT MONUMENTS AND HISTÓRIC BUILDINGS
IN THE CARE OF THE
MINISTRY OF PUBLIC BUILDINGS AND WORKS

0   Miles   60

• Admission charge

o Admission free

■ Admission charge
   more than 10,000 visitors in 1967

ISLES
OF
SCILLY

Fig 61. Ancient monuments and historic buildings in the care of the Ministry of Public Building and Works (data from the Ministry of Public Building and Works).

NATIONAL PARKS

In the types of land and property so far discussed, conservation has been seen in absolute terms, involving direct ownership or control and recreation as almost an additional accrued benefit. In the remaining categories of resource to be discussed the concept of conservation is a very different one, the preservation of visual amenity largely through planning designation and not through the positive management which ownership makes possible. Indeed ownership on this scale would scarcely be feasible, for the area concerned is some two-fifths of the country as a whole (Figure 62).

National Parks have been a reality in England and Wales for only two decades but the vision they embody goes far further back in time. In 1835, Wordsworth could declare that 'the Lake District should be deemed a sort of National property in which every man has a right and interest who has an eye to perceive and a heart to enjoy'.[23] The heart of the problem however lies in the very phrase 'National property': with no great reservoir of land in national ownership, any concept of a park in the direct sense of land primarily devoted to outdoor recreation is, except on the smallest of scales, beyond the realms of financial and political expediency. In 1892, Yellowstone Park was established in the USA, but with an area of 3,350 square miles (almost half the size of Wales) of virtually uninhabited forest it could form no prototype for a British counterpart.

In the nineteenth century, concern was with specific abuses and, with the founding of the National Trust, the acquisition of land and property with high amenity value. Unsuccessful attempts were made from 1884 to secure the passage through Parliament of legislation to give access to mountains and moorland but there was no concerted attempt to secure the visual preservation of large tracts of terrain. After 1918, increased mobility not only posed new threats, but brought a more widespread awareness of rural areas as a scenic resource. The formation in 1926 of the Council for the Preservation of England created what has been aptly termed 'the conscience of a nation confronted with the increasing disfigurement of its countryside',[24] and from its earliest days the Council was an enthusiastic advocate of National Parks. In 1931 the Addison Committee recommended to the govern-

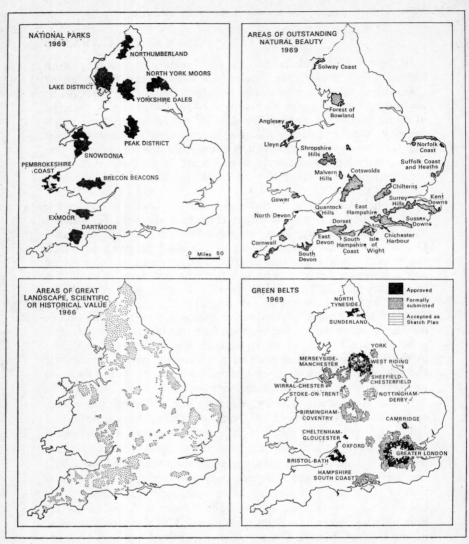

NATIONAL PARKS 1969

NORTHUMBERLAND
NORTH YORK MOORS
LAKE DISTRICT
YORKSHIRE DALES
PEAK DISTRICT
SNOWDONIA
PEMBROKESHIRE COAST
BRECON BEACONS
EXMOOR
DARTMOOR

0 Miles 50

AREAS OF OUTSTANDING NATURAL BEAUTY 1969

Solway Coast
Forest of Bowland
Anglesey
Lleyn
Norfolk Coast
Shropshire Hills
Suffolk Coast and Heaths
Malvern Hills
Cotswolds
Chilterns
Gower
Surrey Hills
Kent Downs
Quantock Hills
East Hampshire
North Devon
Sussex Downs
Dorset
Cornwall
East Devon
South Hampshire Coast
Isle of Wight
Chichester Harbour
South Devon

AREAS OF GREAT LANDSCAPE, SCIENTIFIC OR HISTORICAL VALUE 1966

GREEN BELTS 1969

Approved
Formally submitted
Accepted as Sketch Plan

NORTH TYNESIDE
SUNDERLAND
YORK
MERSEYSIDE-MANCHESTER
WEST RIDING
SHEFFIELD-CHESTERFIELD
WIRRAL-CHESTER
STOKE-ON-TRENT
NOTTINGHAM-DERBY
BIRMINGHAM-COVENTRY
CAMBRIDGE
CHELTENHAM-GLOUCESTER
OXFORD
GREATER LONDON
BRISTOL-BATH
HAMPSHIRE SOUTH COAST

Fig 62. Conservation land (based on a map by the Ministry of Housing and Local Government used with the permission of the Controller of HMSO). No data later than 1966 are available for areas of Great Landscape, Scientific or Historical Value, but such areas have been deleted from this map if they have subsequently been designated as Areas of Outstanding Natural Beauty.

ment in favour of establishing National Parks,[25] but financial crisis effectively shelved the report.

As with conservation in a narrower sense, the Second World War gave welcome opportunity for reviewing the future of the concept in the light of the opportunities of post-war reconstruction. The Scott Committee in 1942 recommended the establishment of National Parks and substance was given to the idea in John Dower's Report of 1945.[26] Dower defined them as

> An extensive area of beautiful and relatively wild country in which, for the nation's benefit and by appropriate national decision and action:
> (a) the characteristic landscape beauty is strictly preserved;
> (b) access and facilities for public open air enjoyment are amply provided;
> (c) wild life and buildings and places of architectural and historic interest are suitably protected, while
> (d) established farming use is effectively maintained.

This report was closely followed by the Hobhouse Report of 1947 which envisaged a National Parks Committee with twelve National Parks each with its own Park Committee as the statutory local planning authority.[27]

Legislative form was given to these ideas in the National Parks and Access to the Countryside Act of 1949. Between 1950 and 1955 ten Parks were designated which between them cover 5,258 square miles, 9 per cent of the total area of England and Wales. There is no need to describe each Park in detail, for their particular beauties are well enough loved and known. With the exception of the Pembrokeshire Coast, they are predominantly upland areas and include most of the extensive tracts of land over 1,000 feet high. Of the areas suggested in the Hobhouse Report, the Norfolk Broads and the South Downs have not been included: there have been no further designations since 1955, though a mid-Wales Park has been mooted.[28]

It is important to emphasise the real nature of the Parks. It has been unkindly said that they are neither 'Parks' nor 'National', and there is a very real sense in which this is true. In the first place, very little of the Parks is public domain. They must support an existing population of some 260,000 in the normal pursuits of rural life; farming, rural industry and forestry. They include much actively cultivated land around their margins and in their valleys, a wider area than John Dower's 'relatively wild country'. It has been estimated, for example, that of the 365 square miles of the Dartmoor National Park, 170 square miles are cultivated farmland[29] where public access is largely restricted to the traditional rights of way; roads, bridle paths and footpaths.

In open country, the position is different though the appropriate legislation is not confined to the Parks alone. Under the 1949 Act, planning authorities were required to make an access survey of land in their area which was technically 'open country', that is 'mountain, moor, heath, down, cliff or foreshore' and then consider what action, if any, should be taken to secure public access to such land either by agreement with owners or by orders if agreement cannot be reached. Cultivated and afforested land was expressly excluded from this definition of open country. These powers have been used sparingly. In many cases the public has long enjoyed de facto access to the uplands with the minimum of hindrance. The problems were greatest where shooting rights were concerned and by far the most widespread use of these powers has been made by the Peak Park Planning Board. Of the 61,347 acres subject to access agreements or acquired by local authorities for access in the National Parks and Areas of Outstanding Natural Beauty, 47,841 are in the Peak Park (Figure 63): the agreements specify that the moorland concerned shall be closed to the public on an agreed number of days during the grouse-shooting season. Many access problems remain and the Ramblers Association has pressed this cause with vigour.[30] Increased numbers seeking remote areas undoubtedly generate and harden opposition by farmers to public use of their land and the review of the need for access rights needs to be a continuing process. But whether access is de facto or de jure, only a comparatively small proportion of the area of National Parks can be considered truly as 'parks' in the usually accepted sense of the term, though their simple visual attraction over a much wider area must not be readily discounted (Figure 64).

Administratively, the Parks are scarcely National in concept. The National Parks Act in no way replaced the existing machinery of planning under the Town and Country Planning Act of 1947. Planning control within the Parks remained in the hands of local authorities, though the care of each park was vested in a local Park committee. These committees take varied forms.

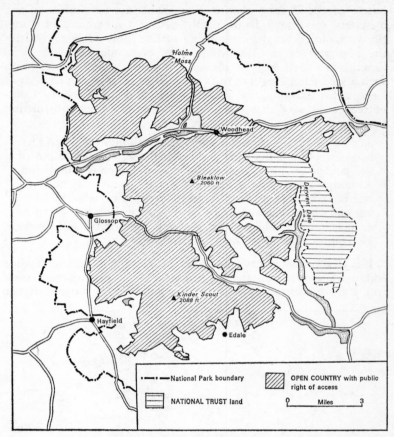

Fig 63.   Access land in the Peak District National Park.

In the first two Parks to be designated, the Peak and the Lake District, a joint planning board with executive powers was created. In the former case a separate planning staff was established and with John Foster as energetic Director and Planning Officer, until his resignation in 1968, a great deal was achieved. In the other Parks which covered parts of more than one county, joint advisory committees were established: [31] in those lying within the bounds of a single county, administration was through a committee of the county council.[32] In each case, two-thirds of the members are drawn from locally-elected councillors, and one-third appointed on the nomination of the Minister as advised by the National Parks Commission. The erstwhile National Parks Commission itself had an advisory, not an executive role. With such a structure, local interests are well to the fore. In its 1967/8 Report, for example, the Snowdonia Park Joint Advisory Committee could aver that one of the functions of its Information Services

. . . is to make visitors aware that, although the Park has been established for their recreational use, the prime use of the land it encloses is to support an indigenous population. Although tourism is an important activity within the Park, and contributes significantly to its economic viability, farming and forestry continue to be of greater importance to its economic life, while more recently electricity and water generation also make their contribution.

It is all too easy to cavil, however. Hamstrung by lack of finance and working through the normal process of development control, the administration of the Parks could be but little different

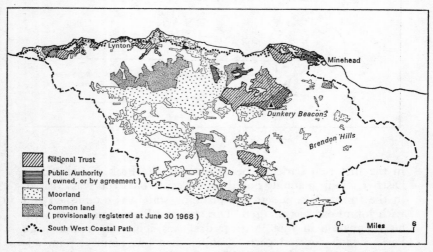

Fig 64. Access land in the Exmoor National Park (after *Access on Exmoor*, special supplement to the *Exmoor Review*, 1969).

from that of surrounding areas. Much of the achievement has been negative rather than positive, but none the less valuable for that in terms of conserving the scenic heritage. The visitor will not see the damage which has been prevented, the many hundreds of unsuitable visual intrusions for which planning permission has been refused. In the Lake District, for example, there were 1,117 applications for planning permission in 1966–7. Of these, 444 were dealt with by constituent District Councils after reference to the appropriate County Planning Officer, the remainder being referred to the Planning Board's Development Control Committee. The Board made 701 decisions during the year, 496 approvals and 205 refusals. Some of the refusals were the subject of subsequent appeals to the Ministry: of those where decisions were made in this year, only six were allowed, twenty-eight being dismissed and thirteen withdrawn. Refusals included applications for new and extended caravan sites, and for the laying out of a golf course on a typical Lakeland fellside at Shoulthwaite. In the last-named case, the Minister decided that

> golf would be an inappropriate use and that the possibility that a man-made change to the landscape would harm the magnificent natural beauty and adversely affect the character of the area was a risk which was too great to take.[33]

All this work involves patient vigilance and a careful balancing of the often-conflicting claims of visual amenity and the economic prosperity of the indigenous community.

RANGES, ROCKS AND RESERVOIRS

Other conflicts are more evident, larger in scale and seemingly intractable. The first group comprises uses to which the land in the Parks was put before designation and which affect both access to and the appearance of the landscape. Dartmoor is a classic instance. Parts have been used since 1875 for firing ranges and military training: more recently, Ministerial planning consent was given in 1948 for the use of some 40,000 acres for artillery ranges and other training purposes and the licence to use the Okehampton training area was renewed by the Duchy of Cornwall in 1956.[34] It was estimated that in 1968 the public was barred from parts of the Park because of Army and Royal Marine exercises for up to 100 days out of 147 during the main holiday

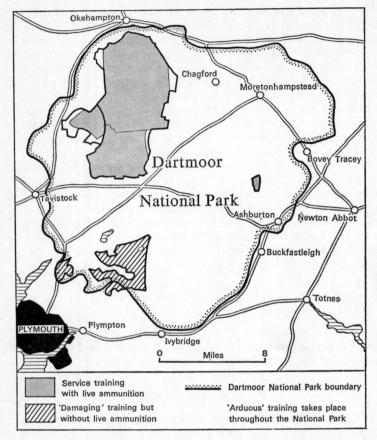

Fig 65. Service training in the Dartmoor National Park (after *Misuse of a National Park*).

season.[35] The Duchy Licences are renewable in 1970, but this present use of the moor denies continuous access to substantial tracts of open country (Figure 65).

The exploitation of mineral and water resources is another vexed issue, not least where existing uses are concerned. The area designated for Snowdonia excluded the three main areas of slate extraction, but in both the Peak District and the Yorkshire Dales limestone quarrying is of major importance. In the Peak, where the scale of operations is particularly great (limestone production increased by 62 per cent between 1954 and 1961), siting aids obscurity, for many workings are on the fringe of the Park or in the dales. The general policy is to approve extensions of existing workings subject to stringent conditions concerning working methods, the character and scale of restoration operations and the times at which blasting is carried out. At Hope, for example, Associated Portland Cement were given permission in 1968 to extend their cement works in order to double output, subject to a measure of landscaping and a scheme for ultimate rehabilitation of the site, to no increase in the volume of distribution by road (the additional cement being carried by rail), and blasting at agreed times: a new 400ft chimney was allowed, but an existing chimney of the same height was to be removed.[36]

Water abstraction generates more concern than any other issue: by means of their generally upland nature, the Parks contain many of the most advantageous gathering grounds in the country. In the Peak District, for example, there are fifty-one reservoirs within the present boundary of the National Park, and twenty-two more just outside: three of these have been made since the designation of the Park.[37] The general problem of reservoir siting and use must be viewed in a much broader context than that of the Parks alone, and will be considered in more detail in subsequent chapters, but outright opposition to all schemes is neither practicable nor desirable. The North York Moors National Park Planning Committee, for example, offered no objection in principle to the Yorkshire Ouse and Hull River Authority's 1969 proposal for a regulating reservoir impounding 8,000 million gallons in Farndale, though 'only quiet recreational pursuits such as fishing, sight-seeing and canoeing should be allowed': they 'doubt whether sailing should be allowed'.[38]

MISSILES AND MINERALS

A further group of conflicts are those which have arisen entirely since designation and which involve matters of major strategic or industrial concern, bringing alien intrusions without precedent into the Parks and against the expressed wishes of the National Parks Commission. These developments have naturally attracted much publicity and are so well known that little pur-

pose would be served in reliving the campaigns in detail. Defence
needs were paramount in the siting of the Fylingdales ballistic
missile early warning station in the North York Moors Park. The
decision to proceed was announced in February 1960: the
Government stated that the limits set by topographical, geographical and operational criteria were extremely stringent and
though the intrusion was 'greatly regretted', they were 'satisfied
that there is no other suitable site in the whole country'. The
special needs of the nuclear power programme led to the building of the Trawsfynydd nuclear power station in the Snowdonia
Park. The only inland station in the first phase of that programme,
it made use of the existing lake at Trawsfynydd to supply the
35 million gallons of cooling water needed hourly and had the
degree of isolation then deemed necessary on safety grounds.[39]
Despite the National Parks Commission's view that 'a nuclear
power station in such a setting could not appear other than a
huge and overmastering imposition' and the Ministry of Housing
and Local Government Inspector's view that 'my own judge-
ment leans strongly to the preservation of the National Park',
construction was authorised in July 1958. Despite careful landscaping, the completed power station dominates the landscape
from many directions, though it has a certain monumental appeal
of its own. Far more disfiguring are the associated pylons of the
overhead 275kV transmission lines.

In Pembrokeshire a resource of a very different kind has
yielded to industrial exploitation, the deep and sheltered waters
of the drowned estuary at Milford Haven. With the advent of
bulk ocean carriers, such relatively remote harbours have an
attraction hitherto gainsaid by their lack of industrial hinterland.
In November 1957 the Esso Petroleum Company was given permission to build an oil refinery, much of which is in the Pembrokeshire Coast National Park. In June 1958 the decision was
made to allow a large iron-ore stocking ground at Angle, south
of the Haven but within the boundary of the Park. Though the
Commission thought this 'totally at variance with the right use of
land in a National Park' the Minister did not feel that 'on the
balance of advantages in the national interest he would be justified
in refusing to grant . . . permission'.[40] Current controversy centres
around the extraction and processing of potash in the North York
Moors. Work began in April 1969 on the site at Boulby, near
Loftus and just inside the Park boundary, by Cleveland Potash,

a jointly-owned subsidiary of ICI and the Charter Consolidated Mining Company. In May 1970 the Minister approved, subject to conditions of 'unprecedented stringency', two further schemes in the Whitby area, schemes which unlike the Boulby mine had been opposed on amenity grounds by the Park Planning Committee.

Potash mining highlights the economic dilemma which underlies the development versus amenity conflict. The Boulby mine alone (which should be productive at the end of 1973) will produce between one and one and a half million tons of potash a year, with an estimated annual saving on the balance of payments of £14 million. Perhaps even more important in an area where the winter unemployment rate is between 8 and 13 per cent, it will provide up to 3,000 jobs during construction and 500 jobs once production begins. There will be visual intrusion—chimneys 200ft high cannot be hidden—though in an area which already has an industrial tradition from iron-ore mining days and is not far from the Skinningrove iron and steel works. The visual problems raised by the other two schemes are even greater.

Amenity is a value more readily perceived by the outside observer who is not in any way economically involved:

'Potash—Whitby's salvation' is how the town's only newspaper headlined its feelings. The unemployed of Whitby cannot exist on the beauty of the surrounding countryside and are prepared to accept this heavy chemical industry with all its drawbacks, both aesthetic and pollutive.[41]

The same writer goes on to say that if the country as a whole wishes to keep its National Parks inviolate it must be prepared to pay the price through the creation by the Government of light industry 'which will not pollute either the sea or the atmosphere and consistent in size and aesthetic appearance with the area'. The solution, however, is rarely so simple for the very isolation and remoteness, which is at the heart of the area's attraction, paradoxically repels industrial investment unless, as in the case of potash, a unique resource exists.

AGRICULTURE AND AFFORESTATION

These strategic and industrial concerns have been the classic conflicts of National Park policy, where the issues are clear cut and a choice, however unenviable, has to be made between conservation in a particular sense or development in the name of wider interests. More insidious but in a way even more important 'have been the widespread changes in appearance which have taken place over large areas of the National Parks in a way which is not only legal but beyond the direct control of their planning authorities.

Agriculture and afforestation were expressly excluded from development control in the 1947 Act, but changes in land-use can have far reaching visual effects. Moorland reclamation has been a particular problem on the North York Moors, Dartmoor and Exmoor. The ploughing and fencing of open country not only mars the attraction of an unbroken sweep of land, but restrains an access which may long have been enjoyed. On Exmoor, this has been of real concern. Here, the open moorland has been used traditionally for rough grazing, but farmers have been increasing the productivity of their holdings by improving this land for more intensive and controlled stocking. Ploughing and reseeding, or conversion of the existing sward by chemical treatment or direct seeding, have changed heather moor to intensively grazed grassland, while fencing permits that grazing to be controlled. The extent of change has been mapped by the Exmoor Society (Figure 66): between 1958 and 1966, the loss of moorland amounted to an average of 1,010 acres a year (898 acres to agriculture, 112 to forestry), or 1·7 per cent per annum of the 1958 total. At this rate, open moorland in private hands would completely disappear by the end of the century.

There are obviously two views of this situation. Farmers resent any 'unreasonable directions . . . which might in any way restrict their right—which is also their duty—to expand their enterprises and to improve their productive capacity to a maximum';[42] lovers of the area deplore the encroachment onto distinctive landscapes and the restriction of access this involves. The access problem was exacerbated by the legal situation under the 1949 Act, for land once ploughed became 'excepted land' and any access agreement was thereby terminated. This position has been changed by the provisions of the 1968 Countryside Act. Six months' notice must now be given of the intention to plough or otherwise reclaim land 'which is moor or heath which has not been agricultural land within the preceding twenty years' (Section 14), and this period can be used to come to some formal access arrangement if thought appropriate by the planning authorities. Additionally, access orders cannot now be abrogated unilaterally by cultivation (Section 17).

Afforestation raises further problems which will be considered in detail when the whole role of the Forestry Commission in outdoor recreation is discussed in the next chapter.

POSITIVE PROVISION

National Parks have so far been viewed only as areas where it is sought to conserve, within the limits of planning powers, land-

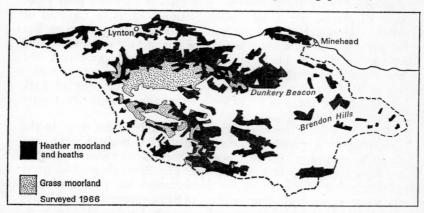

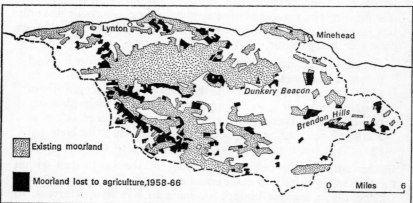

Fig 66.   Moorland losses in the Exmoor National Park (after *Can Exmoor survive?* diagrams II and IV).

N

scapes of high visual appeal. Despite their title, these are areas where positive provision for outdoor recreation is remarkably limited. Access is largely restricted to existing rights of way or to open uplands where the right of entry is de facto only in most cases. The casual motorist or walker will have little immediate evidence to suggest the particular status of the area beyond the signs where main roads are crossed by the Park boundaries. Many Britons have little concept of either the nature or the location of the Parks. In a 1961 survey, a decade after the first Parks were designated, only four of them were known by more than 5 per cent of the people asked 'What National Parks in England or Wales can you think of?' and none by more than 13 per cent. Yet 22 per cent named areas which were not in fact Parks in answer to the question.[43] There are many who would agree that 'the main activities of the park authorities so far have been the provision of car parks and caravan sites, and the erection of park symbols'[44] and that the list of positive schemes is 'impressive only for its modesty'.[45]

Such criticisms, however, ignore two fundamental facts. In the first place, the positive powers available to both the National Parks Commission and the local authorities concerned were, as we have seen, very limited in scope. The Parks themselves grew primarily out of a concern for conservation, the preservation of the more remote and beautiful areas of Britain from the visual blight which had been characteristic of so much development in inter-war Britain. The mass car-borne exodus to the countryside was only just beginning, the implications of the planning legislation of 1947 only just being absorbed. In one assessment .

> . . . the whole atmosphere in which the Commission has had to work has been very difficult for them. They sought to allay the fears of Local Authorities who suspected them initially of making an attempt to take away their planning powers. The Commission have . . . largely succeeded but at a cost of convincing the Local Authorities that the National Parks Act has made little or no difference to them.[46]

In this context, the continuing quality of the landscapes within the Parks is positive comment enough.

Secondly, a meagre budget has been an effective deterrent. In the first twelve years after 1949 an average of about £100,000 a year was spent on the National Parks, this including the costs of the National Parks Commission, Exchequer grants and local authority contributions for developments and the administrative costs incurred by local authorities. As the Commission itself remarked in its *Tenth Report* (1959),

> Over the past ten years, less than one penny per person *per year* has been spent in connection with National Parks. We do not believe that the public would be reluctant to spend, say, sixpence per person per year for the preservation and enhancement of our national heritage in the countryside . . . For in a sense the preservation of our countryside is a matter of pounds, shillings and pence.

Attitudes have slowly changed, a measure of increasing pressure and the Commission's own success in pressing the need for enhancement as well as preservation. The Countryside Act itself, with its emphasis on positive measures, and the transforming of the National Parks Commission into the Countryside Commission are evidence of a changing climate of opinion. In 1967–8, before the effects of impending legislation were felt, the National Parks Commission budget was £167,550 and the Park Authorities themselves spent £601,076,[47] though even these sums are derisory when compared with the opportunities. By the very nature of the administrative structure, partially submerged (except for the Peak Park Planning Board) in the constituent county offices, it is not possible to give a precise total of those employed in the management and development of the Parks, but the Commission's own staff of sixty-seven in April 1968 compares with the Nature Conservancy's 521 in May that year, with a budget of £1,326,000.

Enhancement of amenity however is still low on the national list of priorities. Governments are reluctant to grant finance and powers: as the first report of the Countryside Commission (1968) dolefully declares

> . . . positive action has been much restricted by financial stringency. The year's record contains a more than usually large number of projects which have been unavoidably postponed . . . We cannot . . . but be conscious that our effectiveness must necessarily be circumscribed by the unwillingness of the Government, in spite of repeated requests . . . to allow us an independent budget and less restricted executive powers.

OTHER DESIGNATED AREAS

The National Parks crystallise the problems—and the opportunities—of conservation through planning designation. The Parks, however, are only the apex of a pyramid of categories of designated land. Powers (and their implementation) vary, but it must again be stressed that recreation is often only incidental in these areas for it is the appearance of the countryside rather than its use which is principally at stake.

Areas of Outstanding Natural Beauty have been described as 'a lower tier of National Parks'.[48] Like National Parks, they are selected and designated by the National Parks Commission and its successor but they have no special administrative arrangements for their planning and the provisions of the National Parks Act relating to the development of open-air recreation do not apply, with the exception of access provision and warden service.

There are at present twenty-five areas, covering in all 4,291 square miles, some 7.3 per cent of the total area of England and Wales (Figure 62). They are mostly smaller in extent than National Parks and include less open land and more agricultural land, but many lie much nearer to major centres of population and are therefore subject to enhanced pressure in areas like the North and South Downs, the Chilterns, the Cotswolds and Cannock Chase. Designation is perhaps a formal reminder of their value rather than a positive incentive to action. Grants are available to local authorities of up to 75 per cent of the cost of carrying out improvements. Derelict structures can be cleared, trees planted and tree preservation orders made. There have been access agreements or acquisition of land for access in parts of the Surrey Hills, Cannock Chase, East Hampshire, Dorset and the Forest of Bowland, for example, and there are warden services in Cannock Chase, East Hampshire, the Surrey Hills and the Cotswolds. But over the areas as a whole, positive action has been comparatively small and the main impact (and by far the most important) the maintenance of appearance through development control. The problems and the opportunities these areas afford were underlined by a study of the East Hampshire AONB carried out jointly by the Hampshire Council, the Countryside Commission, the Nature Conservancy, the Ministry of Agriculture and the Forestry Commission[49] where a careful evaluation was made of resources and activities in the broadest sense within the chosen area and a plan developed which recognised 'the need for a more positive and co-ordinated approach to rural planning'.

Lower in the pyramid of conservation are Areas of Great Landscape, Historic or Scientific Value. In this instance, selection and designation were the prerogative of the local planning authority under the 1947 Town and Country Planning Act, who could propose such areas in their development plans for ministry approval. This has only a nominal value as a conservation measure. The areas attract no grants for improvements on amenity grounds, nor need the Countryside Commission be consulted about any proposed development. Designation, however, should be a concern when the planning authority consider the effect on the landscape of any application for development.

Green belts are perhaps the most familiar form of designation, for in encircling towns they impinge most closely on urban living. The basic concept of attempting to contain urban growth by surrounding it with a belt of open land has a long history. In 1580, Queen Elizabeth I forbade by royal proclamation any new building on a new site within three miles of the city gates of London, with the avowed purposes of ensuring abundant cheap food and of mitigating the effects of an outbreak of plague.[50] The growth of London remained a concern, but not until the present century was there effective legislation. The scale of sprawl between the wars demanded action. In 1927 the Greater London Regional Planning Committee was established: their technical adviser, Sir Stanley Unwin, urged the need to reserve land for recreation, to create not simply an agricultural belt but 'a girdle of open space to provide a reserve for the deficiency of playing fields near the centre'.[51] Action was shelved in the ensuing years of economic depression, but in 1935 the London County Council began to use its own somewhat limited powers to establish 'a green belt or girdle of open space lands'. These powers were enhanced by the Green Belt (London and Home Counties) Act of 1938 and by means of these two schemes some 35,500 acres have been kept open.

The 1947 Town and Country Planning Act, with its mechanism of development control, gave added powers. The London Green Belt, embodied in the development plans of the local planning authorities, was extended to between six and ten miles across. In 1955 the Minister of Housing and Local Government asked local authorities to consider establishing clearly defined green belts where they were desirable. The accompanying circular listed three types of situation where a green belt was appropriate:

(*a*) to check the growth of a large built-up area;
(*b*) to prevent neighbouring towns from merging into one another; or
(*c*) to preserve the special character of a town.

Figure 62 illustrates the present extent of Green Belts.

From the point of view of recreation, the prime purpose of a green belt must be clearly recognised. In the words of the Ministry of Housing and Local Government's explanatory book,

> The function of a green belt as a place for the recreation and enjoyment of the townsman is well understood. It differs from, though it does not conflict with, its function as a means of shaping the expansion of a town or group of towns. The former may have more appeal *but the latter is the primary purpose of a green belt.*

The italics are the author's, but their import is clear, for the green belt is primarily a mechanism for the regulation of urban growth. Whether a rigid ring is the best mechanism for this purpose may be open to question, but is beyond the present intention to discuss. The fact remains that 'the inclusion of land in a green belt does not give the public any rights of access which they would not otherwise enjoy'.

Obviously, green belts have an active recreational use and most include commons or other open space.[52] Again, they should provide a valuable visual amenity within easy access. But this usage is largely incidental and only rarely deliberately created, yet this is the very area where a very large segment of demand could most easily be satisfied, as earlier chapters have shown. We shall return to this theme again, for it is one of the most crucial in the whole relationship between the demand and supply of land for outdoor recreation.

THE COAST

In many ways, the coast is Britain's most important resource from a recreational point of view. With no part of England and Wales more than seventy-five miles from tidal water, the coast is easy of access and satisfies a very large part of the total demand for outdoor recreation. As has already been seen, one-fifth of half-day trips, one-third of day trips and three-quarters of all holidays have the seaside as their destination.

To match this demand, there is a coastline some 2,742 miles long.[53] Put more dramatically, this represents a shade over $3\frac{1}{2}$ inches of coast for every man, woman and child in the country. Happily, demand at peak periods is not yet absolute, and the shore itself has breadth as well as length, but it does at least highlight the very real pressures which exist.

These pressures are of two distinct kinds. The first has led to increasingly rapid development and urbanisation. In part this is inimical to recreation. Cases in point are the expansion of port facilities and the growth of associated towns; the use of extensive tracts of estuarine land for oil refineries and other major industrial installations; and the siting of many recent power stations, both conventional and nuclear, on the coast because of the shortage of cooling water inland. Defence needs also take their toll, often with the complete exclusion of the general public: 134 miles of coast are devoted to this and similar Government uses.[54] Other development stems directly or indirectly from recreation itself. The expansion of resorts, particularly many of the smaller ones, has resulted not only from the growth of holidaymaking as such but from the attractions of the resorts as places for retirement[55] and above all from the increasing demand for second homes, whether cottages, chalets or caravans in coastal areas. It is the pace as well as the scale of these developments which is striking. A Lindsey County Council survey, for example, showed that in 1951 there were 4,250 static caravans, shacks and chalets along the Lincolnshire coast: by 1962 the number had increased to 14,250.[56]

The opposing pressure is that which seeks to preserve the coast as far as possible in its natural or semi-natural state. This stems from a desire to conserve scenic amenity, a desire quickened by the rate at which deleterious development has been taking place. Conservation, however, may conflict with recreation. At one extreme, intensive use can lead to increasing disturbance of the ecological balance. One remedy may be the creation of a coastal nature reserve or wildfowl refuge (Figure 56) but this is only possible, or indeed desirable, in a limited number of instances. For the remainder, the resolution of conflict calls for the skilled exercise of development control but, though most of the necessary powers are available to local authorities, they have not always been used adequately or consistently. Indeed, opinions will naturally differ as to the right course to pursue in reconciling pressures, for development may well yield revenue as well as satisfy many interests. In the words of one partisan statement, 'many [local authorities] have encouraged and all have permitted development upon it and thus all have contributed in varying degree to its ultimate total ruin'.[57]

As in so many matters of conservation, isolated action before 1914 was replaced by increasing concern and a more widespread appreciation of the problems between the wars. After 1945, adequate powers became available to control development in a negative sense but more positive and concerted action was a concern of the 1960s.

It is perhaps symbolic that the first property acquired by the National Trust—Dinas Oleu, 4½ acres of cliff-land overlooking Barmouth and donated in 1895 by Mrs F. Talbot—should have been coastal in location, but the Trust controlled less than a mile of coast in 1909. By 1937 that total had risen to 55 miles and to 175 miles by 1965.[58] At the latter date, coastal properties accounted for about one-eighth of all land held by the Trust. In 1965, concerned at the rapidity of coastal development and the relative paucity of areas of high scenic quality still remaining, the Trust launched Enterprise Neptune with the avowed intentions of focusing public attention on the problem of the coast and of acquiring control over those parts of the coast deemed most worthy of preservation. In the event, Enterprise Neptune focused attention on the Trust almost as much as the coast, but despite the stormy waters its encountered,[59] by October 1968 it had resulted in ninety-four miles of coast being added to Trust properties, together with fifty-four miles under negotiation. The majority of these latest acquisitions have been along the west coast of Wales, and in Cornwall, Devon, Dorset and the Isle of Wight.

Development control, as opposed to acquisition, was pioneered so far as the coast is concerned by Lindsey County Council which sought control over random development in the Lindsey County Council (Sandhills) Act of 1932. Adequate powers became available for all authorities after the 1947 Act[60] but the lack of uniform application of these powers and concern for the conservation of a dwindling resource prompted a series of moves on a national scale by the Ministry of Housing and Local Government. In 1963, all local authorities were asked (Circular 56/63) to institute a special

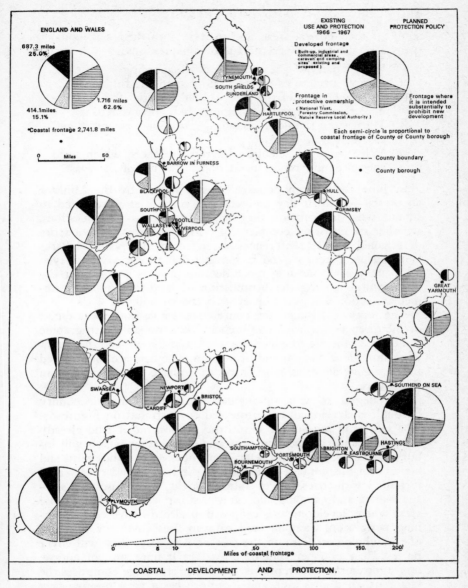

ENGLAND AND WALES

687.3 miles
25.0%

1.716 miles
62.6%

414.1 miles
15.1%

*Coastal frontage 2,741.8 miles

0   Miles   50

EXISTING
USE AND PROTECTION
1966 — 1967

PLANNED
PROTECTION POLICY

Developed frontage
(Built-up, industrial and
commercial areas,
caravan and camping
sites existing and
proposed)

Frontage in
protective ownership
(National Trust,
Forestry Commission,
Nature Reserve Local Authority)

Frontage where
it is intended
substantially to
prohibit new
development

Each semi-circle is proportional to
coastal frontage of County or County borough

-------- County boundary

● County borough

TYNEMOUTH
SOUTH SHIELDS
SUNDERLAND
HARTLEPOOL

BARROW IN FURNESS

HULL

BLACKPOOL
SOUTHPORT
BOOTLE
WALLASEY LIVERPOOL

GRIMSBY

GREAT
YARMOUTH

SWANSEA
NEWPORT
BRISTOL
CARDIFF

SOUTHEND ON SEA

HASTINGS
SOUTHAMPTON PORTSMOUTH BRIGHTON EASTBOURNE
BOURNEMOUTH

PLYMOUTH

0   5   10   50   100   150.   200!
Miles of coastal frontage

COASTAL   DEVELOPMENT   AND   PROTECTION.

Fig 67.   Coastal development and protection (data from *The coasts of England and
Wales: measurements of use, protection and development*).

study of their coastal areas, and to write into their development plans a policy to answer the following questions:

(*a*) Which parts of the coast need safeguarding so that the natural attractions may be enjoyed to the full?

(*b*) In which parts of the coast should facilities for holiday-makers and other developments be concentrated?

(*c*) What steps should be taken to restore lost amenities and to create new ones?

(*d*) What areas of scientific interest are there which need special consideration in relation to the use of the coast?

In June 1965, 'deep concern' was expressed by the Minister about the spread of development and authorities were asked to submit what information they had in answer to the questions, whether studies were complete or not. There was to be a series of regional coastal conferences, arranged by the National Parks Commission. Circular 7/66 recognised that progress was uneven with many areas needing more definite policies and greater co-ordination: pending the formulation of long-term policies, immediate action was asked on existing coastal policies.

The reports of the coastal conferences[61] give not only a digest of the discussion at each conference, but a valuable cartographic summary of the use to which the whole coast is put and the extent of existing development and protection. The data are too detailed for easy generalisation, but Figures 67–70 have been derived from this source.

The degree to which the coast of each county or county borough is developed and protected is illustrated on Figure 67. The left hand semi-circle shows the proportion of land already developed and that held in protective ownership which will inhibit further development. Development is an omnibus term and includes in this context built-up areas; industrial and commercial uses such as quarries, power stations, docks, warehouses and sewage works; and camping and caravan sites: it also includes those areas where development is proposed or already covered by planning permission. Camping and caravan sites cover 3·5 per cent of the whole coastline: in the case of Anglesey, they will cover no less than 15·6 per cent of the coast. It must not, of course, be forgotten that much of this 'developed' frontage comprises the major urban resorts also, and therefore has a very positive part to play in providing recreational opportunity: not surprisingly,

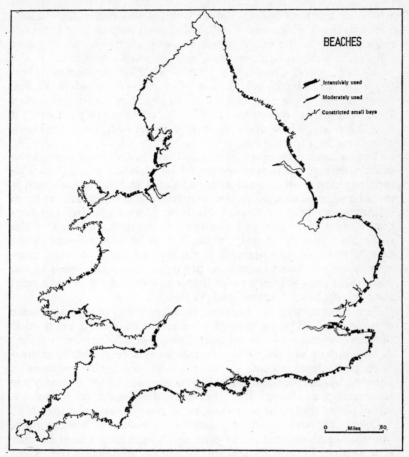

Fig 68. The use of beaches (this map, and Figures 69 and 70, are based on the maps which accompany the reports of the National Parks Commission's Regional Coastal Conferences as listed in note 61. These adaptations are reproduced with the permission of the Controller of HMSO).

most of the county boroughs record more than half their coastline as developed and administrative counties containing several
resorts of less than county borough status also return high totals,
as for example West and East Sussex, with 68 and 50·3 per cent
respectively. At the other end of the scale there are still counties
where the developed frontage is only a small proportion of the
total; in England, Devon (14·7 per cent), Northumberland (15·8
per cent) and the North Riding (16·8 per cent) and in Wales,
Pembrokeshire (10 per cent), Caernarvonshire (15·3 per cent),
Cardiganshire (15·6 per cent) and Merionethshire (16·5 per cent).[62]
For Wales as a whole, the total is only 21 per cent, compared with
26·5 per cent for England.

The protected category as mapped covers only that part of the
coast where protection is conferred by absolute ownership. Fif-
teen per cent of the coastline is protected in this way, though it
must be stressed that protective ownership and access are far from
synonymous. In six counties, Norfolk, Merionethshire, Glamorgan, Devon, Somerset and Cornwall more than one-fifth of the
total falls into this category, rising as high as 28·6 per cent in the
case of Norfolk. In Cornwall, at the date of survey (1966), fifty-
four miles, or almost exactly 20 per cent, was in the hands of the
National Trust—slightly more than one-third of the Trust's total
for the whole of England and Wales.

Actual ownership is, of course, far from being the only measure
of protection. The right-hand semi-circle shows the proportion
of coast where policies of protection have been written into
development plans and where the intention is 'substantially to prohibit new development'. Over three-fifths of the coastline is
covered by this declaration of intent, though as the Countryside
Commission summary dryly remarks 'the degree of protection
afforded by different policies does of course vary considerably'.

Ownership and planning policy is a measure of conservation,
but not of recreational use or capacity. The present use of beaches
is shown on Figures 68 and 69. Figure 68 emphasises the extent
of the coast which is already 'extensively used', however sub-
jective the criteria for this description necessarily are. Use is conditioned in part by the character of the beaches: the coves of
Cornwall's rocky coasts compare with the far more continuous
foreshore of Lancashire or Lindsey. Figure 69 is a better measure
of relative intensity of use for the circles are proportionate to the
number of visitors at peak periods. It must be emphasised that

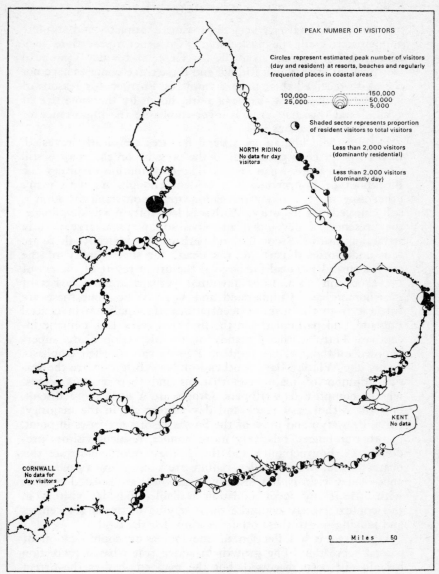

PEAK NUMBER OF VISITORS

Circles represent estimated peak number of visitors
(day and resident) at resorts, beaches and regularly
frequented places in coastal areas

100,000 ———————— 150,000
25,000 ————————— 50,000
————— 5,000

Shaded sector represents proportion
of resident visitors to total visitors

Less than 2,000 visitors
(dominantly residential)

Less than 2,000 visitors
(dominantly day)

NORTH RIDING
No data for day
visitors

KENT
No data

CORNWALL
No data for
day visitors

0   Miles   50

Fig 69. Peak numbers of visitors to coasts.

many of these totals are very approximate estimates and absolute comparisons could be misleading. Two other reservations may be noted. No data are available for Kent, or for day visitors to Cornwall and the North Riding, and these three counties have not therefore received their proper emphasis. Further, for reasons of scale, all numbers less than 2,000 are shown by the same size of symbol and this may visually over-emphasise the importance of some smaller locations.

Despite these limitations, several features are clearly revealed. In the first place, a great deal of the pressure on the coast is still taken by the large urban resorts. The contribution of places like Blackpool or Bournemouth is evident enough. As with many other aspects of outdoor recreation, gregarious concentration is still enjoyed by a majority. With seaside resorts in a fickle climate, the presence of developed amenities still plays a large part in attracting visitors. Secondly, and perhaps paradoxically, there are few under-utilised parts of the coast, for the mobility of the car has spread the load far beyond the urban resort of the era of the excursion train. Least favoured perhaps are the coasts of Northumberland, Cumberland and West Wales, but these are furthest from the main concentrations of population in central England, and particularly in the first two cases, lack climatic incentive. Thirdly, the demands of the day-tripper are superimposed on those of the resident. Resorts vary in their emphasis. Some, like Whitley Bay, Southend or New Brighton are the seaside adjuncts of major conurbations and their visitors almost wholly comprise day trippers. Others are a little more distant, but still within easy reach and day-visitors are in the majority. Rhyl, Prestatyn and most of the Sussex resorts are cases in point. In other instances, relatively more remote, resident visitors predominate: Bournemouth and the Torbay resorts illustrate this characteristic. Many smaller, remote areas also show a predominance of day visitors, but in many cases these are isolated beaches with little if any accommodation available, and 'day visitors' in this context largely comprise those staying in the larger centres and moving out to these other locations for the day.

Figure 70 is a reflection of the increasing sophistication of coastal recreation. The growth in active water-based recreation has already been discussed, but the map emphasises the extent and distribution of one type of facility for it. Concentrations are clearly revealed: the Thames estuary and the Solent are out-

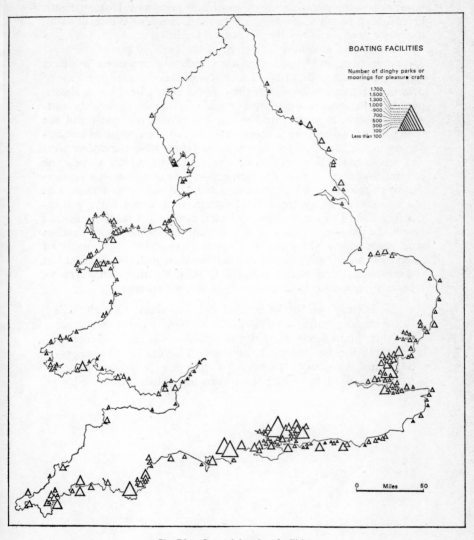

BOATING FACILITIES

Number of dinghy parks or
moorings for pleasure craft

1,700
1,500
1,300
1,000
900
700
500
300
100
Less than 100

0   Miles   50

Fig 70. Coastal boating facilities.

standing, with intensive use also of the coasts of Dorset, south Devon and south Cornwall, Lleyn and Anglesey. But equally, there are few areas totally devoid of facilities.

The maps have shown the extent of the existing use of the coast for recreation, and the degree to which the amenities it offers are being conserved. They cannot, however, show the reality of pressures, the extent to which the capaciy of the beaches to absorb people is being used. Capacity is itself a term with differing meanings—physical capacity, or the absolute limits of beach and sea to absorb varied activities; social capacity, or the degree of crowding users are prepared to accept before they seek alternative sites and environmental capacity, or the extent to which a coastline can be used before visual deterioration sets in or serious conservation problems arise. Capacity too must be linked to access. The use of beaches away from the frontage of urban resorts is inextricably linked to the provision of facilities for car parks and other amenities. In East Sussex, the 1967 survey noted that 'beaches were generally under-used with spare capacity'.[63] The supply of beaches can still, with very few exceptions, match the demand but the same is not true of the means of utilising them. As with so many aspects of resource land, policy is at a cross-roads:

> . . . it is clear that in the coming years planning thought will be increasingly orientated towards not simply the preservation of our limited countryside resources but their increased effective use for human enjoyment. The era of all-out preservation is passing: we must provide for the enjoyment of resources on a far wider scale than previously conceived.[64]

CHAPTER SEVEN

The People's Playgrounds

ACCESSIBILITY AND ACCESS

It may be a truism in recreation terms to assert that 'land is most scarce where cars are most abundant',[1] but of all the paradoxes which bedevil the relationships between leisure and land-use, none is more severe than the locational imbalance between the areas of greatest demand and those of readiest supply. The resources considered in the last chapter are conserved for their character rather than their location: user-oriented land on the other hand is more important for its accessibility than its quality.

The distinction is one of degree rather than of kind, but fundamental nonetheless. To quote but one example, the National Parks, designated largely for the visual appeal of their mountain and moorland scenery, belong to upland Britain: in consequence, south-east England, with more than one-third of the population of England and Wales,[2] has no National Park nearer than Derbyshire or South Wales. It is 120 miles, as the crow flies, from the centre of London to the nearest point on the boundaries of the Peak District or the Brecon Beacons, which may be compared with the average distance travelled in one direction on day trips of fifty miles and on half-day trips of twenty-nine miles (Chapter 4). Other cities may be more fortunate (Sheffield's boundary actually overlaps that of the Peak District National Park) and other areas of coast and countryside may hold equal attraction,

o

but it is obvious that much demand must be met by more local resources with an inherently local appeal.

User-oriented resources are as varied as demand and, reflecting those variations, can be grouped into five broad categories. The first needs only brief mention, for it overlaps with the urban areas discussed in Chapter 3. It comprises land devoted almost exclusively to active sports, with specialised sites where there is little conflict with other uses. In many cases a rural location has resulted not so much from the nature of the particular sport as from the extent of the area required or the availability of a suitable site. Many golf courses fall into this category, emphasising the importance of the urban fringe where accessibility poses few problems but where land values are low enough to make purchase and development financially feasible. More specialised sports are gliding and flying, with land required for the airstrips themselves. There are some sixty private airfields in Britain as a whole,[3] though not all the flying from these is of a recreational nature. Gliding has increased rapidly in popularity, though the total number involved is still comparatively small. There are fifty civilian clubs in England and Wales with a total membership of some 20,000. Launching sites are widely scattered: many use airfields, but there are also some special-purpose gliding fields as at Sutton Bank, high on the edge of the Hambleton Hills overlooking the Vale of York.

Also in this first category are sites for sports with major spectator participation, such as horse- and motor-racing. There are fifty-seven racecourses in England and Wales operating under Jockey Club or National Hunt Committee rules. Most are on the periphery of towns, but their distribution is widespread throughout the country with some concentration around London and in Yorkshire. It has been estimated that when training stables and their extensive galloping grounds are included, the total area of land in Britain as a whole associated with horse-racing may exceed 100,000 acres.[4] In addition, there are point-to-point courses which are in agricultural use for much of the year. Motor and motor-cycle racing facilities range from the seven major international circuits[5] with their formal meetings and full spectator provision, through sprint- and hill-climb meetings to motor-cycle scrambles over rough country, where conditions are more informal and the land is normally devoted to agriculture or other uses. Noise raises problems of compatibility but organised events are less of a threat in this respect than the unorganised and impromptu endeavours of ardent adherents. At Pepperbox Hill, in Wiltshire, for example, 'four young motor-cyclists were high in their praise of the area for scrambles but were greatly outnumbered by those who deplored their ilk and their machines'.[6]

The remaining four categories merit more extended mention and are associated with informal rather than formal activities. The first is *resource land*, extensive in area and widespread in distribution, but where recreational use is incidental to its primary functions. Commons and woodlands are cases in point. The second comprises *rural parks*, nodes where recreational use is paramount and varying from commercialised stately homes to the country parks of the 1968 legislation. The third is the *route network* of roads and footpaths which gives access to the countryside but which with their linear form make small demands on land. The last includes the various types of *inland water*, whether natural in origin like rivers and lakes, or man-made canals, reservoirs and other artificially created water-bodies. These categories are not mutually exclusive and, in many cases, the quality of the resource concerned may raise problems of preservation rather than exploitation, but their dominant characteristic is their ready accessibility in terms of both time and distance, and the access they afford for the townsman in the countryside.

RESOURCE LAND

The whole of rural Britain is resource land in a recreational sense in that it provides a visual amenity of varying quality. Active conservation, as detailed in the previous chapter, is concerned for two-fifths of the area of England and Wales and the 1968 Countryside Act stressed that for the whole country all Government agencies 'shall have regard to the desirability of conserving the natural beauty and amenity of the countryside' (Section 11). But blanket measures of conservation, while they assist aesthetic sensibilities, may do little to satisfy many basic needs of the urban dweller for his day, half-day or evening jaunt into the country. Then access and accessibility may rate as high as visual acceptability.

In this context, land where access is permitted—or at least tolerated—may be divided into land where recreation is the predominant use and that where it is incidental to other functions.

Areally, the latter is by far the more important, and with much recreational use confined to very limited periods of time, as previous chapters have shown, the varied functions may be far from incompatible.

Most rural areas have quite extensive tracts where de facto access to agricultural land is tolerated, indeed, in G. P. Wibberley's words, 'the varied nature of our rural land, in soil, topography and use, means that, except in a few areas like the Fens, there are odd parcels of land throughout all farmed areas where non-agricultural uses such as recreation can occur with little harm'.[7] The identification and mapping of such areas is a virtually impossible task,[8] for many by their very nature are completely informal and the only distinction between them and the surrounding areas of pasture, rough grazing or woodland is the tacit assent (or passive indifference) of the farmer or landowner concerned. Many survive because of the low intensity of recreational use and the lack of resulting conflict with agricultural interest. As pressures increase, paradoxically the supply of these areas tends to decrease as landowners become less tolerant of the additional use.

COMMONS

Two particular categories of land with a subsidiary recreational use deserve additional comment, namely commons and woodland. The former are one of the most widespread and valuable recreational resources, yet also one whose real nature is least understood.

The Royal Commission on Common Lands (1955–8) concluded that there were some 1,505,002 acres of common land in England and Wales, representing 4·03 per cent of the total area of the country.[9] Prior to this report, no estimate of its extent had been made for more than eighty years, and as Sir Dudley Stamp remarked 'with the caution appropriate to a Government department, the Royal Commission when beginning its work was informed that the area of common land in England and Wales was of the order of two million acres with a possible margin of error of one million acres either way'.[10] Even after the work of the Commission, many acknowledged problems remained. This was especially the case in upland Wales. In 1956, Merionethshire County Council returned a total of 12,408 acres of common, including 10,880 acres in the one parish of Trawsfynydd, whereas in evidence to the Commission the Crown Estate Commissioners alone reported that they were the owners of 17,469 acres of common in the county, scattered over eighteen parishes. By mid-1968, provisional registration had been made of 50,000 acres in the county.[11]

The root of the problem lies in the whole concept behind the term. Contrary to popular misconception, commons are neither public property (though individual commons may be publicly owned) nor necessarily unenclosed open land. Rather, common land is a form of land tenure, rooted in agrarian history. It is free-hold land, owned by the lord of the manor or his legal descendant and representative today, but over which other persons have rights exercised together or 'in common'. Common rights are varied: they range from the most generally known and understood right of common pasture, the right to graze animals on the land, to the right to gather wood, dig turf, cut bracken or to fish. More locally there are rights of 'air and exercise' and even, at Pennington in Hampshire, the right of 'hanging out washing'.

Two broad groups of commons can be distinguished. Lowland commons are largely the unenclosed remnants of 'manorial waste' of woodland, scrub or rough grazing remaining after inclosure. The extent of such commons reflects not only tenurial history, but land quality. Where land was good and cultivation continuous, there was little such 'waste' and remaining commons are small in extent. Conversely, when there were large tracts of poor land, 'waste' was extensive, as in the sandy heaths of Surrey, and large commons persist. In upland areas, with settlement and cultivation confined to the valley floors and lower slopes, the division of the higher areas into separate fields by walls and fences was laborious and expensive, and agreement was frequently made to share the open grazing either simply among a group of farmers or by mutual agreement on a basis of shares, termed 'stints' or 'gates'.

These broad considerations are reflected in the present distribution of common land (Figure 71). The majority lies in large blocks of upland Britain, though it must be emphasised that not all upland is held in common, and that there are wide variations in both acreage of commons and common management between otherwise similar areas. This is clearly seen along the Pennines. The Peak District has very little common land, yet on the 'equally bleak and open moors of the Forest of Rossendale . . . common rights are being fully exercised and guarded by well-organised

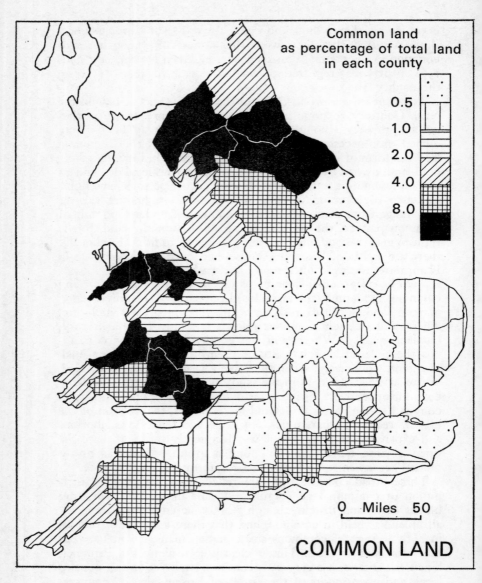

Common land
as percentage of total land
in each county

0.5
1.0
2.0
4.0
8.0

0   Miles   50

COMMON LAND

Fig 71.   The distribution of common land (data from *The Common Lands of England
& Wales*). This is based largely on the returns to the Royal Commission on Common
Lands, 1955–8, as details of commons registered under the Commons Registration
Act of 1965 were not available at the time of writing.

Commoners' Associations'.[12] Much of the fells of the Yorkshire Dales is held in common, but further north towards the Scottish border commons become smaller and more isolated, and almost cease to exist north of Hadrian's Wall. It seems that in medieval times, the scanty population of the border area found little need to assert common rights. Much of the core of the Lake District comprises mountain commons: in 1956, 26 per cent of Westmorland and 11 per cent of Cumberland were reported as commons.

In lowland England, there are evident contrasts between the grassy Midland shires, where commons are small and infrequent, and the tracts of light sandy soils which include such areas of common as the New Forest and the Dorset and Surrey heaths. In 1962, Hampshire had 67,170 acres of common, Surrey, 26,879, the largest totals by far in lowland counties. Other extensive areas are found in parts of the Chilterns and the Cotswolds.

From the point of view of recreation, however, it is not the extent of common land as such which is significant, but the proportion which is available for access by the public at large and not just by restricted categories of commoners.

The commons to which the public has a legal right of access include about 20 per cent of the total. Over the past century, that right has been conferred by the following legislation. Under the Commons Act of 1876, schemes could be made which provided for access and for conservators to manage the common under statutory powers—Ashdown Forest in Sussex and Tebay Fell in Westmorland are instances. Of most widespread importance have been the provisions of section 193 of the Law of Property Act, 1925. This gave firstly a right of access to all commons situated 'wholly or partly within a borough or urban district'. These urban commons, whose importance was emphasised in Chapter 1, form about 10 per cent of the total. Their effective extent was increased both by the wording of the Act and by the empirical nature of the distinction between urban and rural districts. A common had only to lie *partly* within the boundary of the urban district for the whole to be open to access, and many predominantly rural commons were included by this measure. Again, a district which is urban in the technical administrative sense may comprise much rural terrain. The classic instance is the Lake District. As Sir Dudley Stamp has wryly remarked, 'It must strike the foreigner who has struggled to understand the British system of local government as utterly beyond comprehension to find the wild heart of Lakeland designated "the Lakes Urban District" '.[13] But administrative anomaly brings access advantage: as a result of this legislation, the public has the right to walk where they wish over 16,899 acres of Westmorland fells. The other right of access under the Law of Property Act applies to commons in respect of which the Lord of the Manor has executed a deed of access bringing the land within the provisions of the Act.

Other commons have been opened by private Act of Parliament. Under the Malvern Hills Act of 1884, for example, open common on the Malverns was made available for public use: the Malvern Hills Conservators manage the land and have been concerned both to preserve its visual appeal and to provide maintained footpaths with signposts, a few seats and some judicious planting. The 1949 National Parks and Access to the Countryside Act provides for access agreements or orders to be made where necessary to common land which is also 'open country' in the technical sense.

In addition to these instances where the public has a legal right of access, many commons afford de facto access and it is not possible to assess with any accuracy the real acreage of commons used to some degree for recreation. In 1958, the Royal Commission tabulated the primary uses of commons in England and Wales as a whole as follows:

	Per cent of total
Grazing land: stinted	33·0
Grazing land: unstinted or otherwise managed	46·0
Forest and woodland	1·9
Arable	0·3
Bog, fen and marsh	0·6
Scrub and derelict	7·8
Amenity and recreation	10·4

By the very nature of commons, regional variations in these proportions are considerable. Total acreages are much greater in upland Britain but these are frequently no more than areas grazed in common rather than true commons. Rights of public access may be important in individual cases, but there is often little to distinguish them from other areas of rough grazing in visual appearance, in the extent to which public use is tolerated or in their farming role. In lowland Britain, distinctions are much clearer. Sir Dudley Stamp has shown that over the Home Counties and southern England as a whole, 64 per cent of common land had as its prime use amenity and recreation, 18 per cent was scrub and 7 per cent forest and woodland. It is in such areas, close to major centres of population, that commons reach their highest value as open land with access for recreation. They then become very much a user-oriented resource, for there are few people who do not live within ten miles of at least one common.[14]

Their unique character, however, raises problems of both definition and management. The difficulties encountered by the Royal Commission in assembling information have already been noted, but this situation will be largely resolved as a result of the Commons Registration Act of 1965. Under its provisions, all commons and village greens must be registered with the appropriate county council by 1 January 1970 or they will cease to be common land. The registers will show the status of land as a common or as a green, the ownership of the land and the rights of common over it.[15]

Accurate registration of commons and common rights does not solve the problem of managing such land: in far too many cases, 'the public and private restrictions on the landowners' powers, the nature of common rights and the uselessness of many of them in modern circumstances have caused common land to slip out of the hand of active, purposeful management'.[16] It may well be that 'we probably owe some of our most unaltered commons to a few awkward old men here and there, who refused to agree to what seemed a desirable change'[17] but simple preservation in this context may lead to dereliction. At least half of Norfolk's 8,386 acres of common are scrub or gorse or lying derelict: in northeast Essex some commons do little but 'harbour vermin and injurious weeds'.[18] Derelict land may have recreation potential, but it has little recreation attraction.

In more positive vein, the 1968 Countryside Act contained an important provision for the active management of commons to which there is legal access by the public. Under Section 9, a local authority has power to acquire a limited area of the common and construct simple facilities (such as access roads, car parks, toilets and refreshment rooms) to promote the use and enjoyment of the area as a whole.

Ultimately, when commons registration is complete and all objections have been heard, further legislation is envisaged 'to secure the better use of common land—better use in increased produc-

tivity and in wider public access'.[19] This may not be the universal
right of public access for fresh air and exercise on all commons
advocated by the Royal Commission, but it should clear a tangled
legal situation.

WOODLAND

Commons may be an anachronistic survival, but their very
number and location has provided an invaluable recreational resource. Woodland equally, by its widespread occurrence and by
its ability to absorb at least some recreational use as well as fulfil
its prime purpose of producing timber, has an important part to
play in providing land for leisure.

It comes sometimes as a surprise to realise that Britain is one
of the least wooded countries in Europe. For Great Britain as a
whole, less than 8 per cent is covered by woodland and for England and Wales alone the figure drops below 7 per cent.[20] One is
perhaps most aware of this in the uplands of Wales and northern
England, for in contrast the southern counties of England super-
ficially appear well-wooded. To some extent this appearance is
illusory, for much of the effect is created by wooded hedgerows,
small spinneys and park trees, but their importance in economic
as well as visual terms must not be underrated. It has been estimated that such sources constitute one-third of the growing stock
of hardwoods in England and Wales, and that 10 per cent of the
total annual increment of Britain's timber resources was being
provided in 1962 by trees standing outside managed forests.[21]

The visual importance of seemingly wooded lowland can
scarcely be overrated. Apart from its role in providing shelter and
shade for stock, it is an essential element in the townsman's vision
of the country. Hedgerow, tree and copse enclosing neat fields of
arable and pasture give for many a feeling of peace and rural solitude, illusory though it may be. Yet this may well be a transient
feature of the rural scene: few realise how recent is this 'natural'
yet ordered element of so much of lowland England, the product
of eighteenth and nineteenth century parliamentary enclosures.
Prior to that period, in the Midlands and eastern England in particular, the landscape was one of contrast between sweeping open
fields, and the woodland and scrub of heath and 'waste'. Enclosure changed them both: W. G. Hoskins has calculated that
between 1761 and 1844, more than four million acres of open

fields were enclosed and from 1760 onwards more than two million acres of heath, moor and commons were brought, or
attempted to be brought, into cultivation.[22] This new landscape,
so beloved today, had its detractors. The passing of the open fields
brought no lament in literature 'for it was above all a peasant
world and the peasant was inarticulate',[23] but the impact of heath
reclamation stirred deeper feelings. John Clare, born in 1793 and
brought up on the edge of the heath country of northern
Northamptonshire wrote of

> *Swamps of wild-rush beds and slough's squashy traces,*
> *Grounds of rough fallows with thistle and weeds,*
> *Flats and low vallies of kingcups and daisies,*
> *Sweetest of subjects are ye for my reed.*

But soon to the 'commons left free in the rude rags of nature'
came the improvers:

> *The spoiler's axe their shade devours,*
> *And cuts down every tree.*
> *Not trees alone have owned their force,*
> *Whole woods beneath them bowed,*
> *They turned the winding rivulet's course,*
> *And all thy pasture's plough'd.*[24]

But the naked, raw landscape of the new enclosures matured
and in so much of Britain became not only accepted but treasured.
Tree-dotted hedgerow and the grassy verges of enclosure were
of high visual importance: hedges alone throughout Great Britain
cover almost 450,000 acres and are some 616,000 miles in length.[25]
To their visual appeal must be added their importance as a sanctuary for the flora and fauna of the countryside.

To the new improvers of today, hedgerows are as much an
obstacle as they were an asset to such men as Bakewell. As permanent pasture comes under the plough, hedges are not necessary
as barriers or shelter for stock. Even where stock remains, a fence
requires much less maintenance and takes less land. Wide open
tracts of land, unencumbered by hedges or any other barrier, enable machinery to be exploited to the full: the new arable sweeps
restore a sense of space, but reduce shadowed intimacy. In parts
of the arable eastern counties in particular, hedgerow destruction
has been absolute. Figure 72 records the situation in one area
of Huntingdonshire, studied by the Nature Conservancy, where

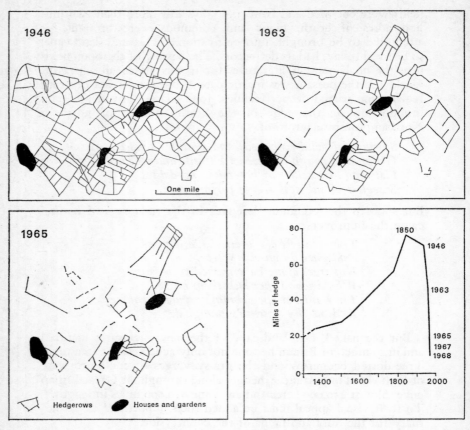

Fig 72. The loss of hedgerows in three Huntingdonshire parishes (after *The Nature Conservancy: progress 1964–1968*, Figure 5).

between 1946 and 1965 alone the mileage of hedges had dropped from over seventy to twenty—the latter figure the same as in 1364![26]

Nor is the change simply in mileage. The widespread use of pesticides and herbicides radically changes the ecological balance. Mechanical cutting prevents the effective regeneration of hedge-row timber, for existing saplings have been shown to be insufficient to replace existing mature trees. Indeed, it may not be too drastic to assert that, without much conscious planting 'ordinary farmland may become largely treeless within the next century'.[27]

This stress on the visual role of wooded landscape in the broadest sense is a necessary reminder not only of recurring change in the rural scene but of its inherently 'created' rather than 'natural' form. Preservationists are all too apt to forget it is the works of man they endeavour to preserve, and not of an intangible 'nature'.

This is nowhere more true than in woodland as a whole. To British—or at least English—eyes, the terms woodland and deciduous are almost synonymous in terms of visual appeal. The reason may indeed be in appearance, and deciduous trees please 'because they are delicately patterned, softly outlined, varied in form and colour, scumbled in texture, seasonal in foliage, tolerant of undergrowth',[28] but preference stems at least as much from innate conservatism. The Forestry Commission may be arguing a special case when they claim that 'scenery . . . is largely a matter of taste and habit of thought. The same person may admire the Black Forest in Germany but not Kielder Forest in Northumberland. Why? Perhaps the simplest explanation is that the former is thought to "belong" whilst the latter is new and strange'.[29] But the day may yet come when 'the russet brown of the Japanese larch in winter, or the silvery sheen of Sitka spruce or noble fir, will be regarded with [no] less delight than . . . the golden autumnal tints of the birch and aspen'.[30]

The role of woodland as a resource, however, lies not only in its visual enhancement of the rural scene and its widespread occurrence in varied forms, but the opportunities it affords for recreation within its bounds. The sheer acreage of woodland may be comparatively small in terms of the total land available but as with commons (with which indeed there is some overlap) its importance lies in both its physical and recreational accessibility. Love of woodland for its own sake is not as deep-rooted as amongst the peoples of hotter and less damp climates, who may seek the shade rather than the sun, but wooded glades, with their filtered light and rustling undergrowth, retain a real appeal.

Distinction must be made between private woodlands and those under the control of the Forestry Commission. The former cover some 1,800,000 acres in England and Wales, though this includes a whole range of woodland types, from coverts and remnants of scrub in tiny parcels, to major forests managed to yield an economic return. In Wales, for example, of 220,000 acres of private woodland in 1967, no less than 120,000 acres cannot be regarded as productive of timber.[31] No accurate data exist to show the extent to which this private woodland is available for public access. Some already, as common or as National Trust property, is fully open and its prime use is recreational: the role of Epping Forest or Burnham Beeches among London's open spaces needs no emphasis, or of the Trust's woodlands on their Ashridge, Blickling or Clumber estates. Some 50,000 acres are available in this way.[32] Of the remainder much is used though, as with other agricultural land, by tacit consent of the owner rather than with express permission.

Forestry Commission woodlands provide not only a major potential resource but in many parts of Britain have been responsible for fundamental landscape changes, in particular on the lower slopes of the uplands of the West and North. Their extent, their appearance and their use must be related to their history. The Commission itself was spawned by the dire lessons of World War I. By 1914, the exploitation of woodland as a whole had left less than 5 per cent of Britain under woodland cover, some 3 million acres in all.[33] Wartime blockade resulted in the felling of 450,000 acres and Lloyd George admitted that we came nearer to losing the war through lack of timber than through lack of food. In 1919, the Forestry Commission was created to remedy this deficiency and for forty years the basis of its policy was the creation of a growing stock of timber as quickly as possible in case of a comparable emergency.

In acreage terms, the result is clearly evident. By 1967, the Forestry Commission controlled 2,802,818 acres in Great Britain as a whole, 751,352 in England and 379,372 in Wales. Of this total, 1,960,978 acres was land either under plantations or earmarked for planting, 563,970 in England and 329,163 in Wales. In addition, private afforestation had been stimulated by financial inducements under the Dedication or Approved Woodlands schemes to the tune of a further 1,048,168 acres, 587,575 in England and 59,895 in Wales.[34]

The scale of this change must be emphasised and also its nature. Although more than half the total of both acquisition and planting was in Scotland, it was no less important in England and Wales. There was at least one forest in virtually every county (Figure 73), although the major plantings were on the uplands of

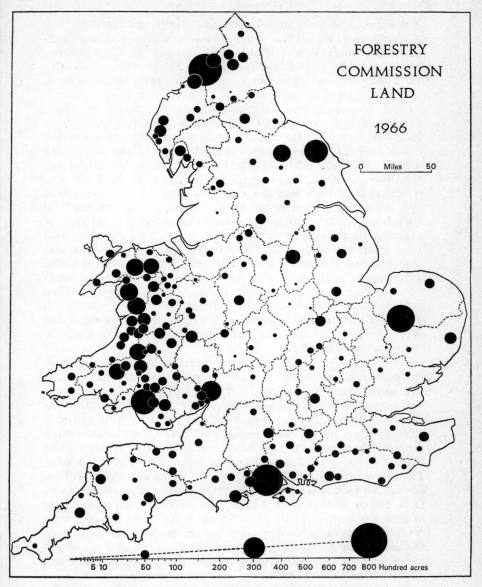

FORESTRY
COMMISSION
LAND

1966

0   Miles   50

5 10   50   100   200   300 400 500 600 700 800 Hundred acres

Fig 73.   Forestry Commission land (data from *Forty-Seventh Annual Report of the Forestry Commissioners*).

Wales and the North. Individual forests cover vast tracts by any
standards—Kielder in Northumberland with 49,000 acres, Thet-
ford Chase on the sandy Breckland of Norfolk with 48,000 acres,
Allerston on the flanks of the North York Moors with 32,000 acres
and Coed Morgannwg in Glamorgan with 39,000 acres, to name
only the largest.[35]

Land development on this scale attracts real attention. There
are arguments against afforestation as such, often, illogically, from
those who seek to retain 'natural' landscapes and ignore the reality
of a former widespread forest cover. A proposal to afforest land
in upper Langstrothdale, in the Yorkshire Dales National Park,
by private interests brought anguished protest from those who saw
in 'the typical high Pennine country—hungry, treeless ground
covered with a pelt of rough grass, reeds and bracken' the 'real
Yorkshire'.[36] But more protest is aroused by the manner of
afforestation than by its extent. The initial need for the rapid
build-up of a strategic reserve of timber dictated the almost exclusive use of fast-growing conifers, which on the land available
and over the same time-span yield six times the volume of hardwoods. Apart from the inherent disdain of conifers as such, alien
and exotic to English eyes (though no more exotic than such
species as the chestnut!), planting in regimented rows regardless
of terrain, punctuated by the harsh lines of straight rides, alienated
much public sympathy.

Prior to about 1958 therefore, forestry in Britain, even if
accepted as economically desirable, was viewed as visually intrusive and inimical to the needs of recreation. True, forest parks
had already recognised something of the problem. Much Com-
mission-owned land was too high for successful planting and such
areas of open upland were designated Forest Parks, with camp
sites and ready access to the upland areas. The first, in Argyll, was
opened in 1935, but was followed by others south of the Border.
The Snowdonia Forest Park, 23,800 acres in the Gwydyr and Bed-
dgelert Forests, was designated in 1937, and the 35,000 acres of
Dean Forest Park in 1938. The Border Forest Park, 126,000 acres
in extent with the North Tyne valley at its heart, lies largely in
Northumberland, while the New Forest, with 65,730 acres controlled by the Forestry Commission, is not a Forest Park in the
technical sense, but with some 60 per cent in open heath and
grassland has long been a noted recreation area.[37]

The Forest Parks made available much upland wilderness to the public as of right, but involved little diversion of effort from the Commission's prime function, for there was little positive provision outside the campsites as such and the land in question was of little economic use. In the last decade, however, there has been a broader concept of the Commission's role and not in recreation terms alone. The dominating concept of the strategic reserve has shifted to one of afforestation as a source of employment and other social benefits in marginal upland areas particularly in Wales and Scotland. Production forestry as almost the sole motivation was usurped for less tangible benefits.

It is beyond the present scope to discuss the motives for such change and the rate of economic return which may be expected, whether judged in the light of forestry alone, by the cost of timber imports or by agricultural alternatives.[38] In recreation terms, however, there has been a twofold change. In the first place, and symbolised by the appointment of Sylvia Crowe as landscape consultant in 1964, there has been a greatly increased concern for visual amenity and a much wider appreciation of the role sympathetic planting can have for the preservation, and indeed the enhancement of scenery.[39] Secondly, there has been a more positive attitude towards recreational use as such. Access on foot has always been permitted along forest roads and paths, even though with little positive encouragement. Now picnic sites proliferate—over 100 adjacent to public roads—campsites are created in greater numbers and positive measures taken for the conservation of wild-life. At Grizedale in the Lake District, with 7,300 acres of woodland on an estate purchased in 1936, facilities include not only a camping site, picnic sites, car parks in a wood adjoining Coniston Water, nature trails and forest walks, but a wild-life centre and deer museum, a tree-top watch-tower for ten people and smaller 'photo-safari' high seats. Even to *The Guardian*'s critical country diarist, this is a 'kindly invasion', as some twelve square miles of 'pleasant rolling country of sleepy farmsteads and bare hillsides' has reverted again to forest,

> for here are no harsh lines and ugly regimentation but rather a sensitive use of the contours so that already the new landscape fits quite happily into the mountain backcloth behind. And to the forest to find sanctuary have come back the animals and the birds so that the area now teems with more wild life than anywhere else in the district.[40]

P

Grizedale, under the enthusiastic management of Bill Grant, is a positive example of what can be achieved with less unimaginative and restrictive terms of reference to marry forestry, amenity, conservation and recreation.[41] It may involve some narrow financial sacrifice (and the Government has yet to recognise in tangible form the financial restraints imposed by recreation demands on productive forests)[42] but emphasises the value of a widespread resource in not only yielding some financial return and assisting the balance of payments but also in giving respite and solitude to walker, nature-lover and even, where appropriate, the motorist.[43]

RURAL RENDEZVOUS

Commons, woodlands and forests, anachronistic survivals or strategic acquisitions, owe their importance for leisure to their scale rather than their function: covering between them some four million acres of England and Wales their prime use is only rarely recreation but they have an immense value as a reservoir of land for this purpose, widespread in location and easily accessible in some degree by most.

Other facilities cover far more restricted areas and yet absorb an even greater share of leisure activities. In recreation jargon, these are 'honeypots', nodes of attraction for the gregarious pleasure-seeker. The focus may indeed be a resource of high quality, but its prime asset lies not so much in that quality as such, stimulant though it may be, but in its ability to satisfy demand on a large scale but in a small compass.

The basic idea is, of course, far from new. Pleasure gardens, Victorian parks and seaside resorts were the urban precursors, with 'company and diversion' hand in hand. Focal points of attraction within the resources already considered fulfil the same purpose in a rural setting; the crowded viewpoints and access areas within the National Parks; the most frequented beaches, commons and other open spaces; forest car parks and picnic sites and thronging monuments and stately homes. But these are almost nodes despite themselves, nodes yielding to demand whether gladly or with reluctance rather than nodes whose very purpose is to stimulate demand, to seek out patronage for profit or for less material motive.

Many rural 'attractions' are obvious and need little comment. Some capitalise the ownership of a natural resource—Swallow

Falls in Snowdonia, or Stump Cross and White Scar Caves in the Craven Pennines for example. Others create an artificial resort, like Chester or Whipsnade Zoos, where the space requirements can be more cheaply satisfied in a rural setting. Yet others turn resources of a very different character to recreational use: railway enthusiasts, whose schemes for the preservation of erstwhile branch-lines can be used for commercial advantage as well as personal pleasure, are a case in point. Along the Welsh coast, for example, the 9½ mile long narrow-gauge Festiniog Railway carried 294,000 passengers in 1968, the Talyllyn Railway 122,167 and even British Rail's own steam-worked Vale of Rheidol line 48,532.[44] While these owe much of their success to being situated in a major holiday area, other lines such as the Bluebell Railway in Sussex or the Keighley & Worth Valley in Yorkshire are much nearer to major centres of population. The latter carried 4,500 passengers over the five days of the Easter holiday alone in 1969. At a transport attraction of a rather different kind, the Crich Tramway Museum in Derbyshire, 116,286 tickets were sold for tram rides in 1968. Such enterprises are perhaps far removed from more general concepts of recreation in the countryside, but the part they play in absorbing pressure must not be under-estimated.

Steam-worked railways or electric tramways thriving on nostalgia are only one small fragment of the capitalisation of historical attachment, for 'love of the past complements English devotion to the open air'.[45] This lesson has long been learned by the owners of stately homes. Many buildings have already been secured as a heritage through the National Trust or the Ministry of Public Buildings and Works, but here the prime accent is on preservation rather than exploitation. Whether through economic necessity or the genuine desire to share the privilege and pleasure of their own inheritance, country-house owners open their properties to the public to a remarkable degree (Figure 74). Though the distribution is widespread, there is an evident concentration in lowland England, a concentration reflecting not so much the major grouping of urban population—the prime market—as the greater abundance of such properties in the richer agricultural shires.

Data for the number of visitors are not consistently available (some, like the Duke of Bedford 'do not disclose our figures to anyone'[46]) but the extent to which the property is open on a weekly and a seasonal basis gives some indication of the part

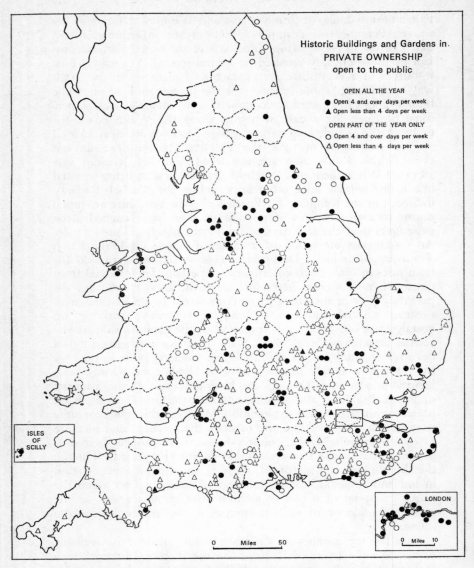

Historic Buildings and Gardens in.
PRIVATE OWNERSHIP
open to the public

OPEN ALL THE YEAR
● Open 4 and over days per week
▲ Open less than 4 days per week

OPEN PART OF THE YEAR ONLY
○ Open 4 and over days per week
△ Open less than 4 days per week

ISLES
OF
SCILLY

LONDON

0   Miles   50

0   Miles   10

Fig 74. Historic buildings in private ownership open to the public (data from
Historic houses, castles & gardens in Great Britain and Ireland, 1967 edition).

played by visitors in the whole functioning of the estate. To some owners, the weekend visitor is a useful but scarcely essential economic increment, to others the sole focus of enterprise. Lord Montagu of Beaulieu, for example, recorded 552,794 visitors in 1967, and the Marquess of Bath 220,000 to the house at Longleat and 500,000 to the Lion Reserve in the same year.

The Longleat lions emphasise that in the manner of display there is wide distinction and dissent. Some owners seek unashamedly to promote attendance by spicing history with popular entertainment. Beaulieu, with its motor museum, model railway, go-karts and periodic rallies, as well as its Abbey and Palace House and gardens, is a classic instance, deliberately substantiating a claim of 'wet or dry, the finest day's family outing in the south'. Others are more restrained or idealistic in their approach. Of Blenheim, the Duke of Marlborough has declared that 'my home is an education, not an entertainment'.[47]

There is no simple right or wrong in such a choice, for the paradox of preservation or promotion is the familiar one which threads so much of conservation. For some properties, there may well be a stage when too many visitors can defeat the purpose and the process of preservation, when owners should heed the warning that

> The moment you feel impelled to asphalt the second lawn for parking the charabancs, and to convert the old coachhouse into a cafeteria, I beg you to pause and reflect. The more cups of tea required, the more imperative the need for public lavatories. So the potting shed will next have to be sacrificed. There is no end to a vicious circle. Your little haunt of ancient peace will soon become a hurly-burly of struggling, cross humanity.[48]

But many properties, and their parkland setting, can readily accept large numbers and both entertain and educate, to the mutual benefit of owner and visitor. The landscaped vistas of Repton or Capability Brown may be as artificial as an urban park, but they can satisfy the urge of many for a day in the country.

COUNTRY PARKS

Stately homes and other rural rendezvous are the longstanding prototypes of the new generation of 'country parks'. Formally enunciated in the 1966 White Paper *Leisure in the Countryside in England and Wales* (Cmnd 2928), they were envisaged as fulfilling a three-fold function.

> They would make it easier for town-dwellers to enjoy their leisure in the open, without travelling too far and adding to congestion on the roads; they would ease the pressure on the more remote and solitary places; and they would reduce the risk of damage to the countryside—aesthetic as well as physical—which often comes about when people simply settle down for an hour or a day where it suits them, somewhere 'in the country' . . .

They were defined in the Countryside Act as 'a park or pleasure ground for the purpose of providing, or improving, opportunities for the enjoyment of the countryside by the public'. In amplification, the Countryside Commission consider that the area of land (or of land and water) should be not less than 25 acres in extent, though 'the area as such is less important than the capacity to absorb a considerable number of people or to provide a variety of recreational activities'.[49]

The concept is deliberately vague. It is not the idea which is new, for there are ample rural as well as urban precedents, but the recognition of the need to apply public funds at national level to such schemes. The Victorian park was a municipal answer to a municipal need. A century later, the cross-currents of the new mobility have not only shifted demand from an urban to a rural setting but, with the existing fragmented pattern of local government, mean that that demand is often exercised beyond the bounds of the authority which receives the participants' rates. Rural counties with a sparse population are sometimes expected to bear a financial responsibility for facilities used mainly by inhabitants of wealthier county boroughs. Some assistance has hitherto been given for work in National Parks and Areas of Outstanding Natural Beauty, but under the 1968 legislation exchequer grants of up to 75 per cent may be made towards the cost of country parks. Nor is this assistance confined to local authorities: in the words of the Act, grants can be given 'by way of payment towards capital expenditure incurred by an owner of land which, under arrangements made with the local authority, is used as or as part of a country park' (Section 33 1c).

The effectiveness of this approach in creating new resources must obviously depend upon the scale of the finance which is made available. Present indications are that the Countryside Commission is thinking of aid to the tune of some £2 million annually, supporting perhaps ten major projects each year.[50] Achievement must rest upon the economic health of the nation as a whole, for amenity cannot command high priority in times of financial stringency, but even at this level of support, it will be many years before a coherent system of country parks can emerge. Recognising this, the Commission has established three basic priorities for grant aid, namely:

(a) encouraging the provision or improvement of country parks where the present facilities appear inadequate. Indications of need are a deficiency of recreation areas within easy reach of large city regional populations, pressure of use on existing facilities, traffic congestion, and damage to the physical environment of the countryside.

(b) encouraging the improvement of areas already in use for recreation which could be converted into country parks with a modest investment from central funds.

(c) encouraging development of country parks on land at present derelict or under used, particularly where publicly owned. The use of high quality agricultural land should be discouraged.[51]

The enunciation of priorities is easier than their practical application. Twenty-five per cent of the cost must still be found by the authority or private agency concerned, and not all counties feel disposed to pursue an active policy in this direction. It is no coincidence that the five counties[52] putting forward the first six schemes recommended for approval by the Commission are known for their vigorous promotion of countryside recreation, but their enthusiasm is not universally shared.

The diverse character country parks can assume is well illustrated by three of these early schemes. The first to receive a grant, in March 1969, was Cheshire's Wirral Way.[53] This imaginative plan is based on the conversion of a disused railway into a new right of way for walking and riding, the linear form being supplemented by nodes of development, with car parks, information centres and picnic areas, on the sites of former stations (Figure 75, A and B). It provides much-needed additional recrea-

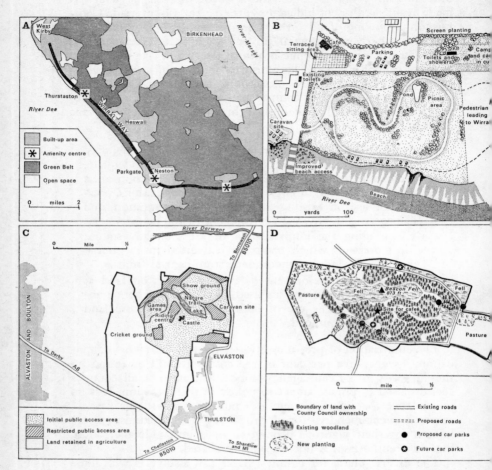

Fig 75. The first country parks under the Countryside Act of 1968; A The Wirral Way, Cheshire; B Detail of envisaged development on the site of the former Thurstaston station on the Wirral Way; C Elvaston Castle, Derbyshire; D Beacon Fell, Lancashire (based on outline development plans supplied by the County Planning Officers of Cheshire, Derbyshire and Lancashire).

tional facilities on the immediate fringe of the built-up area of Merseyside; it runs for the most part through areas of attractive if not spectacular scenery, flanking the Dee estuary for much of its length; and it effectively removes a potential eyesore in the derelict remains of the railway itself. The development of such a fortuitous site inevitably involves compromise: the linear form dictated by the railway gives less varied opportunity for walks which begin and end at the same place, while the gentle curves and gradients of a railway track bed are more monotonous for the walker than the twists and turns of a field path. Again, the station sites are themselves restricted, and for the motorist will offer little relief from congestion unless he is prepared to leave his car and walk some way through the Park. Costs are also high: for the advocates of wholesale conversion of disused railways to rural footways it may come as a shock to realise that the capital cost of this scheme will be of the order of £250,000 for some 12 miles of route, including the cost of land acquisition, the creation of a grassy footpath and bridleway and the landscaping of the station sites.

The second scheme, at Elvaston Castle in Derbyshire (Figure 75C), is nodal rather than linear and instead of creating a completely new facility, seeks rather to conserve and secure access to an existing parkland site with extensive woodlands and mature planting. The Castle itself dates largely from 1817, but the particular value lies not so much in the building as in the surrounding gardens and parkland, the work of a local landscape architect, William Barron, who introduced examples of every known species of European conifer. The whole site covers 390 acres, but 200 of these are in agricultural use. The remainder 'affords a variety of scenery and landscape ranging through mature woodland, lake and heathland to formal gardens and avenue vistas . . . The extent of the estate and the manner in which it is landscaped should ensure that large numbers of visitors will be enabled to be accommodated without giving the impression of overcrowding'.[54] In form, it thus differs but little from the grounds of many stately homes in private or public ownership, but the interest lies in the use of this mechanism for securing an accessible and desirable open space.

Lancashire's first country park is an open space of a very different character. Beacon Fell is a 269-acre site rising as an isolated hill to 873ft at the south-western extremity of the Forest

of Bowland (Figure 75D). It was planted in the 1930s and 1940s
as a water-gathering ground, but the plantations are now
neglected and overcrowded. The County Council bought the Fell
for £9,250 in 1968: it plans to thin the plantations, and gradually
introduce belts of deciduous trees to relieve the solid wedges of
conifers. Access roads will be provided, with car parking eventually for up to 400 cars, but the summit, with its magnificent views,
will be retained as natural open heathland. The aim, in the formal
language of the management plan, is 'the creation and maintenance of a balanced composition of woodland, field and open fell
conducive to . . . outdoor leisure pursuits of a quiet and informal
nature . . . whilst at the same time giving the public access to
prominent viewpoints not usually easily accessible by motor
car'.

Green belt footpath, landscaped country house and wooded
fellside are contrast enough, but they illustrate the varied character of these new nodes of recreation in the countryside. That
newness, however, lies not in form, for they have innumerable
precursors, well-loved and well-used, but in their financing and
administration and above all in the promise they afford of the
ultimate creation of a carefully conceived pattern of recreational
opportunity rather than a sporadic and haphazard response to
demand. To some, leisure and planning may appear diametrically
opposed and mutually incompatible, the Commission's country park
emblem symbolic of 'two adults and a child who managed to
get into a Country Park and are clamouring for a lift to get out
of it',[55] but to most gregarious townsmen their 'amalgam of
clarity, order and accessibility'[56] will give what he largely seeks
of the rural scene.

FOOTPATHS

As earlier chapters have shown, most people's enjoyment of the
countryside is compounded of three distinct elements: visual
appreciation of the rural scene; active enjoyment on restricted areas
of land and water; and movement along clearly defined corridors
of access. These last, the networks between the recreation nodes,
have not always received the attention they deserve, whether
footpaths, bridleways or roads, yet their effective development
and use are fundamental in the overall quality of enjoyment of
outdoor recreation.

Footpaths are the real Cinderellas, yet as the Minister of Housing and Local Government once remarked

Everybody's idea of the English countryside is the right to walk across a field and sit under a tree, to walk along a track through unspoilt woodlands or over fells, to sit by a lake and fish, or to take the dog for a walk across the common . . . Other countries offer magnificent panoramas, mountains and lakes, rivers and coasts, but in Britain one can be part of the countryside. At all costs we must preserve this unique quality.[57]

The footpath network itself has a complex origin and fulfils varied functions. The pattern evolved in a casual way over the centuries in response to both local and national needs: '. . . some were deliberately planned, many evolved as simple accommodation routes, from farm or cottage to village, and by usage they have acquired the status of legal rights of way. Others developed as drove roads or pack horse routes and often cover long distances'.[58] But patterns of movement change, and as the Gosling Committee declared 'it is now generally accepted, and much of the evidence before us confirms, that the majority of footpaths today have a recreational purpose in sharp contrast to the utilitarian purpose which gave rise to many of them'.[59]

In this context, the aristocrats of the network are the Long Distance Footpaths created by the National Parks and Access to the Countryside Act of 1949. The aim was the development of a national system of public rights of way through some of the most striking upland and coastal scenery (Figure 76). The financial responsibility was entirely the Exchequer's, designation that of the National Parks Commission, but implementation falls to local authorities.[60] In the event, practical execution has fallen far in arrears of intent and designation. By mid-1969, formal approval had been given to ten paths with a combined length of 1,273 miles and seven other schemes were in varied stages of preparation. But of these only two had been completed with formal rights of way throughout their length, the 250-mile Pennine Way opened in April 1965 after fourteen years of negotiations, and the 93-mile Cleveland Way in May 1969. The Pembrokeshire Coast Path should be complete in early 1970, and Offa's Dyke Path along the length of the Welsh borders by 1971. The root of the problem lies in the complex negotiations for the necessary rights of

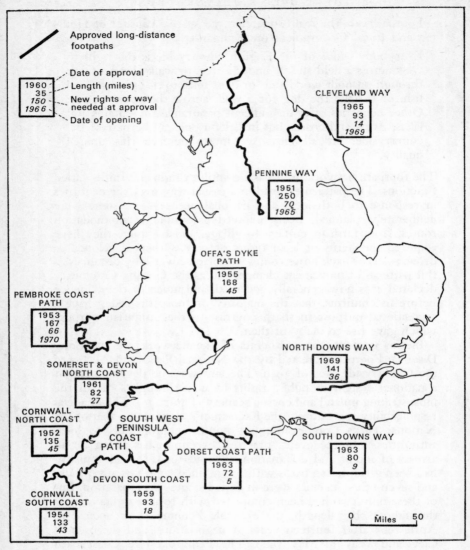

Fig 76. Long Distance Footpaths (based on a map by the Ministry of Housing and Local Government used with the permission of the controller of HMSO).

way. Of the approved schemes, new rights of way were needed over 340 miles of their length, and agreement has still not been reached for some 78 miles: the Pennine Way involved no less than thirty-three separate local authorities and the Offa's Dyke Path thirty-six. Even formal completion does not mark the end of the problems: on the day the Cleveland Way was opened by Arthur Skeffington MP, the *Yorkshire Evening Post* tartly remarked, 'it is earnestly hoped that he does not volunteer to walk the first 500 yards. The mud would be over his boot-tops in no time'.

These paths are perhaps more a symbol of opportunity than an incitement to achievement. Parts are well frequented and open up incomparable vistas of great swathes of moorland and lowland, villages and coast, but only a tiny minority of walkers or riders follow them consistently throughout their length. Nevertheless, the publicity surrounding their establishment has focused attention on wider problems of countryside access and footpath networks.

The changing role of the footpath has already been evidenced, but it has led to wide variations in the degree of use. In many rural areas, away from towns or outstandingly scenic areas, demand is slight, as the East Hampshire Study bore witness.[61] With so much outdoor recreation in the country tied closely to the car, innumerable paths have become unusable either by ploughing up, or through lack of sign-posting, maintenance or use. In addition to such informal losses, some 1,500 legal closures and diversions are being confirmed annually.[62]

There are signs, however, that the nadir of use has been reached and that it is not only the ardent enthusiasts of the Ramblers Association and kindred bodies who would agree with John Dower's assertion in 1945 that 'ample and assured footpaths and bridleways, adequately maintained and equipped with sign-posts, stiles, gates, bridges, etc. are a national need extending to all parts of the country—from the immediate vicinity of built-up areas to the remotest rural districts'. Legislation for assurance was embodied in the 1949 Act which, for the first time, required local authorities to prepare definitive maps of rights of way, though in 1968 the Gosling Committee could legitimately express concern 'that nineteen years after the passing of the Act there are still fourteen counties in England and six in Wales which have not completed the definitive maps for the whole of their areas . . .' Nevertheless, the gradual appearance on Ordnance Survey one-inch maps of the red symbols for 'Public paths and roads used as public paths' marks a major advance on the traditional warning that 'the representation on this Map of a Road, Track or Footpath is no evidence of the existence of a right of way'. Many groups are actively clearing and waymarking paths. In 1968 the Oxfordshire branch of the CPRE enlisted the aid of school children to examine the state of rights of way throughout the county, and subsequently to begin clearing away obstructions.[63] In 1967–8, the Society of Sussex Downsmen recorded that no less than 268 bridleways and footways had been cleared or otherwise made usable in the course of the year, the vast majority by the Society itself, and that 325 footpath signs had been erected in the previous eighteen months.[64]

But while such partisan activity may preserve or elaborate an existing network, it does not necessarily assert its viability. Concern in this respect was voiced in the 1966 White Paper *Leisure in the Countryside in England and Wales* (Cmnd 2928) which felt that radical changes might well be needed to 'permit the development of a system of footpaths and bridleways, some based on existing routes, but others newly created, which would be more suited to modern needs. Such a system might ideally consist of a carefully planned network . . .' The Gosling Committee tartly retorted that 'we approach suggestions of a "system" and a "carefully planned network" with great caution because much of the value and charm of footpaths lies in their waywardness'. The Ramblers Association made the point with even greater vigour in declaring 'we would not like to see the present system of meandering paths replaced by theoretically determined routes. Most users of footpaths today are not seeking a Euclidean progression. They do not require the shortest distance between A and B . . .'

Nevertheless, the fundamental problem remains. On high-grade agricultural land the presence of a right of way can be a very serious handicap to the farmer and many existing paths even where access is unobstructed are virtually unused. But the footpath network remains the place where most of all the quietude and peace, the softness and the savour of being at one with the countryside can best be experienced. Their sheer number—in Kent alone there are over 10,000 rights of way[65]—is a reasonable guarantee of solitude: such enjoyment in a mobile society may be a minority pursuit but its value is increasingly recognised.

ROADS

The paradox of footpaths is repeated with far greater intensity in the case of roads. With these, the utilitarian purpose in their creation remains, indeed has been intensified beyond recognition with the advent of car and lorry. Recreational use is superimposed upon the utilitarian, and though the intensity of impact is far from coincidental in time and place, the pressures are evident and need no further repetition.

But conflict here is not only between those to whom the countryside is workshop and those who seek in it their playground, but between the varied attitudes of recreation seekers themselves. The dominant role of the car in so much recreation experience was discussed at length in Chapter 4, and not simply as a means of transport into the countryside, but for many as the very real focus of their activities there. Yet often those who fight most vigorously for the right of access to rural land oppose most strenuously the right of the motorist to have unfettered access to their rural preserve: '. . . the dirt, noise and sheer un-aesthetic appearance of non-stop motor traffic can do irreparable harm to environment . . . It is a question of making a choice be-tween the motor car, and our precious, shrinking countryside'.[66]

The choice is not perhaps as clear cut as the preservationists would claim. In the first place, despite our intricate network of minor roads, much truly wild country remains really inaccess-ible except on foot. If one makes the arbitrary assumptions that few motorists will wish to move more than a ten-minute walk from their vehicles and that only a tiny minority will venture away from metalled roads, surprisingly large tracts of country will remain inviolate in this sense (Figure 77). In other words, the road network itself as a resource must be examined more closely, and its inherent form as a corridor through an area rather than a blanket coverage of it more clearly stressed.

The purely aesthetic argument is a harder one to counter, for roads and traffic are visually and audibly intrusive. But here again, the effect is often exaggerated. Interests which would ban or severely restrict road traffic deplore the almost complete passing of the rural railway: a plume of steam on the hillside above Maen-twrog (or even on the upper slopes of Snowdon) arouses romantic nostalgia and railways are seen as 'the obvious and ideal "Rapid-transit" system able to take large numbers of people to the heart

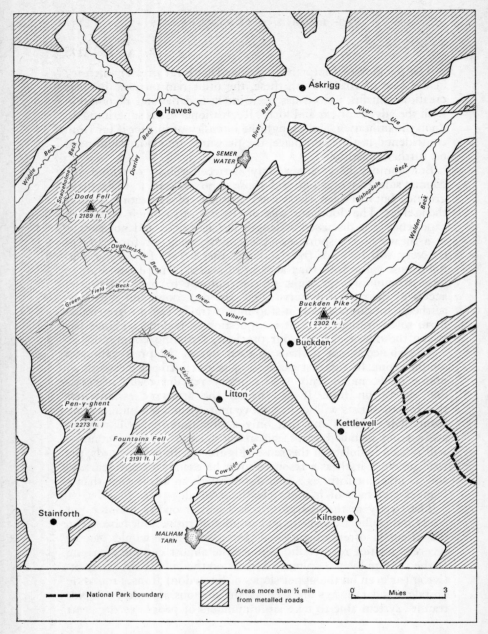

Fig 77. Areas more than half a mile from metalled roads in the Yorkshire Dales.

of the countryside with the minimum of damage to the environment'.[67] All this is not to deny that real problems exist. The sheer pressure of road traffic in such Lakeland valleys as Langdale and Borrowdale needs no further emphasis: in the Yorkshire Dales, 22,000 vehicles were recorded entering the National Park on a July Sunday in 1968 between 11 am and 8 pm, with flows of 2,983 vehicles on B6160 at Bolton Abbey and 1,826 on the B6265 between Skipton and Grassington. But these flows are confined to the corridors that the roads themselves represent (and to very limited periods of time), and a more universally satisfying answer may be sought in improving the corridors than in purely restrictive measures. It is not without significance that proposals for traffic restrictions in Langdale and Borrowdale were opposed most vigorously by the Langdale Residents Committee themselves.[68]

This whole theme of the car in the countryside is perhaps the most critical and hotly debated of all aspects of outdoor recreation, and one where opinions are most entrenched and violently opposed. Proposed solutions will be more speculatively discussed in the following chapter: suffice at this stage to have examined the scale of demand and to stress the linear character of the resource which seeks to satisfy it. Horizontal segregation yet holds hope for conservation and the satisfaction of gregarious and solitary demand.

INLAND WATER

Despite the problems they engender in a recreational sense, roads are at least a widespread resource, the network universally spread throughout the country with areal differences of degree and not of kind. With water resources, the problems are of a very different order, for the supply is both finite and restricted in location yet demand continues to mushroom—and not for recreation alone, for this is only one aspect of water use.

Consumption for industrial, domestic and agricultural use currently averages some 5,000 million gallons a day, and by 30 September 1967, river authorities had authorised the abstraction from all sources of 8,800 thousand million gallons a year.[69] Simple totals of abstraction and consumption, however, are only the beginning of the story, for they ignore both the re-use of water within a river system and the geographical location of that system

Q

in relation to rainfall, run-off, and the major sources of demand. There is no overall shortage of water in England and Wales in this context: the problem is to make it available at the right time in the right place.

Locational imbalance is an even greater problem for recreational use. Water bodies are sporadic in occurrence and bear little correlation to the distribution of population. Again, their suitability (and availability) for the different forms of water-based recreation varies widely. The wetter uplands of the West and North might seem initially to offer the opportunity in this respect that their open moorland and mountains afford to walker and climber. But run-off in tumbling streams, with waterfalls and rapids, is of value to the angler alone, or, in more limited stretches, to the more adventurous canoeist. Natural lakes, the Lake District itself excepted, are surprisingly few and upland reservoirs only rarely available for access.[70] Figure 78 illustrates for a county of varied relief not only the sporadic distribution of water available for recreation, but the widely differing uses to which individual water bodies are put because of either their inherent nature or restrictions imposed by their owners.

The most widespread resource and for this small insular nation in the long run the most important is, of course, the sea, but the contribution of the coast was considered in the previous chapter. Inland waters can be grouped into two broad categories, natural and artificial, with rivers and lakes belonging to the former, canals, reservoirs and wet gravel pits to the latter. As with land-based activities, further distinction can be made between those resources which provide a network for movement and those which satisfy an activity happily confined to a specific location, though the distinction is not always clear cut. The contrast in this respect between cruising and angling is obvious enough, but many water sports require the use of a body of water of considerable extent, and may in that use give rise to serious problems of compatibility (Chapter 4).

RIVERS AND LAKES

Estimates of the available inland water in England and Wales vary between 205 and 325 square miles,[71] but not all of this is available for recreation. The most widespread resource are rivers and streams, but despite the extensive network they form, their

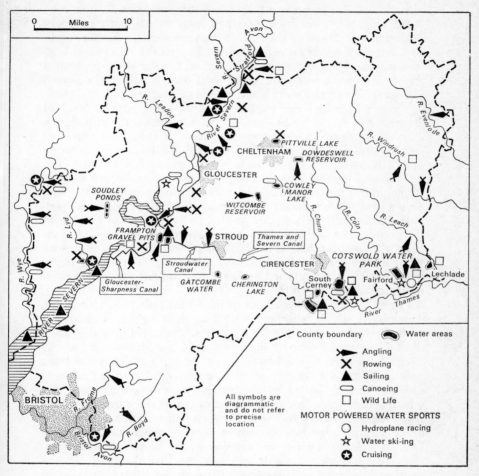

Fig 78. Water-based recreation in Gloucestershire (after Gloucestershire CC *Outdoor Water Recreation*, Figure 2).

recreational use is limited to comparatively few activities, except in their broader and more fully navigable stretches.

Perhaps their most important role is as an adjunct to scenery in themselves. Much of the lure of water is visual, whether sparkling, gurgling mountain torrent or the lazy stealth of a placid lowland stream. Many an urban exile echoes Rupert Brooke's lament 'for water sweet and cool, gentle and brown, above the pool'[72] and searches out the river bank for picnic and for play.

To this informal use is allied that of angling. The level of demand for this sport has already been emphasised: although it may vary greatly in character and extent, it is evident wherever water yields fish of any quality. Industrial effluent may decrease potential—often in urban areas where demand is keenest—but measures of control have increasing impact. To take but one example, in the Irwell in Lancashire whose murky waters have long been a byword for industrial filth, pollution levels have been dropping dramatically. The upper reaches to Bury have only one-fifth the pollution of five years ago, and even between Bury and Manchester it has been halved in the same period. Fish have been seen as far downstream as Agecroft and fishing rights are being negotiated for its tributary, the Croal, where clubs have released 17,000 roach, rudd and perch.[73]

For all these uses, it is access to the banks rather than on to the water itself which is important.[74] The right to fish is associated with the bed of the river: the owners of the bank usually own the bed to mid-stream though this need not necessarily be the case. Many owners are helpful over access, but this is far from universally true. Useful powers were conveyed by the Countryside Act which added to the category of 'open country' for which access orders could be agreed or enforced, waterways, land adjoining waterways and access strips to them. Such powers are, of course, discretionary but their very existence should underline an existing climate of opinion. One of the newest long-distance footpath proposals, perhaps the first designed for the gentler rambler, is a 73-mile walk through the Yorkshire Dales to the Lake District and following for the most part the banks of the Wharfe, the Dee, the Lune and the Kent.

Widespread river navigation is possible only by canoe where passage can be secured with a depth of only nine inches and a width of two feet. On broader, deeper stretches, rowing, sailing and cruising become possible, and the lower reaches of most rivers

are an invaluable part of the network of navigable waterways.
Depth requirements have been quoted as 3ft 6in for motor cruisers
and 4ft for yachts, but this is affected in detail by the particular
type or class of vessel concerned.[75] It is interesting to recall that
in 1724 1,160 miles of river were navigable for commercial craft,[76]
and though the total used in this way has now shrunk to a tiny
fraction,

> On a summer day the punts, the canoes and the motor
> launches rise in Boulter's Lock on the surge of water from
> the gates, till they are released to explore Cliveden Reach and
> the approach to Cookham. The pleasure craft, and the holiday
> makers in them, seem to suit the river, as if it had been
> dredged for ease of holidaying.[77]

The heritage of larger natural water bodies is far more restricted.
Apart from mountain tarns and meadow ponds, invaluable though
they may be in their scenic setting, there are few lakes of any size
outside the Lake District and the Broads. In the whole of Wales
there is no natural stretch of water bigger than Bala Lake, with
an area of 1·7 square miles, little over half the size of Liverpool's
reservoir at Lake Vyrnwy.

The scarcity of resources intensifies the pressures on those
which do exist. As frequent references have already shown, parts
of the Lake District suffer perhaps the most intensive use of any
area of Britain for both land- and water-based recreation. Pressures are equally evident in Broadland, the largest fully-linked
network of separate rivers and major inland waters in Great
Britain: navigable waterways here extend for some 120 miles, the
freshwater broads up to the 300-acre expanse of Hickling Broad
and Breydon Water in the estuary of the Yare to 2,167 acres at
high spring tides.[78] But even a resource on this scale is hard
pressed to accommodate demand. The first boat-hire firm was
created in 1878, but by 1938 the annual number of holidaymakers
in the region was estimated at 100,000[79] and by 1964 over one-
quarter of a million.[80] In 1964, there were 9,247 licensed craft
of all kinds on the Broads, and of these 4,740 were for hire.
Growth has been particularly rapid in power-driven craft, with a
four-fold increase between 1947 and 1964. It was estimated that
some 10,000 berths were available in cabin-craft at the latter date
and that some 10,000 people a year were regularly sailing in the
area.

CANALS

The increasing popularity of water-based recreation and the relative scarcity of sheltered stretches of natural water inland for its satisfaction, has focused attention on the available artificially created alternatives. Of these, the canals are in many ways the most interesting, an historical survival finding a totally new justification. Commercially, 'the real problem of the waterways . . . is simply the difficulty of an older form of transport competing with newer ones which may be cheaper, more expeditious or more flexible in operation'.[81] The commercial vicissitudes of a 200-year-old system, spawned when the competitor was the carrier's wagon and the pack-horse, are not the present concern. Suffice to say that by 1962, it had an annual deficit of some £2 million, over 40 per cent of gross revenue. In 1965, the new and vigorous British Waterways Board published *The facts about the waterways* which provided an invaluable account of the actual and potential uses of the network. These uses are summarised in Figure 79, but from this study emerged the conclusion that only a very small proportion of the network was commercially viable by any reasonable criteria.

For the remainder, the financial outlook was grim indeed. To adopt for each such waterway the cheapest possible solution (elimination where practicable, or the cheapest form of water channelling) would cost a minimum of £600,000 a year at 1965 prices. Maintenance of this non-commercial network to a standard suitable for pleasure cruising would cost an additional £340,000 a year. To put these figures in perspective, net annual income from recreational uses was amounting to only some £20,000 from angling and £70,000 from pleasure craft.

Faced with these unpalatable facts, the Government took a bold decision. The 'inescapable' deficit of £600,000 a year was recognised but the intention was further announced 'to retain for pleasure cruising substantially the existing network available for this purpose' and that 'this recreational purpose of the nationalised waterways should be recognised by public Act of Parliament'.[82] This decision, subsequently passed into legislation, was remarkable in more ways than one. It not only secured a network of 'cruiseways' freed from the uncertainty of regular review, but marked the beginning of a more creative attitude towards recreation and amenity in general. A public body was charged with 'a

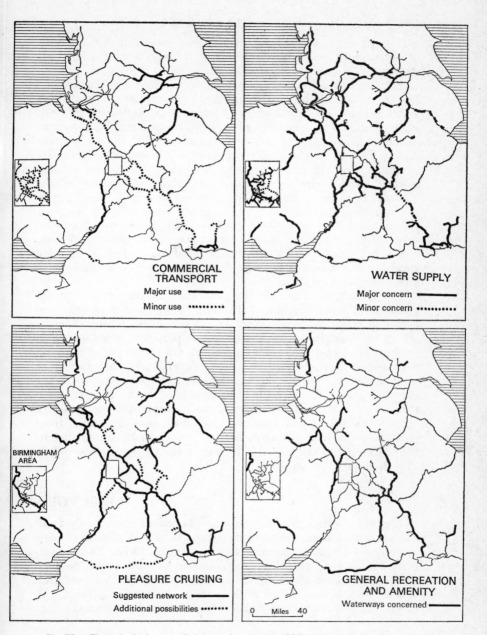

COMMERCIAL
TRANSPORT
Major use ━━━━━
Minor use •••••••••

WATER SUPPLY
Major concern ━━━━━
Minor concern •••••••••

BIRMINGHAM
AREA

PLEASURE CRUISING
Suggested network ━━━━━
Additional possibilities •••••••

0   Miles   40

GENERAL RECREATION
AND AMENITY
Waterways concerned ━━━━━

Fig 79. The principal uses of the canal network, 1965 (data from *The facts about the waterways*).

new and positive role to play in the development of this potential' of the waterways, a role backed by the necessary financial resources.

The 'cruiseway' network covers some 1,400 miles (Figure 80). Its importance lies both in its inherent character as a unified route system and in the location of the areas it serves. Reflecting its commercial origins 'to take coal, china clay, timber, etc, from port to inland town and from one town to another',[83] the network is closely related to the pattern of population and thus is readily accessible for its present users. Visually, 'contrast is of the essence' for though 'the pleasure they give is sharpened by the glimpses of urban landscape and industrial history . . .' yet ' . . . on the waterways, countryside begins much sooner than it does for the harassed road user. Only a mile or two away from the town centre there is, very often, a sanctuary from noise and confusion . . .' while further still 'hundreds of miles of small peaceful rural canals insinuate their way through the glories of the English and Welsh countrysides'.[84]

The attraction of the canals is not only visual, for part of the pleasure of canal cruising still stems from their relatively uncrowded state. In 1968, there were some 12,000 craft afloat or ashore on a single day[85]—less than nine per mile, compared with an average of 59·2 road vehicles per mile for the whole of the road network of Great Britain in 1967.[86] Nevertheless, the number of craft licences showed an increase of 12·6 per cent over the previous year and it remains to be seen how the waterways retain their appeal as numbers increase and congestion more nearly approaches conditions obtaining on the roads. Revenue from pleasure craft was £146,616 in 1968, more than double that of four years previously, but reflecting a change in pricing policy as well as a growth in traffic.

RESERVOIRS

The use of canals for recreation has benefited enormously from the present statutory requirement of the British Waterways Board actively to promote amenity and recreation. Other bodies concerned with the control and exploitation of water have no such duty, and this has given rise to increasing conflicts and pressures. It must be said that not all such conflicts arise from inherent lack of sympathy towards potential recreational use by river authorities

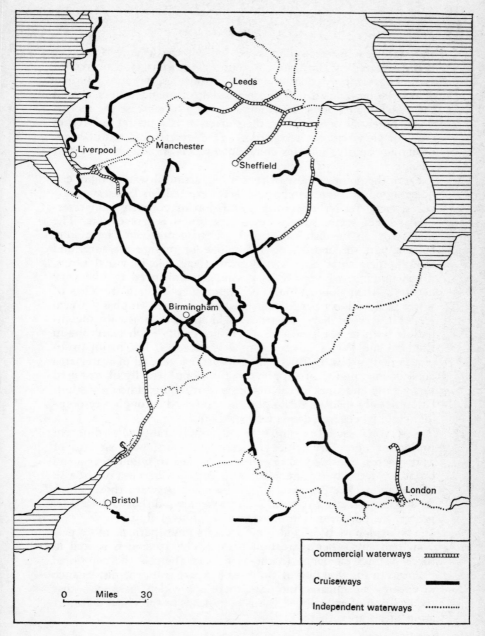

Fig 80. The cruiseway network (data from *British Waterways: recreation and amenity*).

Commercial waterways
Cruiseways
Independent waterways

Leeds
Liverpool
Manchester
Sheffield
Birmingham
Bristol
London

0   Miles   30

and statutory water undertakers. Indeed, the Water Resources Board, created by the Water Resources Act of 1963, is on record as feeling strongly that 'the river authorities, because of their direct responsibility for the management of inland waters, should themselves be empowered to initiate action to increase the recreational potential of waters in their areas. It is a matter for regret that our view was not accepted . . .'[87] Nevertheless, attitudes are changing rapidly, and this comment itself is an indication of that change.

From the point of view of recreation, artificial water bodies can be grouped into five categories: lakes created for landscape purposes; canal feeder reservoirs; regulation or compensation reservoirs; direct water supply reservoirs; and wet gravel pits. The first two can be dismissed briefly. Ornamental lakes have long been a part of landscaping for public or private pleasure, and though their total area is not great, their role in visual terms, for swimming, rowing or even sailing is enhanced by the very nature of their conception. The importance of such stretches of water as London's Serpentine needs no further emphasis. Canal feeder reservoirs have a purpose which is not normally incompatible with recreational use. There are eighty such reservoirs in England and Wales, covering some 3,318 acres. The major problem in their use is the fluctuation of water level and of water area consequent upon their supply function, but virtually all are used for angling and those of adequate size for sailing. The only stipulation usually made is that rights are exercised through a responsible club, to ensure adequate supervision.[88]

Reservoirs used for public water supply raise very different problems. There are some 550 such reservoirs, with an area of 35,000 acres, but many are completely closed to public access and on others recreational use is severely curtailed because of the risk of pollution. The distinction must be made between those which feed water directly to public supply systems and those whose purpose is the compensation or regulation of river flow.

The exploitation of land for reservoirs raises perhaps more passion than any other recreational issue. This passion is rooted in three distinct elements. In the first place there is the emotional reaction to the flooding of rural land. Apart from the disturbance of existing agricultural interests, there is a widely held view that the creation of an artificial water body leads to the visual deterioration of an area, that

. . . a reservoir is an urban service and in that sense is an extension of the town into the country. It carries with it the characteristics of the town and thereby suburbanises the country. In our national parks, which contain the last remaining and very limited reserves of wild country in England and Wales, to reduce either the extent or the quality of it is to squander a part of our environmental capital for ever.[89]

While there is a real measure of truth in such reactions, a water body need not be without its own inherent attraction and an artificial Lake District can have much to commend it.

But reaction is intensified by the total area necessarily involved, and not only by the area of water surface but by the whole catchment area. In the Peak District, for example, too conveniently near to surrounding conurbations, nearly 30 per cent of the area is used as gathering ground for reservoirs.[90]

Both these objections, however, would have had much less impact if reservoirs and catchment areas had not long been effectively restricted for other use, whether agricultural or recreational. This has been the case in areas of high landscape value. Manchester's inroads on the Lake District are a classic instance. Mardale was virtually sterilised when Haweswater became a reservoir; at Thirlmere 'one can do no more than drive round it at a respectful distance'; and more recently the schemes for Ullswater and Windermere have provoked bitter and prolonged legal battles. It is equally the case in areas of far less inherent quality, but closer to the urban areas they serve, when a potential source of pleasure is seemingly standing idle and unapproachable. Sheffield, for example, a fairly liberal authority, allows sailing on only 343 acres of the 2,057 acres of reservoirs situated within sixteen miles of its town hall.[91]

The roots of the problem are historical and technical. The creation of a pure water supply for burgeoning urban areas became a major preoccupation in the nineteenth century, but at a time when the inherent value of land as a scarce and frequently beautiful resource was not adequately appreciated. 'The foresight of Victorian engineers who built for posterity is often commended, whilst the truth may be that some of those who built large water projects did not take sufficient account of the resources they were pre-empting and set a rigid pattern of development for too far ahead.'[92] The technical need was to 'provide a sufficient and wholesome supply of water'.[93] Pollution can be minimised by filtration and chlorination, but the traditional view of water authorities has been that the best defences are the elimination of possible sources of pollution and long storage and that these can best be maintained by excluding humans altogether from reservoirs and from vast tracts of catchment areas. Increased access means improved processing, and water undertakings 'cannot be expected as a general rule to incur heavy expenditure arising from the provision of recreational facilities . . .'[94]

In the last two decades, however, methods and attitudes have changed. In the first place, it is increasingly rare for major storage schemes in remote areas to be linked directly by pipelines to consuming areas. Rather, the policy has been 'that water should move naturally and cheaply from one part of the area to the other by using the rivers themselves so that the maximum benefit from the conservation accrues to all users'.[95] Reservoirs thus become regulatory in function and there need be no inhibitions about contamination. This new generation may be exemplified by Liverpool's Tryweryn reservoir, inaugurated in 1965. Two and a half miles long, and three-quarters of a mile wide, it is used to regulate the flow of a tributary of the Dee: actual abstraction is some seventy miles away, from the Dee near Chester. In consequence, this new sheet of water within the Snowdonia National Park is not only a visual attraction in itself, but sailing and fishing are encouraged, car parks, laybys and lavatories have been provided and a camping and picnic site developed.

But changes in attitudes have been just as important as changes in techniques. The White Paper, *Leisure in the countryside: England and Wales* recognised that 'access to many reservoirs is still restricted and sometimes forbidden without sufficient reason' and that for new reservoirs '. . . arrangements usually are, and certainly should be made, at the planning stage so that the full recreational possibilities can be taken into account and the appropriate facilities . . . included'. The Institution of Water Engineers itself, in its report *Recreational Use of Waterworks* (1963) emphasised '. . . that no risks should be taken with the quality of water supply to the public . . .' but added that 'access to many reservoirs and waterworks lands, from which water is filtered and sterilised, could be permitted if reasonable regulations for control are applied'.

Government policies were underlined by the 1966 circular *Use of reservoirs and gathering grounds for recreation.* For regulatory and compensation reservoirs 'the Ministers know of no sufficient reason why . . . the public should be denied recreational access . . .' For supply reservoirs 'there is still scope in many areas for reviewing the existing rules': the Institution of Water Engineers' advice is accepted that sailing, angling and bird-watching are wholly compatible with the use of water for public supply, providing adequate control is exercised. Administration is best practised through recognised clubs, and the return in fees should cover the necessary additional expenditure. A typical example of such arrangements is seen in the case of Leeds Corporation's new Thruscross Reservoir in the Washburn Valley, where the Leeds Sailing Club has been permitted to sail up to 100 sailing dinghies at any one time for a trial period of two years.

Older attitudes, too, are changing. Manchester's restrictive policy in the Lake District has been modified with the building of water treatment plant at Watchgate in Long Sleddale through which water from Haweswater, Ullswater and Windermere will pass. In Mardale, there will be 'a new life of guarded hospitality to the holidaymaker',[96] with hostel, caravan and camping sites, car parks and footpaths. Existing rights of access on Ullswater and Windermere will be preserved. In a time of land hunger, water storage can no longer be regarded as the sole rightful use of large areas of land: indeed, as one water engineer has recently stated, 'multi-purpose use, under skilful and unified control, should be expected to convert at least some . . . conflicting interests into compatible or even beneficial ones'. Indeed '. . . multi-purpose use might make the construction of a new reservoir an economic possibility in a case where no single-purpose reservoir would be economic'.[97] Recreational use figures high amongst such purposes.

GRAVEL PITS

Important as this new attitude towards reservoirs and recreation may be, it is important not to over-emphasise it. The numbers of potential sites are comparatively few and many too small in area for uses other than angling. It has been estimated that the effective capacity of a water body for sailing lies between one boat to half an acre to one boat to two acres, depending in part on the class of boat concerned.[98] Indeed, perhaps the only major body of inland water on which real expansion could take place are wet gravel pits, the flooded remnants of excavations for sand and gravel on low ground or in river flood plains. In 1964, some 90 million cubic yards of sand and gravel were being produced from some 1,350 pits,[99] the industry as a whole presenting a major problem of land reclamation. Wet pits are in particular demand for recreation in south-east and midland England, where other water bodies, apart from rivers, are comparatively scarce. A survey of twenty-seven counties showed 5,500 acres of wet-pit lakes being used for recreation by 168 fishing, sailing, water ski-ing and canoeing clubs.[100] However, such lakes may be relatively transitory features. They may not only be considered a nuisance by local opinion, but are economically valuable for tipping of building or industrial waste.

One example of the potential of such areas is seen in the Cotswold Water Park of the upper Thames Valley. Here, gravel working is concentrated in two main areas, south and west of South Cerney and between Fairford and Lechlade; the two areas being linked by the Thames. At present there are some 700 acres of water, but ultimately 3–4,000 acres may be available for water sports. The area is already intensively used for a wide range of activities—rowing, canoeing, fishing, sailing, hydro-planing, water ski-ing and motorboat racing. In 1967, a joint committee of Gloucestershire and Wiltshire County Councils, and Cirencester, Cricklade and Wootton Bassett Rural District Councils was established to advise on the maintenance and development of the Water Park. Their intention is, in due course, to acquire some of the pits 'and arrange for their ordered development in accordance with a Master Plan, which will ensure the continuation of water sports already established in the area and provide for further recreation facilities as the pits are extended or new pits created'.[101] The involvement of local authorities in the development of facilities on this regional scale is indeed a tribute to the lure of water and the winds of change.

CHAPTER EIGHT

Problems and Prospects

LEISURE AND RESOURCES

At this period of time, the population density has reached the critical level, and the choices before the community lie between the over-exploitation of resources to the long-term detriment of the system, the planning of new systems of resource use . . . and population control.[1]

SIR JOSEPH HUTCHINSON'S assessment is applicable to a far greater range of resources than those devoted to recreation alone, but even in the limited context of the use of land for leisure it has an inexorable ring. Much of this book has been concerned, explicitly or implicitly, with pressure, the pressure of an escalating demand for outdoor recreation on finite resources of land and water. In the long run other pressures may be more critical, but few are as intimately involved with the potential quality of life in town and country.

In part, the pressure arises from sheer weight of numbers. England and Wales already have a mean density of population more than double that of India, and it is tempting to agree with Sir Joseph that 'this country is in fact over-populated now, and will inevitably be more heavily over-populated in the future, whatever we may decide to do about it'.[2] But speculation as to optimum population (Sir Joseph's target figure was 40 millions) brings no solution to the problems presented by such numbers and by their seemingly inevitable increase.

So far as recreation is concerned, numbers alone are only the beginning of the problem, as earlier chapters have shown. As mobility and affluence have become no longer the prerogative of the few but the expectation of the many, so demand has become more widespread in its areal impact and tastes more varied and sophisticated. Within a generation there has been change of kind as well as of degree. As in so many other respects, the Second World War marked a fundamental watershed: though many trends were clearly evidenced between the wars, only since 1945 have they become really widespread. Along with burgeoning demand has grown increased development control and the widespread recognition (if not always ready acceptance) of physical planning as the inevitable concomitant of increasing pressure on land resources.

It is in this context that the present pattern of leisure and land use, the focus of this book, must be viewed. Existing pressures pose problems enough, but it must never be forgotten that the situation is essentially dynamic and solutions must be sought which anticipate both the direction and the scale of change. The prediction of that change is no easy matter, indeed

. . . it is only over the short term that predictions about changing leisure patterns may be made with any confidence or projections calculated geared to present associations . . . The longer term of the next two or three decades is one in which radical change may overtake and overturn conclusions derived merely from the present trend, and in which therefore the process of prediction—in the ordinary sense—may have little validity.[3]

But though precise prediction may be hazardous and even premature, the reality of existing pressures remains and in conclusion some further means of alleviating those pressures will be considered, means which underline the need to use resources of land and water to the full. It is not intended to draw up a planning blueprint or to presage revolutionary change, but rather to highlight processes already taking place, the wider acceptance of which would ease some problems of outdoor recreation and enhance the enjoyment of leisure for many.

TIME AND SEASON

Recreation pressures are limited in both time and space. The analysis of demand clearly demonstrated that most outdoor leisure pursuits are characterised by extreme seasonality and periodicity. Peak demand is limited in most cases to a few fine summer week-ends and to Sundays in particular, and even in the major holiday areas to a high season of no more than two months. Outside these periods, demand for the majority of activities can be readily satisfied under most existing conditions. Such concentration not only lessens satisfaction at a time when most are seeking it but makes economic viability for many recreation enterprises much harder to achieve. Yet of all problems in recreation, this is the least tractable, for any solution affects patterns of living far beyond recreation alone. Life is not yet sufficiently leisure-oriented for the demands of leisure to dictate its rhythms.

The situation has some hopeful trends. Holidaymaking is becoming a little more flexible. The incidence of school holidays still restricts the main holiday period for many to some six or eight weeks in July and August, but late May, June and September are little less suited for the purposes from a climatic point of view and more drastic staggering of holidays from both classroom and workshop should be encouraged. One major educational constraint is the timing of public examinations: the coming overhaul of the school examination system might well consider as radical a review of timing as of syllabus.

Patterns are also changing as long holidays become more widespread. When a single fortnight ceases to be the focus of the holiday experience and second and even third holidays become more widespread, the timing of the main holiday becomes less critical. The increasing number of second holidays has already been indicated (Chapter 5) and the spread of this habit may bring important repercussions on the intensity and the duration of the holiday season as a whole.

More rapid progress may perhaps be achieved in blunting the existing distinction between the working week and the weekend. As a truly five-day week becomes more universal, and as continuous processing in industry focuses attention on a four- or five-shift week regardless of the actual days involved, there should be a lessening emphasis on Sunday as the major opportunity for a continuous period of recreation away from home. Such changes may spread rather than lessen the load, but when a ready alternative is available to the Sunday outing there may be less inclination to tolerate congested roads and crowded facilities.

It would be less than realistic, however, to assume that major changes in the timing of recreation will either come quickly or bring extensive relief to the intensity of peak demands. Pressures may be spread but scarcely lessened, for any relief which may accrue in this way will be more than countered by the general upsurge of demand. It is through more effective use of space rather than through more widespread use of leisure time that reduced pressure and increased pleasure must be sought.

SEGREGATION AND CONSERVATION

Some forms of outdoor recreation make but small demands on space, and demands that can easily be calculated. Team games, such as tennis and bowls, are all 'compact' pursuits with relatively slight rates of growth. Many are primarily urban or urban fringe in location. The provision of adequate pitches, courts and greens makes comparatively little demand on land: there may be many difficulties in particular locations, but overall the problems in making adequate provision are relatively small.

This is far from the case with rapidly growing open country pursuits, whether passive recreations such as driving, picnicking and view-gazing or the more active endeavours of golfer, hiker, climber, rider or sailor. Almost all these activities are hungry for land and for many the desire for relative solitude still further lowers the effective capacity of rural areas to absorb the consequent pressures. Tracts of remote country, moorlands and mountains

. . . offer the last illusion, in Britain, of escape from the civilised world. Presumably this is what the 'serious' visitor seeks from them, but if his view from the upland slopes is of the ribbon development of picnic parties along the valley road he leaves dissatisfied.[4]

To date, the reactions of many planning authorities to increased pressures have been comparatively simple. As roads become clogged, improvements are made to remove bottlenecks and raise capacity: such improvements generate further demand and the end product is all too rarely a solution and all too often undesired

and more intense congestion. The fundamental problem remains, of a finite (indeed with urban and industrial growth, a shrinking) resource measured against a burgeoning demand, and a demand which is not that of outdoor recreation alone but of all forms of rural land use.

Any approach to a solution must be vitally concerned with two major factors which have been constantly reiterated in earlier chapters. In the first place, there is the paradox inherent in so much countryside legislation which seeks to improve access while at the same time promoting conservation. 'Given that towns-people ought to be able to spend their leisure in the country if they want to . . . the problem is to enable them to enjoy this leisure without harm to those who live and work in the country, and without spoiling what they go to the countryside to seek'.[5] In the resolution of this paradox, full regard must be paid to the second factor, the spatial pattern of demand, its concentration into intensively used nodes, with linear linkage of roads, bridle tracks and paths. The vast majority want simply a view of 'un-spoiled' countryside while driving, walking or riding, and their physical contact with the countryside is confined to the routeway they have chosen.

Hitherto, there has been little positive management of this de-mand, except in areas of most acute pressure, but the scale of demand is now such that a simple laissez faire attitude can no longer suffice. Management involves planning, and planning in this context the acceptance of what to many are unpalatable principles of direction and control. Freedom in leisure may well have to be relative rather than absolute if a real measure of enjoyment is to remain.

The spatial pattern of demand suggests that management should begin with the horizontal segregation of the varied demands on rural land, a segregation already characteristic of much existing use. To be effective, segregation must be founded upon a careful evaluation of resources, based on physical characteristics, visual quality, existing use and ultimate potential. One classic approach was that of the Outdoor Recreation Resources Review Commis-sion in the USA which sought to delineate recreation zones based upon relationships between physical resource characteristics and public recreation needs.[6] Six broad classes were outlined (Figure 81) and management principles laid down for each. The ideas developed in the ORRRC report have a much wider application

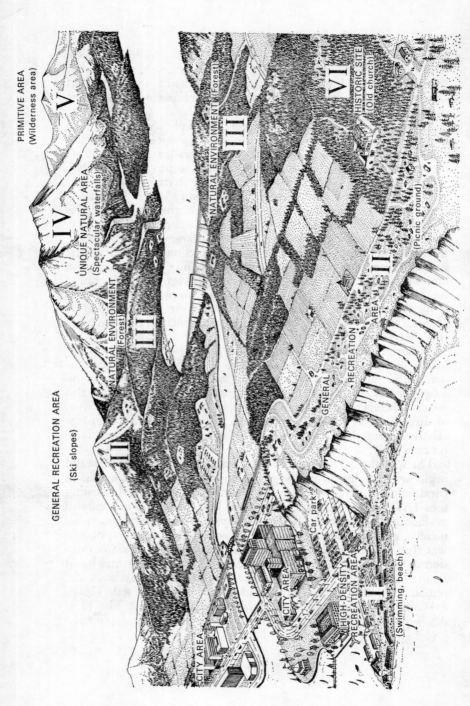

Fig 81. The classification of recreation areas in the USA (based on a diagram in *Outdoor Recreation for America*).

than to the USA alone, but their relevance to the British situation is limited in two ways. In the first place, they were designed for a country where pressure on land resources is far less acute and where extensive tracts can be developed for recreation or conservation alone. Only one of the six categories (Class III, natural environment areas) was envisaged as being 'usually in combination with other uses'. Secondly, as a logical corollary, they exclude all 'land not suited or available for recreation' along with roads and other means of access. In England and Wales, where virtually the whole rural area is farmed or forested to some degree, the aesthetic appeal of the developed landscape is no small part of the rural contribution to visual pleasure.

Despite these reservations, the basic principles are still important. Areas must be identified where conservation should be the paramount concern, where recreation interests should be dominant or where existing ways of life can be pursued unchallenged. In part, of course, such principles already lie entrenched in existing legislation and planning practice. But a finer appraisal of resources is needed and a more positive attitude to management and control. Techniques have been evolved,[7] but they need more universal application, and designation must be matched by effective and appropriate action.

RURAL HEARTLAND

Most at risk are those areas of the highest scenic quality whose attraction is national rather than regional or local. Their appeal may be largely visual or may lie also in a sense of remoteness and wildness instilled by their sheer extent. Most of these areas are already embodied in National Parks or Areas of Outstanding Natural Beauty yet it is in these areas that the paradox induced by the need for conservation and the desire for access is most intense.

The very existence of this paradox suggests a twofold approach to the problem, and one which is reinforced by existing patterns of use. In the first place, areas should be identified where conservation is the prime concern. These would be far more limited in extent than existing conservation areas (Figure 62) and more specialised in purpose, more akin in fact to the larger National Nature Reserves. Many would coincide with John Dower's 'relatively wild country', their aim to keep as unspoiled as possible existing sweeps of moorland and mountain, rough watershed country away from established roads and other means of mass access. Access would not be prohibited, but would only be possible by those prepared to walk considerable distances. There can be few more effective means of ensuring relative isolation. In some parts, there would be freedom to roam at will; in others it might be necessary to restrict access to marked paths.

Much upland country away from roads already falls into this category but areas designated in this way would be regarded as inalienable so far as intrusive developments are concerned. They would, of course, continue to be farmed: the aim would not be to create an empty wilderness, but to preserve the visual and spiritual quality of isolation and desolate beauty. It might well be that farming would need more rigorous control than has hitherto been acceptable, both with regard to land use and building development, but again the aim would not be to fossilise an existing pattern but to ensure that change is sympathetic to the character of the area as a whole.[8] Such control would be an added financial penalty to farming in what are already marginal conditions, but the corollary would be a recreation subsidy as compensation. An interesting precursor of this principle was initiated by the Countryside Commission in 1969 with payments to farmers on the western slopes of the Rhinogs in Snowdonia and in Martindale and Patterdale in the Lake District towards such tasks as marking paths (and thereby discouraging trespass), clearing rubbish, tree planting and repairing walls and fences broken by thoughtless visitors.[9]

The extent of such areas would be conditioned by public attitudes and available finance. Not all, however, need be in classic upland areas. Many relatively undistinguished stretches of moorland would benefit in this way in areas such as parts of mid-Wales or the eastern Pennines (the watershed country both east and west of upper Nidderdale springs readily to mind), and so too would other lowland farming areas of high visual quality, with a 'rural' rather than a 'wilderness' appeal. The overall aim would not be strictly that of nature conservation, but the preservation of remoteness against all except the determined walker.

The corollary of such conservation areas would be positive development of access in other areas of high quality, but access tempered by control on the routeways followed and the viewpoints used. It seems unduly selfish to preserve as the walker's prerogative all the best panoramas: Lliwedd or Crib Goch may be the rightful heritage of the energetic, but for many the Snowdon Railway fills a heartfelt need. If conservation areas of the kind discussed may be considered Class V areas in the American categorisation (primitive or wilderness areas), then Class IV areas (unique natural areas) are those to which effective access should be secured while preserving their uniqueness. This would mean powers to purchase land, build laybys and car parks in selected areas not just to absorb cars but to give easy access to worthwhile viewpoints, or even to build new roads with an avowedly recreational purpose.

One example may suffice of the possibilities envisaged. The Malham area is one of the major nodes of attraction in the Yorkshire Dales National Park. At present, the motorist leaving Malham village on the road to the west of Malham Cove is enjoined by stern notice not to halt despite the stirring views of the Cove which open up. The paths to the Cove and Gordale Scar are unmade, but pressure of numbers wears grass bare. Despite the new car park in Malham village, the present situation neither gives really adequate access nor preserves rural quietude. How much better it would be to accept that enjoyment can in this instance best be served by building adequate overlooks, perhaps coupled with one-way traffic on a rebuilt loop of road between Malham village and Malham Tarn, access to the Cove and Gorge on made footpaths with explanatory displays as to the origin of these features, and perhaps fields devoted to picnicking south of the village along the banks of the stream. The development of such a node would be designed more as a true park for both enjoyment and instruction: it would imply some change in land ownership and extensive capital outlay. To the country lover horrified at such a thought, one can only point to the very small area actually involved, and the much vaster sweeps of surrounding upland from Kirkby Fell through Fountains and Darnbrook Fells to Kilnsey and Malham Moors which could be preserved in the ways outlined earlier.

Conservation and access areas would be the opposing poles of development in the rural heartland, catering for very different needs, but between them they are far from co-extensive with the whole of existing National Parks and AONBs. Shortage of finance and existing agricultural interests would preclude such sweeping change. Much would remain subject to existing development control, lightly conserved, with positive provision for recreation largely confined to relatively minor improvements along the main corridors of movement, with the attraction of the area being the general quality of the intervening rural scene. It may rightly be made easier to view from a passing car, but its overall character (and overall recreational capacity) would not be greatly changed except at the selected nodes.

Inevitably therefore, with increasing pressures some measure of constraint will have to be applied at peak periods, however limited these may be. Such constraints can be of various kinds. The most widespread is that of simply curbing demand to match supply. On a small scale, the principle is familiar enough with those facilities which have a finite capacity, as for example when all seats are occupied in the sports stadium or all boats hired on the boating lake. It is less easy to apply in an open country situation, though road congestion and limited parking impose crude filters. Ultimately, indeed, the capacity of the corridors determines the pressure of use. Size of car parks is more frequently the determinant of 'crowded' or 'empty' beaches than the nature of the beach itself. In the Forest of Bowland it was noted that on a peak summer Sunday afternoon 'in many cases car parking counts represent the existing physical capacity of the centre'.[10]

Although such a constraint may limit pressures to an acceptable level, it is both negative and frustrating in operation. One alternative is the more extended use of pricing mechanisms. The principle is already well established. Club subscriptions for various sports both restrain and sort demand: golf is a prime example of price restraint. It is no coincidence that golf is of negligible significance for those with incomes much below £1,200 per annum (Chapter 2). Entry fees to stately homes and other 'attractions' provide a basis of commercial viability and the price can be adjusted to restrain or stimulate demand to an acceptable level. Traditionally, the countryside is 'free' though not in many privately-owned parts to which there is public access. It is possible to envisage many further extensions of price restraint as an instrument of policy as well as a means of ensuring an economic return for the high cost of providing facilities. Car parks with prices graded according to the attraction of the hinterland, scenic routes with tolls charged at peak periods[11] or admission charges to view major natural features are all possibilities however abhorrent to present opinion.[12]

COUNTRY CONCENTRATIONS

Previous discussion, whether concerned with development or constraint, has focused on those areas of countryside or coast which afford the most attractive opportunities, the 'heartland' of rural recreation experience. But such areas of England and Wales cater for only a small proportion of total demand. Many are difficult of access from the South East in particular and it is towards rural areas nearest to the major urban areas that the greater volume of demand is directed. More adequate provision here not only satisfies existing demand, but helps in filtering off some of the pressure on the high resource areas. In some counties, the creation of attractions to 'intercept' those who would otherwise visit more popular areas is already declared policy,[13] and the same thinking lies behind the current promotion of country parks.

In more intensively farmed areas the potential clash of interest between agriculture and recreation is even greater but again capable of resolution when the inherent nature of recreation demand is considered. The actual demands of leisure on land remain comparatively small: in the East Hampshire study, it was shown that ideally by the early 1980s an additional 1 per cent of the whole area would be needed for recreational purposes (Chapter 4). Urban man is still concerned primarily with the *appearance* of the countryside—a compelling concern, with many implications for agricultural practice and conservation as such,[14] but one adding little to actual pressures on land use. Demand remains linear and nodal: it is what he sees from his chosen viewpoint, whether overlook, footpath or moving car, which is important for his enjoyment not actual physical contact with the land. Roads may be congested on summer Sundays, but adjacent fields remain relatively inviolate.

Along the corridors of movement, roads and footpaths, contrasts in use are also evident. While pressures do indeed mount on country lanes, most are well able to cope even at times of peak loading. The average motorist (to the joy and benefit of the minority) still concentrates on A and B roads, the average walker to a few well-known and well-trodden paths: sophisticated map-reading is still an unfamiliar exercise to many. In one sense, such unfamiliarity preserves remoteness for many rural areas, but in another it deprives many people of a more satisfying recreational experience.

Such considerations suggest the need to manage roads as consistently as land, and to integrate the planning of the two. At present, road improvements which do not affect the boundary of the highway are 'permitted development', and the Highways Committee can go its own way without reference to the Planning Committee. Minor roads are subject to parochial pressures.

With insufficient funds, at times insufficient for maintenance, and demands from every corner of the county, the County Surveyor can all too easily be forced into sprinkling the countryside with isolated small improvements. It is the minor road which gets these because they are 'local' and because they achieve the maximum peace at minimum cost.[15]

It must be remembered that the recreational use of minor roads is only one part of their overall function: nevertheless selective improvement and selective restraint can do much on the one hand to relieve pressure on other roads yet on the other to preserve a tolerable level of quietude.

The development of a broad strategy is obviously necessary. New corridors of movement can be created by the promotion of scenic drives. Gloucestershire envisages the development of such a route along the Cotswold escarpment, with ready access to viewpoints and parking facilities, including a series of small car parks immediately adjoining the road where the view can be enjoyed without leaving the car.[16] Similarly, the Forestry Commission hope to publicise a circular route through the Forest of Dean, using existing roads to link picnic places and beauty spots, and with information centres explaining the work of the Commission and local history and ecology as an integral part of the design.[17] Apart from the merits of such routes in focusing movement, the provision of adequate laybys at viewpoints is of major assistance in easing traffic flow.

Such examples use existing routes and a particularly attractive setting. In some places, scenic quality may justify new road construction. The Blue Ridge Parkway of the Appalachians of the eastern United States could have its counterpart here in a Plynlimmon Skyline Drive, for example, which by building eight miles of new road from Cwmbiga to Nant y Moch would provide a continuous route from Llandidloes to Tal y Bont.[18] Such routes could well be narrow, with a low maximum speed and a ban on stopping except at designated points: they could also be toll roads to recoup something at least of the price of enjoyment.

Schemes of this kind would be the aristocrats of the system. At the opposite end of the scale many areas of comparatively modest attraction, but readily accessible from the major concentrations of population, could be threaded by designated scenic routes, carefully if unobtrusively sign-posted to create an effective network but using existing minor roads. Enjoyment would be enhanced by adequate laybys: in many areas, the broad margins characteristic of many roads aligned at the time of enclosure could be used for this purpose. In some cases, further emphasis could be given to the route by providing a focus of interest other than scenery alone. 'Heritage highways' could link places associated with people and events of our rich history. In the USA, Illinois has its Lincoln Trail, existing roads with signs and information markers added to trace the journeys of young Lincoln in the State. British counterparts are too numerous to need extended mention, but include themes as diverse as the classic campaigns of the Civil War and the newly-recognised heritage of industrial archaeology. A carefully routed tour of industrial sites in the Staffordshire potteries, of the cotton industry in south-east Lancashire or of the iron workings of the North Riding would certainly add interest and variety to recreational as well as educational experience.

Such developments should be matched by deliberate lack of emphasis in other areas: absolute closure of roads is rarely possible because of the needs of local traffic, but dead-end signs can be reasonably effective deterrents. Throughout, the stress should be on conscious management, with clearly defined policy objectives in channelling recreation traffic as well as matching existing needs. Positive provision is obviously appreciated, at times embarrassingly so. Stockport and District Water Board's Errwood reservoir in the Goyt valley, opened in 1968, was designed with picnic sites and overviews on the fringing road, but increased use soon brought the need for one-way traffic, and, in 1970, the creation of an experimental motorless zone at summer weekends.[19] But guided use is better than misuse and frustration, a comment that applies as much to the footpath network as the roads.

The Errwood reservoir focuses attention on the concentrations as well as on the corridors. In the previous section, the need was emphasised to provide new nodes to intercept those who would otherwise visit more popular areas, to create 'honeypots' of attraction in the contemporary jargon. The role of country parks, and other user-oriented resources was emphasised in Chapter 7: it remains to stress the variety of attractions which can fulfil this need.

Country parks, whether specifically created with grant aid under the new legislation or the many older facilities which serve the same purpose, comprise land devoted almost entirely to recreation. There is much scope for developing leisure attraction in other areas whose prime use is very different. Integrated, multipurpose schemes make full use of resources of land and water: the problem very often is a financial one with the principal user unable or unwilling to provide the necessary capital for recreational development.

The potential of reservoirs, and in particular of compensating or regulatory reservoirs where problems of pollution are much less, deserves reiteration. Water is an attraction whether as an adjunct to scenery or for sailing and other aquatic activities. But recreation provision, even when permitted, is often half-hearted in scope, a reluctant addition rather than an integral part of the initial scheme.

We can learn from what has been achieved elsewhere. An American example is illustrated in Figure 82. Dillon Reservoir in the state of Ohio was created as a flood control reservoir on a tributary of the Muskingum River. Though the water level fluctuates, it covers some 1,300 acres, and the area suitable for boating is some five miles in length. The lake margins and the reservoir itself were seen to have obvious recreation potential in an area of rolling but scenically undistinguished terrain. Accordingly, a comparatively narrow strip around the reservoir was leased by the Ohio Department of Natural Resources, some 1,400 acres being considered usable for park development, though the presence of a railway and relative isolation has limited development on the west side of the park to hunting and fishing. On the east side the land has been laid out for intensive use. Differing activities are segregated (as are different types of craft on the water itself), but facilities are provided for day use (with swimming as a major feature) camping and vacation cabins, marinas, picnic sites, trails and paths for walking along the wooded slopes, shooting practice, and an amphitheatre where in the season nightly illustrated talks are given on the wild life and other features of the area. The total area involved in this intensive use

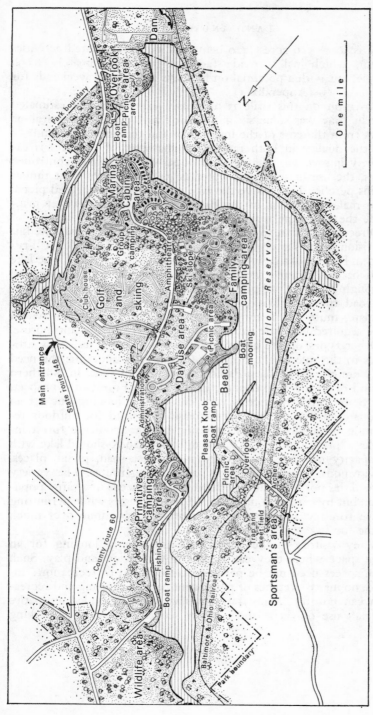

Fig 82. Dillon Reservoir State Park, Ohio (data from State of Ohio, Department of Natural Resources, Division of Parks and Recreation).

zone is some 550 acres (220 being for golf and related activities alone), which will provide facilities for approximately 8,000 people, but with a potential on holidays and special weekends for up to 24,000 (Appendix 1).

Provision on this scale is obviously expensive—the estimated cost in 1965 was some six million dollars for the facilities alone apart from the cost of the initial dam and the associated land[20]— but the quality in both range and character of facilities is extremely impressive. The wooded slopes with carefully controlled vistas, the use of trees and water as scenic foci, the neat timber cabins perched high above the lake and the fully-equipped picnic areas make recreation in the Park a real pleasure however man-made the landscape may be.

Direct translation to a British setting may not be feasible, but provision on this scale compares with that, for example, at Try-weryn, Liverpool's new regulatory reservoir above Bala. The lake itself has pre-empted the best farm land in the valley floor, and although laybys in fair profusion have been provided on the fringing road, the upper slopes and surrounding areas remain bleak and desolate, mute testimony to a missed opportunity which would have required but little extra land removed from agricultural use.

Other types of site afford additional opportunities. New attitudes to the role of the Forestry Commission underline the need for more effective Forest Parks, on the lines of those in Northern Ireland or in the Netherlands. In the Dutch Forest of Nunspeet, 'the State Forest Service is very consciously looking out for an adequate answer to the ever-increasing demand for outdoor recreation possibilities'[21] and provision in the 3,700-acre forest includes a 'playing pond' or 'Zandenplas'—a sandy-shored lake with a capacity of some 4,000 visitors—a forest road, picnic places, playgrounds, day-camping sites and walking routes. This variety of facilities not only satisfies the recreation needs of a large population but by careful zoning caters for most tastes while permitting active forestry and nature conservation to continue over much of the forest.

Many visitors to the countryside are simply looking for an open space where they can park, enjoy the view and play. Such open spaces need not be permanently devoted to recreation: indeed, on many stretches of permanent pasture, grazing and recreation can co-exist. Many farmers have a well-founded antipathy to such use of their land: others seek by imposing a parking charge to make it economically worthwhile. There may well be scope for a recreation subsidy which would encourage farmers to make small parts of their farms available for informal recreational use on a limited number of days each year. Simple sign posting would be needed and such use need not cause significant damage to the sward. This kind of area would be especially valuable where there is a dearth of such open spaces as commons and woodland.

All the nodes so far discussed cater for informal recreation of a general nature. More specialised 'attractions' also absorb much recreation pressure, often in locations which would not otherwise contribute to satisfying leisure demand. The plethora of stately homes is the classic case. But other aspects of the national heritage have a contribution to make. The growing concern for the preservation of monuments of the industrial revolution can be channelled in this direction, whether the simple museum based on the early furnaces at Coalbrookdale, the textile museum in the 1789 Higher Mill at Helmshore in Lancashire, or the far more ambitious proposals for an open-air museum of past industrial, urban and rural life at Beamish Hall, in 270 acres some six miles from Newcastle-upon-Tyne. The emphasis in this last instance is on activity: it is envisaged as 'a collection of material which works if it's machinery, which is open for a look round if it's a shop, which will generally be available for a ride if it's transport'.[22]

The heritage of nature is as varied as the heritage of man, and the establishment of nature trails is not only an attraction but a valuable education. Although the idea has long been recognised, they have only recently been seen in this country on any scale, the first being established in 1961.[23] While especially appropriate at popular beauty spots, on designated nature reserves or Forestry Commission property, they can also fill a useful role in far less likely places. In Yorkshire, for example, there were nature trails in 1968 in Wilton Park, Batley, less than a mile from the Town Hall and in the Rivelin valley at Sheffield, accessible by five Corporation bus routes. The Wilton trail alone was followed by some 8,000 people in fourteen months.[24] Another trail is in the grounds of Drakelow power station near Burton-upon-Trent.

Such seemingly unlikely sites are a reminder that not all recreation nodes need occupy high quality rural land, whether that quality is in terms of visual amenity or agricultural potential.

Indeed, recreation is often a viable use for derelict or semi-derelict land. The Chasewater scheme in Staffordshire was developed from a 230-acre canal reservoir surrounded by wasteland within a railway loop. At Druridge Bay in Northumberland, a country park is to be created from an opencast mining site. The contribution flooded gravel pits can make to water-based recreation has already been noted.

One particular type of derelict site has attracted considerable attention. The contracting railway network leaves many routes with some prospect for alternative use. Several are already used as footpaths in rural areas. A mile of the erstwhile Glyn Valley Tramway near Glynceiriog has been a riverside path in the ownership of the National Trust since 1948. Cheshire's Wirral Way country park has as its focus the former railway between Hooton and West Kirby, and in Derbyshire, the Tissington Trail has been created along the route of the erstwhile Buxton-Ashbourne line. This potential has stimulated a special study by the Countryside Commission,[25] though it must be emphasised that the cost of acquisition, development and maintenance of disused railways is a formidable obstacle to their widespread conversion to recreational use.

METROPARKS

Recreational nodes, both actual and potential, are distinguished by variety of site and purpose. The Countryside Act, offering financial assistance in the creation of country parks, has stimulated many local authorities to examine the potential of their areas in this light bringing forth far more schemes than can be supported in the immediate future. One consequence is an enriching of opportunity (not least by increased awareness) but another is the danger of a fragmented pattern inadequately related to the direction and the level of demand for recreation on a regional scale. Here the limitations of existing local government structures are immediately apparent. Most new provision is being made by county authorities, but catering in the main for the denizens of the larger county boroughs.

In terms of general opportunities for outdoor recreation in the countryside this is of comparatively little moment in a land where distances between major urban centres are rarely great and where there is a great deal of overlap between even short-range patterns of movement (Figure 39). The real problem comes in the immediate environs of the major conurbations, in the areas at present frequently designated as Green Belts or in the 'living space' of Cracknell's concept. Time and inclination restrict much recreation to short distances from home, to areas of only moderate attraction and with only moderate facilities.

A similar need brought forth the Victorian park. Movement then was on foot or by rudimentary forms of urban transport, and on the periphery of the tightly-packed town the formal, ordered landscape of the city park provided the accessible opportunity for recreation. It is no coincidence that the first street tramway in Britain ran from the gates of Birkenhead Park through the town to the Liverpool ferry. The needs now have changed. The older city parks still have a valid role, and there is still a place within the city for facilities for a varied range of outdoor sports (Chapter 3). But for most informal recreation new patterns have emerged. The mobility afforded by the car is spreading rapidly and is already available to more than half the households of the country. Part of the pleasure of recreation is the making of a journey, but that journey is rarely far afield. High quality of surroundings is demanded for full satisfaction on long trips, but at other times standards will be less exacting. All the evidence suggests that demand is inversely proportional to distance, but that much demand is relatively unsophisticated and can be satisfied close to its origin.

Such considerations again focus attention on the urban periphery, not the immediate periphery of Victorian times, but that area within range of half an hour or an hour's drive. Many regional parks already exist in such locations, either remnants of open space such as Cannock Chase or Epping Forest, or new creations such as the Lee Valley Regional Park. Equally, many of the new generation of country parks are in similar situations to match available opportunities: Cheshire's Wirral Way is on the threshold of suburban Merseyside. But the need intensifies for a recognised system of such parks both for the satisfaction they can themselves offer and for the protection they may afford to areas of rarer quality further afield by absorbing pressure close at hand. Such parks should not haphazardly seize available opportunities, but be a planned and recognised system. The reorganisation of local government recommended by the Maud Commission with a structure based on the concept of the city region would assist such planning immeasurably.

s

There are many prototypes for such systems, and one deserves brief mention, the Metroparks of the Huron-Clinton Metropolitan Authority serving the greater Detroit area of the USA. The Authority was established by a referendum in 1940 of the five counties which include Detroit and the major surrounding settlements (Figure 83) and was created purely to provide recreational facilities on a regional scale, complementing those already available in city and state parks.

Three elements of the system are worth emphasising: its financing, its location and the nature of the facilities it affords. Financially, the principal source of income is a local tax levy

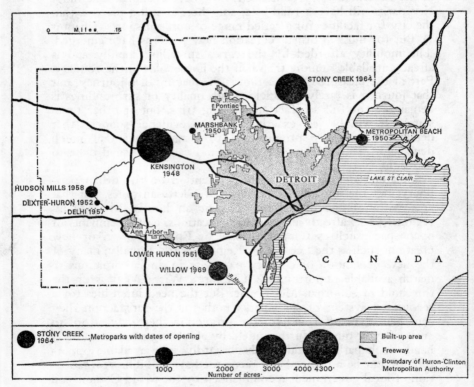

Fig 83. The Metroparks of the Huron-Clinton Metropolitan Authority (data from HCMA).

based on the proportion of one-sixtieth of the county property tax (Appendix 2): the residents of the area having willed the end, have in this case also willed the means. There is no entrance charge to the parks (except for parking during the season at the intensively-used Metropolitan Beach), though obviously such facilities as boat hire and golf are made to yield an adequate return.

The location of the parks is related to three factors. In the first place, they are conceived entirely as day-use facilities, and are sited within forty-five minutes drive of the centre of the conurbation. Secondly, they are directly related to the pattern of freeways and designed so that each sector of the conurbation has a park within easy reach. In 1965, 95 per cent of park users were residents of the Authority's five-county district. The variety of facilities afforded by the various parks and their situation on radial routes from downtown Detroit means that most parks are well-used by residents from all parts of the conurbation though on week-days in particular each is used more by adjacent residents.[26] Thirdly, they utilise the opportunities afforded by the presence of the Huron and Clinton river valleys. In several of the parks, the river is itself the focus of attraction; at Kensington and Stony Creek artificial lakes have been created as the centre point of design. Land acquisition proceeds well in advance of park development: much has been on damp, marshy ground with little agricultural potential. Elsewhere, as at Island Lake south-west of Kensington or near the mouth of the Huron river, gravel is being extracted from land appropriated by the Authority: such operations not only provide a valuable source of income, but greatly assist in the subsequent creation of lakes and landscaping.

Facilities are widely varied. While the overall aim was to provide 'large, easy-to-get-to picnic-type facilities' with, paradoxically, 'well-prepared ,"natural" picnic sites'[27] and ample scope for water-based activities, each park has a character of its own (Figure 84). Thus, Metropolitan Beach is an intensively used resort-type facility, with interest concentrated on an artificial beach fifty-five acres in extent stretching 1¼ miles along a former swamp on the shores of Lake St Clair. Kensington centres on the wooded shores of the artificial Kent Lake, but with a wide range of facilities for open-air enjoyment—sailing, boating, canoeing, fishing, swimming, golfing, picnicking and walking, together with nature trails and a nature centre staffed by the Authority's naturalists. In contrast, Dexter-Huron is much simpler, both

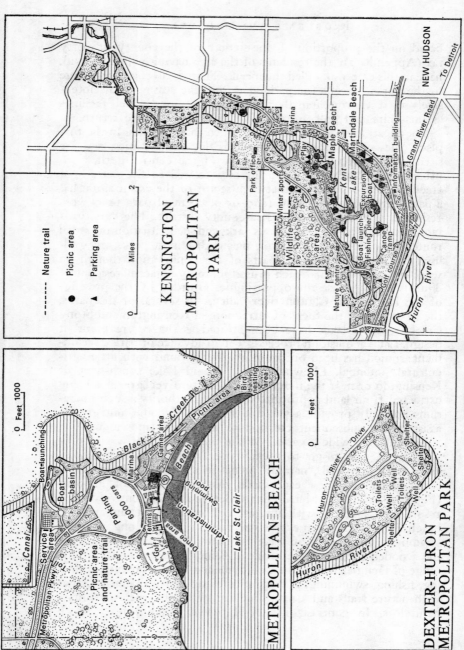

Fig 84. Specimen park layouts, Huron-Clinton Metropolitan Authority (data from HCMA).

smaller in size and providing only facilities for picnicking and open-air play along the wooded, picturesque (and in this instance completely natural) banks of the Huron River.

These parks are intensively used, receiving over six million visits in a normal season. On a typical July Sunday in 1965, four parks alone received 115,400 visitors (41,000 at Metropolitan Beach), and a July Wednesday saw 34,600 visitors. The intensity of weekday use is interesting, for it reflects the accessibility of these parks for recreation on a summer evening.

Such a system is not, of course, capable of direct translation to British conditions. It is prodigal of land in a setting where land is far more readily available than in our own crowded island. Kensington alone covers 4,200 acres with 1,200 acres for Kent Lake. But much of this land is the extensive matrix for the intensively-used core, a matrix which could well be farmed land or woodland if land pressures were greater. The facilities are geared in part to a hotter summer climate, where open-air swimming and picnicking are activities that can be pursued more readily than in our own fickle weather.

However, the system has real lessons to teach—planned provision, careful location and adequate financing give a variety of recreational opportunities for intensive use close to the built-up area of the conurbation. Many other examples could be invoked of provision for recreation deliberately planned on a regional basis, the essence of such provision being conservation in the broadest sense. By satisfying much intensive demand in this fashion, pressures elsewhere are more effectively controlled and a fit hierarchy of facilities established, delineated according to both distance and desire. Many British conurbations, of course, already have such a ring of parks in all but name. Merseyside has its beach resorts of varying character at West Kirby, New Brighton, Formby and Southport, its country parks at Delamere Forest and the Wirral Way with the adjacent open spaces of Caldy and Thurstaston Hills, but these lack co-ordination. Planning will be necessary to seize such further opportunities as may be presented by the creation of a barrage across the Dee and the securing of more effective access to the Clwydian Hills.

The financing of such systems pose problems, but realistic provision demands realistic payment. Intensive-use parks can be financed through user charges, through taxation or through realising increments in land values. The last principle was the basis of financing many Victorian parks, by the sale of fringing land for housing, with site values being enhanced by park vistas and facilities. Similar development on a limited scale in premium green belt locations could be more attractive in appearance than some mediocre farmland. The same principles could, indeed, be applied in more remote country park locations, however much such ideas may offend the precepts of rigid rural conservationists.

CONCLUSION

The opening chapter invoked the contemporary challenge of leisure. Subsequent chapters have examined the kaleidoscopic patterns it assumes on the threshold of the 1970s. Many issues have been omitted, the intention being to identify and focus upon patterns of demand and supply. The priorities recreation should assume in the face of alternate claims on land and finance are policy decisions beyond the present discussion, but the time is long past when such decisions can go by default, for pressures of leisure on land are now such that there can be no laissez faire alternative to some measure at least of public direction. That direction should be not only balanced but bold, so that the quality of living as well as the quality of both rural and urban landscapes may be enhanced. There can no longer be a dichotomy between town and country: each is workshop and playground and each should be employed and enjoyed to the full. With a rich heritage to conserve, in a compact island with a large and growing population, the challenge of leisure is immediate and insistent demanding effective and inspiring solutions. Rural as well as urban planners should heed the words of Daniel Burnham, the American architect-planner, written shortly before his death in 1912:

Make no little plans; they have no magic to stir man's blood and probably themselves will not be realized. Make big plans; aim high in hope and work, remembering that a noble, logical diagram once recorded will never die, but long after we are gone will be a living thing, asserting itself with ever-growing insistency ... Let your watchword be order and your beacon beauty.[28]

APPENDIXES

1. Dillon Reservoir State Park Design Criteria

Area or facility	Control	Area in acres	Estimated use per day
Swimming beach	100sq ft per person	4·5	2,000
Family picnic	15 locations per acre	15·0	1,000
Ski slope (temporary)	1,000 lin ft rope tow	5·0	350
Family camping	10 sites per acre	24·0	960
Primitive camping	8 sites per acre	5·0	200
Vacation cabin	30 cabins	145·0	150
Marina	80 boat slips	10·0	250
Administration and Maintenance	Office, storage, toilets, garages, shops, yards	11·0	25
Parking	150 spaces per acre	12·0	1,800 cars
Sportsmen area	target, skeet, trap, archery	44·0	250
Day camp	2 groups per acre	15·0	200
Overlooks	2	20·0	500
Controls	2	3·0	25
Golf course, club house and related facilities	18 holes, tennis, swimming	220·0	1,000
Ski slope (permanent)	2,000 lin ft	10·0	700
Camping (additional)	10 sites per acre	15·0	600

Source: Chas. T. Main Inc, *Preliminary Report and Master Plan, Dillon Reservoir State Park* (1965), 10

2. Huron-Clinton Metropolitan Authority Finances

Accumulated balances, 1942-67

Income		Dollars
Revenue from County taxes		55,378,099·55
Federal Government participation		602,424·92
State Government contribution		1,000,000·00
Other grants and bequests		455,826·12
		57,436,350·59

Expenditure	Per cent	Dollars
Land acquisition	16·8	9,670,238·60
Park development	40·8	23,417,827·09
Parkway construction	5·8	3,345,472·01
General planning	1·6	929,609·01
Equipment	2·8	1,576,502·92
Administration	8·9	5,128,702·67
Park operation (less revenues)	19·8	11,340,232·43
Appropriations and reserves	3·5	2,027,765·86
		57,436,350·59

Operating balances, 1967

Income	Dollars
Balance carried forward	192,444·57
Taxes	3,655,579·21
Park operating revenues	691,496·58
Grants from Federal Government	410,133·00
Grant from State agency	26,631·92
Interest	57,540·81
Miscellaneous	36,247·40
	5,070,073·49

Expenditure	Dollars
Appropriations for projects	1,684,401·99
Administration	697,509·78
Operation and maintenance	2,050,317·86
Balance carried forward	637,843·86
	5,070,073·49

ACKNOWLEDGEMENTS

I MUST first express my deep appreciation to the British Academy, whose award to me of the Thank-Offering to Britain Fund Research Fellowship made possible the initiation of the work upon which this book is based. The continued interest of the Academy and the encouragement of successive Secretaries, Sir Mortimer Wheeler and Mr Derek Allen, have been a real stimulus. I hope that this book may be some return at least for that interest and in considering a problem of growing importance to the quality of life in this country may also be a fitting expression of my thanks to the generous donors of the Fund, whose concern for 'the well-being of the people of the British Isles' was roused by the welcome they found here when refugees from Nazi oppression.

My interest in land and leisure was stirred by the pioneer writings and the teaching of Professor E. W. Gilbert, and in particular by his eloquent plea for a geographical approach to the problems they present in his lecture to the Oxford Preservation Trust in 1964, *Vaughan Cornish and the advancement of knowledge relating to the beauty of scenery in town and country*. He has given me continual encouragement in both a personal and an academic sense, his comments on the initial draft of the book saved me from many errors, and I am grateful not least for the preface he has so willingly contributed.

This work, however, would not have been feasible without the generous and unselfish assistance of Professor R. W. Steel and my colleagues in the Department of Geography, the University of Liverpool. They gladly shouldered the additional burdens incurred by my leave of absence, and were unstinting in comment and advice.

Many individuals working in the field of recreation have exchanged ideas and information. I am especially grateful for much valuable discussion to Mr C. D. Barnard (British Tourist Authority); Dr T. L. Burton (Michigan State University); Professor J. T. Coppock (University of Edinburgh); Mr Michael Dower (Dartington Amenity Research Trust); Miss M. Fulcher (University of Lancaster); Mr J. Gittins (Snowdonia National Park Survey); Miss J. Hartley (Countryside Commission); Dr P.

294 ACKNOWLEDGEMENTS

Lavery (Birkbeck College, London); Mr I. Masser (University of
Liverpool); Mr D. D. Molyneux (Sports Council); Mr J. A. Noble
(Cheshire County Council); Professor H. B. Rodgers (University
of Keele); Mr W. J. Slater (University of Liverpool); and Mr M.
F. Tanner (University of Birmingham) who also read and commented upon parts of the manuscript. I would also thank all those
individuals, County Planning Officers and their staffs, and other
organisations, far too numerous to mention by name, who have so
readily responded to my requests for information, often going to
very great lengths to unearth what I required. During my visit to
the USA, I received ready hospitality and much assistance from
Dr D. E. Christensen (Southern Illinois University); the late Mr
E. Mallonen (Recreation Planner, Huron-Clinton Metropolitan
Authority); Mr R. Ramey (Recreation Supervisor, Division of
Parks and Recreation, State of Ohio); Dr H. A. Stafford and Mr
K. Corey (University of Cincinnati); Dr J. Velikonja (University
of Washington); and Dr B. T. Wilkins (Cornell University).

The book itself owes a great deal to the cartographic skill of the
staff of the drawing office of the Department of Geography, the
University of Liverpool, Mr A. G. Hodgkiss, Miss P. J. Treasure
and Miss C. A. Roby. They have an enviable ability to turn the
roughest of sketches into maps of clarity and meaning. Mrs K.
Rawsthorne has undertaken all the secretarial work connected
with this project. Her unruffled patience and her ability to translate my scrawl into an ordered manuscript have been invaluable.
Mr K. Balmer has willingly undertaken the laborious task of compiling the index.

I am grateful to the following persons and organisations for their
assistance in supplying data used in the maps and for their permission
to reproduce copyright material: Dr D. C. Nicholls (1, 21);
Central Electricty Generating Board (4); British Travel Association (5, 9, 10, 11, 13, 18, 31, 43, 45, 47, 48, 49, 52); County Planning Officers, Cheshire and Lancashire (17, 23); D. D. Molyneux
(19); Greater London and South East Sports Council (20, 22);
Greater London Council (24, 25, 26, 27, 28); County Planning
Officer, County of Lincoln—Parts of Lindsey (32); County Planning Officer, Wiltshire (33); Liverpool Corporation (36); The
Marquess of Bath, Liverpool Corporation, Ministry of Public
Building and Works, Montagu Ventures Ltd, National Museum
of Wales, National Trust, World Methodist Council (37); Dr B.
Cracknell (39); Lake District Planning Board (40); Youth Hostels

Association (41, 53); County Planning Officer, Gloucestershire (42, 78); County Planning Officer, Caernarvonshire (44); County Planning Officer, Devon (46); County Planning Officer, Cornwall (50); Montagu Ventures Ltd (51); Snowdonia National Park Survey (54); National Trust (57, 58); C. H. D. Acland (59); Ministry of Public Building and Works (61); Map Librarian, Ministry of Housing and Local Government (62, 76); Peak Park Planning Board (63); Exmoor Press (64); Dartmoor Preservation Association (65); Exmoor Society (66); Nature Conservancy (72); County Planning Officers, Cheshire, Derbyshire and Lancashire (75); Department of Parks and Recreation, State of Ohio (82); Huron-Clinton Metropolitan Authority (83, 84).

It has been a pleasure to work with the series editor, Professor R. Lawton, and I am grateful to him for his careful and patient reading of the text. Last, but very far from least, my thanks are due to my wife and family for their long and glad forbearance with the labours of leisure.

J. ALLAN PATMORE

Oxton, Birkenhead
January 1970

NOTES

No detailed bibliography has been included with the book for two reasons. First, the notes to each chapter deliberately contain a good deal of bibliographical material, and much of a formal bibliography would be repetitive. Second, good bibliographies have already been published (see Chapter 1, note 6) and outdoor recreation is such a rapidly expanding field of interest that any bibliography would be woefully out of date by the time of publication. For more recent work, the reader is referred to the monthly issues of *Recreation News*, published by the Countryside Commission, which contain notes on recent books and articles and a summary of research in progress.

CHAPTER ONE

1 Dower, M., *The Challenge of Leisure* (Civic Trust, 1965), 5
2 Amos, F. J. C., 'Approach to planning—a planning officer's view of the next ten years', *Journal of the Town Planning Institute*, 55 (1969), 141
3 Central Office of Information, *Britain 1969, an official handbook* (HMSO, 1969), 417
4 *The Guardian*, 11 April 1969
5 Central Office of Information, op cit, 416
6 See, for example,
Burton, T. L. and Noad, P. A., *Recreation research methods, a review of recent studies* (University of Birmingham Centre for Urban and Regional Studies, Occasional Paper No 3, 1968)
Greaves, J., *National Parks and access to the countryside and coast: trends in research* (Countryside Commission, 1968)
Palmer, J. E., 'Recreational planning—a bibliographical review', *Planning Outlook*, 2 (1967), 19–69
Research Register No 2 (Countryside Commission, 1969)

7   Lowenthal, D. and Prince, H. C., 'English landscape tastes', *The Geographical Review*, 55 (1965), 187

8   Ibid, 190

9   Pimlott, J. A. R., *The Englishman's Holiday* (Faber and Faber, 1947), 211

10 Burton, T. L. and Wibberley, G. P., *Outdoor recreation in the British countryside* (Wye College, 1968), 2

11 Demangeon, A., *The British Isles* (Heinemann, 2nd edition 1949), 380–1

12 Quoted in Gilbert, E. W., *Brighton, Old Ocean's Bauble* (Methuen, 1954), 18

13 Ibid, 152

14 Quoted in Robbins, M., *The Railway Age* (Routledge and Kegan Paul, 1962), 56

15 Grinling, C. H., *The history of the Great Northern Railway* (Methuen, 1903), 103

16 Joy, D., *Cumbrian Coast Railways* (Dalesman, 1968), 78

17 Quoted in Gregory, L. F., 'View-hunting with Geneviève', *Town and Country Planning*, 33 (1965), 151

18 The total quoted is that given by Burton and Wibberley, op cit, 13, and refers to 1962–3. This is the best estimate which can be obtained from available evidence, though a range between a minimum of 1·3 million acres and a maximum of 4 million is suggested

19 See, for example, M. L. Bazeley's map, reproduced in Darby, H. C. (Ed), *An historical geography of England before 1800* (Cambridge University Press, 1951), 177

20 Hoskins, W. G., *The making of the English landscape* (Hodder and Stoughton, 1955), 129

21 See the discussion in Thorpe, H., 'The green villages of County Durham', *Transactions of the Institute of British Geographers*, 15 (1949), 153–80

22 Hoskins, W. G. and Stamp, L. D., *The common lands of England & Wales* (Collins, 1963), 28. This book also contains a map showing the distribution of greens

23 Ibid, 63–4

24 Hoskins, W. G., op cit, 1955, 221

25 See, for example,
    Gilbert, E. W., 'The growth of inland and seaside health resorts in England', *Scottish Geographical Magazine*, 55 (1939), 16–35 and Patmore, J. A., 'The spa towns of Britain'

in Beckinsale, R. P. and Houston, J. M. (Eds), *Urbanization and its problems* (Blackwell, 1968), 47–69
26 Quoted in Pimlott, J. A. R., op cit, 43
27 G. Cowling, Blackpool's Chief Assistant Planning Officer, in National Parks Commission, *The coasts of North-west England* (HMSO, 1968), 9
28 Darby, H. C., 'British National Parks', *The Advancement of Science*, 20 (1963), 307
29 *Power and the countryside* (Central Electricity Generating Board, 1965)
30 *Use of reservoirs and gathering grounds for recreation*, Ministry of Land and Natural Resources circular 3/66, Department of Education and Science circular 19/66
31 Black, J. N., 'Responsibility in resource management', *The Advancement of Science*, 25 (1968), 128

CHAPTER TWO

1 Outdoor Recreation Resources Review Commission *Outdoor Recreation for America* (Washington, 1962), 25
2 This work was the responsibility of H. B. Rodgers of Keele. Report No 1 contains tables and commentary relating to the sample as a whole; Report No 2, published in 1969, gives a regional breakdown of the data. In the latter case, the problems engendered by small sub-samples are particularly evident
3 The author of the report was K. K. Sillitoe. It was undertaken on behalf of the Department of Education, but also took into account the special interests of the Ministry of Housing and Local Government and the Inner London Education Authority
4 Op cit Table 1. This refers to activities on an average Sunday. Detailed discussion of sampling errors is beyond the present purpose but some measure of their importance can be seen from the following figures quoted in the Northern Region survey:

Activity	Number taking part	Sampling error + or −
Walking (not using transport)	225,000 (Sunday)	30,000
Playing cricket	25,000 (Saturday)	10,000

On Saturdays, twenty-three listed activities had fewer participants than playing cricket and 'the need for caution on figures smaller than this, is obvious'

5 Op cit, 37

6 In addition to the surveys already mentioned, which are the basis of this section, see also the BBC Audience Research Department's *The people's activities* (BBC, 1965)

7 Other surveys yield somewhat different results. In the BTA survey, active outdoor recreation on a summer weekend was recorded by only 7 per cent of those interviewed, and such pursuits as driving for pleasure and watching live sport by only another 8 per cent. These figures however refer only to those mentioning the activity, not to the total proportion of time spent in its pursuit. More comparable is the Northern Region survey, which showed 20 per cent participating in outdoor recreation on an average summer Saturday and 32 per cent on an average summer Sunday. The equivalent figures for summer weekends in *Planning for Leisure* are 42 per cent for men and 34 per cent for women, though again these refer to the proportion of time spent rather than the proportion participating

8 For a further discussion of differences between the three countries see Burton, T. L., 'Outdoor recreation in America, Sweden and Britain', *Town and Country Planning*, 34 (1966), 456–61

9 See Burton, T. L., *The classification of recreation demands and supplies* (University of Birmingham Centre for Urban and Regional Studies, 1967)

10 Graham, J. A. M., 'The big business of dig business', *Reader's Digest*, 93 (July 1968), 67–71

11 Wibberley, G. P., *Agriculture and urban growth, a study of the competition for rural land* (Michael Joseph, 1959), 121. Chapter 7 contains a useful, if slightly dated, discussion of the uses of land in gardens

12 This figure agrees remarkably well with the known figure for total ownership. In 1965, 41 per cent of all households had one or more cars, in 1966 45 per cent. The BTA survey was conducted late in 1965. By 1968, 49 per cent of British households had one or more cars, 6 per cent two or more. Ministry of Transport, *Highway Statistics, 1968* (HMSO, 1969), Table 56

13 Masser, I., 'The use of outdoor recreation facilities', *Town Planning Review*, 37 (1966), 41–54

14 Margetson, S., *Leisure and pleasure in the nineteenth century* (Cassell, 1969), 211

15 Based, with modifications, on Nicholls, D. C. and Young, A., *A report on recreation and tourism in the Loch Lomond area* (University of Glasgow, 1968), 16

16 The following indices were used, the number of years from which the average was calculated being indicated in brackets:
　Adult clubs affiliated to the Rugby Football Union (5)
　Clubs affiliated to the Grand National Archery Society (7)
　Sale of golf balls (5)
　Cycle Touring Club Membership (4)
　Affiliated groups of the Ramblers Association (5)
　Admissions to Ancient Monuments and Historic Buildings, England and Wales (4)
　Gliding hours, British Gliding Association groups (3)
　Clubs affiliated to Amateur Rowing Association (6)
　Angling licences issued by river authorities (7)
　Clubs affiliated to Royal Yachting Association (5)
　Clubs affiliated to British Canoe Union (4)
　Branches affiliated to British Sub-Aqua Club (5)
　Sources: *Britain 1969 An official handbook* (HMSO, 1969)
　　　Molyneux, D. D., 'Working for recreation', *Journal of the Town Planning Institute*, 54 (1968), 149–57
　　　Basic Road Statistics, 1969 (British Roads Federation, 1969)
　　　Unpublished data from Ministry of Building and Public Works

17 In contrast, tennis is now estimated to be one of the faster-growing sports in the USA and this may herald a revival in Britain. *US News & World Report*, 22 July 1968

18 Northern Advisory Council for Sport and Recreation, *Survey of Golf Facilities* (North Regional Planning Committee, 1967)

CHAPTER THREE

1 Quoted in Briggs, Asa, *Victorian Cities* (Pelican edition, 1968), 10

2 Dower, M., *The challenge of leisure* (Civic Trust, 1965), 19

3 Williams-Ellis, C., *England and the octopus* (Bles, 1928), 39
4 These estimates, and those of transfers of land from agricultural use, are based on Best, R. H., 'Extent of urban growth
   and agricultural displacement in post-war Britain', *Urban
   Studies*, 5 (1968), 1-23
5 See, for example, Ministry of Housing and Local Government, *Housing standards, costs and subsidies*, Circular 36/67
   (1967)
6 Best, R. H., op cit 5. Doubts have been expressed about the
   acreage recorded as transferred to forestry, for the Forestry
   Commission's own estimates are somewhat lower, but they
   are unlikely to change the relative positions of forestry and
   towns as acquirers of agricultural land
7 Best, R. H. and Coppock, J. T., *The changing use of land in
   Britain* (Faber and Faber, 1962), Table VII
8 Best, R. H., *Land for New Towns: a study of land use,
   densities, and agricultural displacement* (Town and Country
   Planning Association, 1964), 18
9 For a recent discussion of problems in classifying urban open
   space, see Burnett, F. T., 'Open space in new towns', *Journal
   of the Town Planning Institute*, 55 (1969), 256–62
10 Liverpool Corporation *Review of City Development Plan
   Report No 15, Open Space* (1964), 4
11 These 'initial appraisals' are as follows:
   Cheshire County Council *Recreation in Cheshire: Survey
   of existing facilities for sport and physical recreation—1.
   Preliminary Report* (1967)
   Eastern Sports Council *First appraisal of major facilities and
   field games* (1967)
   East Midlands Sports Council and Technical Panel *Recreation in the East Midlands, an initial appraisal of major
   facilities* (1967)
   Greater London and South East Sports Council *Sports
   Facilities, Initial appraisal*, Volume 1 (1968)
   County of Lancashire *Survey of existing facilities for sport
   and physical recreation, Preliminary report* (1967)
   County of Lancashire *Survey of existing facilities for sport
   and physical recreation, an appraisal:*
       Volume 1, *The County* (1967)
       Volume 2, Parts 1–8 Sub-regional reports (1967)
       Volume 3, *Swimming Baths* (1967)

T

North East Advisory Council for Sport and Recreation *Provision for sport and recreation in the North East* (1965)
Northern Advisory Council for Sport and Recreation *Public Swimming Baths in the North East* (North Regional Planning Committee, 1966)
Northern Advisory Council for Sport and Recreation *Water Sports in the Northern Region* (North Regional Planning Committee, 1967)
Northern Advisory Council for Sport and Recreation *Survey of Golf Facilities* (North Regional Planning Committee, 1967)
Southern Sports Council *Major Sport and Recreation Facilities, a first appraisal* (1967)
South Western Sports Council *Initial appraisal of major facilities* (1967)
South Western Sports Council *The use of coastal waters for recreation* (1967)
The Sports Council for Wales *Major sports facilities, an initial appraisal* (1967)
West Midlands Sports Council Technical Panel *Regional recreation* (1966)
Yorkshire and Humberside Sports Council *Sports facilities, an initial appraisal* (1967)

12 Derived from Burnett, F. T., op cit, Tables 1 and 3
13 Ibid, 259
14 Ben Whitaker MP, 'Grass and trees are not enough', *Evening Standard*, 27 April 1968
15 Gooch, R. B., *Selection and layout of land for playing fields and playgrounds* (The National Playing Fields Association, 1963), 95–8. For a wider discussion of the implications of the NPFA standard, see Gooch, R. B., 'Planning for recreation', *Town and Country Planning*, 32 (1964), 480–4
16 Studies in Kent, at Paddock Wood and Maidstone, suggested less than half the NPFA's assumed proportions of participants. See Liverpool Corporation, op cit, 6
17 Gooch, R. B., op cit (1964), 480
18 Greater London Council Planning Department *Surveys of the use of open space, Volume 1* (Greater London Council, 1968), 7
19 Chadwick, G. F., *The park and the town* (Architectural Press, 1966), 374

20 Dewhurst, E., 'Outdoor sports come in from the cold', *The Guardian*, 7 January 1969

21 For detailed examples, with construction costs, see The Sports Council *Planning for Sport* (Central Council of Physical Recreation, 1968), 60–5

22 Gilmour, O. W., 'Harlow's Sportcentre', *Town and Country Planning*, 35 (1967), 69-72

23 For participation rates in indoor sports see The Sports Council, op cit, 88–90

24 Ibid, 21. The participation rates quoted in this section are derived from this source and from Molyneux, D. D., 'Working for recreation', *Journal of the Town Planning Institute* 54 (1968), 149–57

25 National Opinion Polls Limited *Major County Cricket* (1966)

26 Willis, M., 'Provision of sports pitches', *Town Planning Review* (1968)

27 For further details of this provision, and the assumptions on which it is based, see The Sports Council, op cit, 30–2

28 County of Lancashire, op cit., Volume 1, 16

29 National Playing Fields Association *School playing fields— Dual use policies in operation* (1964)

30 Frost, D., 'Manchester shows the way for ailing clubs', *The Guardian*, 14 January 1969

31 Precise figures are not available, but this estimate is based on an average of 100 acres for each 18-hole course and 50 acres for each 9-hole course. In Lancashire, the average is 5·6 acres for each hole—108 acres for an 18-hole course. In the Northern Region, the 'most usual size' for an 18-hole course is 90 acres, and almost three-quarters of the courses cover the equivalent of between 72 and 126 acres per 18 holes

32 Quoted in Greater London and South East Sports Council, op cit, 19

33 Northern Advisory Council for sport and recreation *Survey of Golf Facilities* (North Regional Planning Committee 1967), 12. County figures vary more widely, but must be viewed with greater reserve. In the North, the range was from Lancashire with 3·7 members per thousand to Cumberland and Westmorland with 8·4

34 Work is at present in progress on a study of golf on a national scale by Dr D. C. Nicholls of the University of Glasgow's Department of Social and Economic Research

35 *The Observer* (colour supplement), 12 November 1967
36 Widdup, C., 'Fairways in the Green Belts?' *Town and Country Planning*, 34 (1966), 124
37 The cost of a new 18-hole golf course was estimated as between £80,000 and £100,000 in 1967 by the Northern Advisory Council for Sport and Recreation
38 Quoted in Chadwick, G. F., op cit, 100
39 Abernethy, W. D., 'The importance of play', *Town and Country Planning*, 36 (1968), 472. The October-November issue of this journal contains an important series of articles on providing for the play needs of children
40 Based on a stratified random sample of 2,015 adults in thirty-three wards of the former County of London. See Greater London Council Planning, op cit. All material relating to London in this section has been derived from this source
41 Masser, I., 'The use of outdoor recreation facilities', *Town Planning Review*, 37 (1966), 41-54
42 In the London survey, the following figures were obtained for at least one visit to a public park:

	Per cent of total	
	Previous week	*Previous month*
Adults	39	70
Children 1½-9	46	81
Children 11-16	51	81

CHAPTER FOUR

1 *Thirteenth report of the National Parks Commission* (HMSO, 1962), 73
2 *Traffic in the Lake District* (The Friends of the Lake District, 1964), 4
3 'William Small', 'Conservation for whom?' *Town and Country Planning*, 35 (1967), 49
4 Colin Buchanan and Partners, *South Hampshire Study, Supplementary Volume 2, Methods and policies* (HMSO, 1966), 143
5 Personal communication from H. B. Rodgers
6 Greater London Council Planning Department, *Surveys of the use of open space, Volume 1* (Greater London Council, 1968), 36

7 British Travel and Holidays Association *Survey of Whitsun Holiday Travel* (1963)
8 *Highway Statistics 1968* (HMSO, 1969), Table 56
9 Mansfield, N. W., 'Traffic policy in the Lake District National Park—some general considerations', *Journal of the Town Planning Institute*, 54 (1968), 267
10 National Parks Commission *The Coasts of Kent and Sussex* (HMSO, 1967), 48
11 National Parks Commission *The Coasts of North Wales* (HMSO, 1968), 41
12 National Parks Commission *The Coasts of North-West England* (HMSO, 1968), 36
13 *Peak District National Park Survey* (British Travel Association, 1963, unpublished)
14 Colenutt, R. J., 'Modelling travel patterns of day visitors to the countryside', Area, 2 (1969), 45
15 Furmidge, J., 'Planning for recreation in the countryside', *Journal of the Town Planning Institute*, 55 (1969), 62–7
16 Studies at particular sites continue to proliferate from T. L. Burton's pioneer work at Box Hill. Many results are not directly comparable because of wide differences in definitions and approach, and reliability varies because of widely differing sample sizes and statistical approach. The following list incorporates the principal ones used in this section:
Peak District National Park Survey, op cit
Burton, T. L., 'A day in the country—a survey of leisure activity at Box Hill in Surrey', *Chartered Surveyor*, 98 (1966)
Burton, T. L., *Windsor Great Park—a recreation study* (Wye College, 1967)
Colin Buchanan and Partners, op cit (New Forest)
Countryside Commission *The weekend motorist in the Lake District* (HMSO, 1969)
Duffell, J. R. and Goodall, G. R., 'Worcestershire and Staffordshire Recreational Survey 1966', *Journal of the Town Planning Institute*, 55 (1969), 16–23
Furmidge, J., op cit (East Sussex)
Hampshire County Planning Department *The use of county open spaces* (Hampshire County Council, undated): surveys conducted in 1966
Kilpatrick, C. S., *Public response to forest recreation in*

Northern Ireland (Ministry of Agriculture for Northern Ireland, undated): surveys conducted in 1964. Beyond the strict area of study, but methodologically useful

Lancashire County Council, *Lancashire Coastal Survey— Formby area report* (1966)

Lindsey Countryside Recreational Survey, *A survey of the public use of the Lincolnshire Wolds and adjacent areas* (Lindsey County Council, University of Nottingham, 1967)

Mutch, W. E. S., *Public recreation in National Forests: a factual survey* (Forestry Commission Booklet No 21, HMSO, 1968)

Ross, J. B., *Tourism in Northumberland* (Northumberland County Council, 1966)

Wager, J., 'Outdoor recreation on common land', *Journal of the Town Planning Institute*, 53 (1967), 398–403

Wiltshire County Council, *Leisure in the countryside— survey of the use of selected public open spaces* (1967)

In subsequent discussion, no specific reference is made to these surveys where the source used is obvious from the context

17 Figures include 3,637 people who stayed overnight in tents, caravans, etc, and 1,235 cars parked overnight

18 Hampshire County Council et al, *East Hampshire AONB, a study in countryside conservation* (1968), 56

19 Ibid, 21

20 Law, S., 'Planning for outdoor recreation in the countryside', *Journal of the Town Planning Institute*, 53 (1967), 384

21 These proportions should be accepted with some caution, as they not only assume an accurate knowledge of mileage covered, but are also based on a fairly small sub-sample

22 Although the survey was conducted during a Saturday and Sunday in the holiday season, few holidaymakers appeared to visit these inland sites: only 28 out of 552 people questioned gave a different home address to the one from which they had travelled that day, and only 10 of these had travelled from the holiday resorts

23 Twenty-seven per cent of visitors reached this site on foot: 88 per cent of all journeys to all twenty-nine sites were made by car

24 Law, S., op cit, 384

25 These figures refer to holiday addresses in many cases, as the purpose is to emphasise the role of the *day* excursionist. Forty-six point two per cent came from *permanent* addresses within the Poole-Winchester-Portsmouth triangle

26 Cracknell, B., 'Accessibility to the countryside as a factor in planning for leisure', *Regional Studies*, 1 (1967), 148. The paper includes a graph of traffic flows on Sundays in September 1961 on five A class roads some twenty miles out of London: as might be expected these show an earlier build-up of traffic and rather later peaks for they are concerned with movement to and from destinations, rather than the situation at the destinations themselves

27 The figures plotted here deliberately exclude the effect of organised school parties

28 Epworth 36·0 per cent, Fountains 38·9 per cent, Longleat 40·7 per cent, St Fagans 44·8 per cent, Beaulieu 46·4 per cent, Bodiam 48·8 per cent. The figures for Bodiam and Longleat are slightly distorted by their closure at the end of 1967 because of the threat of foot and mouth disease and the consequent total lack of December visitors

29 Wager, J., op cit, 400

30 Quoted in Manley, G., *Climate and the British scene* (Collins, 1952), 3

31 Ibid, 121

32 Brooks, C. E. P., *The English climate* (English Universities Press, 1954), 200

33 BBC 1, 4 September 1968 and 20 August 1969

34 Wager, J., 'How common is the land?' *New Society*, 30 July 1964

35 Cars could be driven on to all types of site to varying degrees. 'Car parking areas' are sites where the *dominant* character was a car park

36 Lancashire County Council Planning Department *Forest of Bowland Recreational Study Summary Report* (1967), 3

37 Lake District Planning Board *Traffic in the Lake District National Park, Draft report on detailed studies of Borrowdale and the Langdales, August 1967*, (1968)

38 Calculated from design figures in Ministry of Transport *The Layout of roads in rural areas* (HMSO, 1968), 10–11

39 According to the Road Research Laboratory's Technical

Paper No 72, the average road widths in rural areas are as follows:

Trunk roads	23ft
Class 1 roads	21ft
Class 2 roads	18ft
Other roads	14ft

40 op cit
41 The basic formula eventually derived was

$$R \text{ (miles)} = \frac{\sqrt{N}}{50} \text{ approximately}$$

where R is the required radius and N is the population of the settlement. The whole calculation is based on numerous assumptions which require further refinement, but is a most interesting first attempt to quantify this concept in a meaningful way
42 Ministry of Land and Natural Resources, *Leisure in the Countryside England and Wales* (Cmnd 2928, HMSO, 1966), 6
43 Hampshire County Council, op cit, 1968, 56
44 *The Geographical Review*, 55 (1965), 190–2
45 *The place of the horse in recreation* (The British Horse Society, undated). The statistics refer to the situation in 1967
46 *The Guardian*, 26 February 1969
47 Coppock, J. T., 'The recreational use of land and water in rural Britain', *Tidjschrift voor Econ. en Soc. Geografie*, 57 (1966), 81–8. This excellent pioneer paper is the source of much of the material in this paragraph
48 Ibid, and Woollacott, M., 'Grouse groan', *The Guardian*, 9 August 1969
49 61,560 in 1964. Woollacott estimates 100,000 guns using an annual total of 60 million cartridges, but not all these are expended on game birds
50 For maps of areas concerned in the various Field Sports, see Coppock, J. T., op cit
51 *Park and Recreation Information System, Planning Monograph No 2* (The Resources Agency, State of California, 1966), quoted in Law, S., op cit, 386
52 Detroit Metropolitan Area Regional Planning Commission,

Regional Recreational Lands Plan (1966). This is, of course, a relatively low figure and allows the retention of parts in a near 'natural' state. Around Cleveland, land for picnicking, including parking and play areas, has been developed for peak densities of between 10 and 41 persons per acre, according to quality, with a mean of 31 persons per acre. Cleveland Metropolitan Park District *New Gems for the emerald necklace* (1961). This clearly accords with Wager's estimate of peak capacity on commons

53 An Foras Forbartha, *Specimen Development Plan Manual 2–3, Planning for Amenity and Tourism* (1966), 42–8

54 1,274,000 licences were issued by River Authorities in 1966. Other estimates suggest at least 2,000,000 people fish with some regularity

55 British Waterways Board *Annual report and accounts 1968* (HMSO, 1969), 15

56 British Waterways Board *Annual report and accounts 1967* (HMSO, 1968), 16

57 Browne, P., 'Hooked—on line and sinker', *Reader's Digest* (July 1968), 32

58 Based on data in Tanner, M., *Coastal Recreation in England and Wales* (Sports Council SC(67)29, 1967)

59 For specific demands of each activity, see Gloucester County Council Planning Department, *Outdoor Water Recreation* (1968)

CHAPTER FIVE

1 Board of Trade estimates. These figures do not represent *total* expenditure on travel abroad, only that in other than British currency. They also relate to *all* travellers, not just holidaymakers: it was estimated that in 1968 68 per cent of travellers from Britain were going on holiday and 14 per cent on business

2 The survey is conducted for the BTA by Social Surveys (Gallup Poll) Ltd. In 1968, some 3,000 interviews were completed with British people taking holidays in Britain and some 2,000 with people who took a holiday abroad. While this is probably the most sophisticated study of its kind in the world, the statistical errors to which it is necessarily subject must not be forgotten. They vary from plus or minus 1 per cent

on a random sample of 4,000 (for a figure of 12 per cent and at the 95 per cent confidence level) to plus or minus 6·5 per cent for the same figure on a random sample of 100. This qualification is particularly important when considering small regional sub-samples. A summary of the results of the survey in recent years is contained in *The British on Holiday* (British Travel Association, 1969). All data are from this source unless otherwise acknowledged

3 Gilbert, E. W., *Brighton, Old Ocean's Bauble* (Methuen, 1965), 32

4 *Tourism in Wales* (Welsh Tourist Board, 1969), 8

5 A study is at present in progress at Wye College, but results will not be available until late 1970

6 Fairhall, J., 'City dwellers find country cottage bargains elusive', *The Guardian*, 4 February 1969

7 The map is based on one compiled by Caernarvonshire County Council. It depicts properties where

    (*a*) rates are paid by a person residing outside Lleyn

    (*b*) rates are paid by persons residing at an address other than that of the property itself, but within Lleyn, where there seems a strong reason because of its location that it is used for holiday purposes

Many such properties may, of course, be used for holiday letting rather than a second home in the more restricted sense of the term, but it emphasises the problems of definition in this respect

8 *Town and Country Planning*, 33 (1965), 246

9 *The French Tourist Industry* (Ambassade de France, service de presse et d'information, A/56/2/8, 1968), 20. See also Clout, H. D., 'Second homes in France', *Journal of the Town Planning Institute*, 55 (1969), 440–3

10 *Town and Country Planning*, op cit, 247

11 From the poem 'Retirement', quoted in E. W. Gilbert, op cit, 13

12 Ibid, 7

13 It will be noted that these proportions add up to 119, not 100 per cent. This reflects both double-counting (a coastal area adjacent to mountains, for example) and those who stayed in more than one place

14 In this discussion 'holidaymakers' refers to all those taking their main holidays in Britain.

15 Devon County Council *Annual Survey of Holiday Development, 1967* (1967). The 1967 data are used in preference to those from 1968, as the formation of Torbay CB and its consequent exclusion from the area of the Administrative County by the latter date make the later figures of more limited value. The 1967 data include the whole of the geographical county with the exception of Plymouth and Exeter CBs

16 Recent BTA surveys have been complicated by the use of regions for tabulating place of residence which differ from those used for tabulating destinations. It is not therefore possible to construct a simple diagram of the extent of 'in' and 'out' movement in a given region for 1968. See also Burton, T. L., 'Holiday movements in Britain', *Town and Country Planning*, 33 (1965), 118-23 for a fuller discussion of the 1960 situation

17 Northumberland County Council *Report of coastal survey* (1965), 18. Emphasis is also placed on the comparatively low totals of August sunshine received on this coast—about 150 hours compared with 220 at Eastbourne

18 Much depends on the character of the individual resort in this respect. For contrasted examples, of a coastal resort with a restricted hinterland and an inland resort with a far wider appeal, see maps of the origins of visitors in Daysh, G. H. J., *A survey of Whitby and the surrounding area* (Shakespeare Head, 1958), 164 and Patmore, J. A., *An Atlas of Harrogate* (Harrogate Corporation, 1963), 30

19 *The Guardian*, 5 July 1968

20 Cornwall County Council *Survey of the Holiday Industry* (1966), 27

21 Rawnsley, C., 'Preserving the coast', *The Countryside in 1970, Proceedings of the Second Conference* (Royal Society of Arts, 1965), A3

22 Burton, T. L., 'Caravan sites for holidaymakers', *Town and Country Planning*, 34 (1966), 113-9

23 The BTA national figures probably underrate the importance of caravans in Wales for, in regional terms, they are based on very small sub-samples. The Welsh Tourist Board estimates that in 1965, 52 per cent of Wales' tourist accommodation was in caravans (op cit, 24). For a very full study of development and location, see Pryce, W. T. R., 'The location and growth of holiday caravan camps in Wales, 1956–65', *Trans-*

actions of the Institute of British Geographers, 42 (1967), 127–52

24 Absolute growth has not been disallowed, but only up to the limits of the spare capacity previously authorised. The results are seen as follows:

	Static caravans and chalets Increases per year in number of units	
	1954–60	*1960–4*
Saturation areas (excluding Pentewan)	363	227
Remainder of coastal areas	247	354

This may be compared with the situation in Denbighshire where existing development, largely in the Abergele area, was considered to be at maximum desirable capacity

Abergele	*1959*	*1966*
caravans	6,351	6,379
chalets	1,302	1,364

25 Devon County Council estimates suggest 55,000 visited the Park on Sunday, 5 August 1968, and an average of 45,000 on each Sunday in July, August and September. *Annual Survey of Conservation and Recreation, 1968*, 16

26 The Council for Wales and Monmouthshire *Report on the Welsh holiday industry* (HMSO, 1963), 32

27 Lake District Planning Board *Report on traffic in the Lake District National Park* (1965), 2

CHAPTER SIX

1 Outdoor Recreation Resources Review Commission *Outdoor Recreation for America* (Washington, 1962), 49

2 Burton, T. L. and Wibberley, G. P., *Outdoor Recreation in the British Countryside* (Wye College, 1965), 16. It should be noted that the acreage quoted includes only certain categories of land, in particular Statutory Access Areas in National Parks, Nature Reserves, National Trust Properties, Common Land and Forestry Commission and other woodlands. The last two are open to wide variations in the interpretation of 'access land', and these problems are discussed more fully later

3 Town and Country Planning Association Executive Commit-

tee, 'A policy for countryside recreation in England and
Wales', *Town and Country Planning*, 33 (1965), 473

4   Ministry of Land and Natural Resources, *Leisure in the
Countryside, England and Wales* (HMSO Cmnd 2928, 1966),
6

5   For a full history of the development of conservation see
Stamp, Sir Dudley, *Nature Conservation in Britain* (Collins
New Naturalist series, 1969)

6   Ibid, 61

7   *Report of the Committee on Land Utilisation in Rural Areas*
(Cmnd 6378, HMSO, 1942)

8   For full details of the Conservancy and its work, see *The
Nature Conservancy Handbook 1968* (HMSO, 1968)

9   For a detailed discussion of varied habitats and their significance see Stamp, Sir Dudley, op cit, Chapter 4

10 For further details of the recreational use of National Nature
Reserves, see *The Nature Conservancy Progress 1964–1968*
(Nature Conservancy, 1968)

11 The standard history of the Trust, on which this section
necessarily leans heavily, is Fedden, R. *The continuing purpose: a history of the National Trust, its aims and work*
(Longmans, 1968)

12 *The properties of the National Trust* (National Trust, 1969).
These totals refer to England, Wales and Northern Ireland.
They exclude the 63,000 acres of land and buildings for
which the Trust holds covenants. One hundred and fifty-six
buildings are open to the public

13 Fedden, R., op cit, 140

14 Ibid, ix: this is the comment of the Chairman of the Trust

15 In 1955, Clumber Park had an estimated 50,000 visitors on a
bank holiday weekend, and 106,000 in 1964. In 1965 there
were 80,000 cars at Runnymede

16 *The Benson Report on the National Trust* (The National
Trust, 1968), 96

17 Dinton Park, Philipps House, Wilts (181); Dorney Wood,
Bucks (55); Morwen Park, Middlesex (36); Nunnington Hall,
Yorks (397); Ormesby Hall, Yorks (365); Plas-yn-Rhiw,
Caerns (334); Printing Press, Strabane, N. Ireland (134);
Stoneacre, Kent (191); The Weir, Hereford (154); West
Green House, Hants (282); West Wood Manor, Wilts (490)

18 Benson Report, op cit, 97

19 Fedden, R., op cit, 90–1
20 See the detailed list in *Ancient Monuments and Historic Buildings in the care of the Ministry of Public Buildings and Works* (HMSO, 4th edition, 1966). Monument in this discussion is used as a generic term to cover all properties in the care of the Ministry
21 Hampton Court, Kew, and Queen's Cottage, Kew
22 In addition to those named, the following monuments in the London area exceeded 100,000 visitors in 1967: Tower of London (over 2,000,000), Osborne House and Hampton Court (over 500,000). For further details see the annual statement of admission figures to Ancient Monuments
23 Quoted in Blenkinsop, A., 'The National Parks of England and Wales', *Planning Outlook*, 6 (1964), 10. This is a particularly valuable summary of the origins and legislative structure of the parks
24 Darby, H. C., 'British National Parks', *The Advancement of Science*, 20 (1963), 307
25 *Report of the National Parks Committee* (HMSO Cmnd 3851, 1931)
26 *National Parks in England and Wales* (HMSO Cmnd 6628, 1945). John Dower died shortly after the production of this report, but his widow became a founder member of the National Parks Commission, and subsequently its Deputy Chairman
27 *Report of the National Parks Committee (England and Wales)* (HMSO Cmnd 7121, 1947)
28 See, for example, *Eighteenth Report of the National Parks Commission for the year ended September 30, 1967* (HMSO, 1968), 8
29 Standing Committeee on National Parks of the Councils for the Preservation of Rural England and Wales, *The case for control of afforestation of open land in National Parks* (1961), 17
30 Recent cases have been in the Nantlle valley in Snowdonia and in the Forest of Bowland. See the statement by the Executive Committee of the Ramblers' Association *Access in Snowdonia* (E.0179, 1969)
31 Snowdonia, Yorkshire Dales, Exmoor and Brecon Beacons
32 Dartmoor, Pembrokeshire Coast, North York Moors and Northumberland

33 *Lake District National Park Fifteenth Annual Report 1966–67* (Lake District Planning Board, 1967)

34 *Misuse of a National Park: military training on Dartmoor* (Dartmoor Preservation Society, 1963) and The Standing Committee on National Parks of the Council for the Preservation of Rural England and the Council for the Preservation of Rural Wales, *National land use and the Dartmoor National Park: the case for the removal of damaging military training* (1965)

35 Dartmoor Preservation Association *Newsletter No. 51* (March 1969)

36 *Nineteenth Report of the National Parks Commission and first report of the Countryside Commission for the year ended September 30, 1968* (HMSO, 1968), 40

37 *What price water?* (The Voluntary Joint Committee for the Peak District National Park, 1969), 3

38 Minute 132 of the North York Moors National Park Planing Committee, quoted in personal communication from the Clerk of the County Council

39 For a detailed discussion of the siting of the Trawsfynydd station, see Mounfield, P. R., 'The location of nuclear power stations in the United Kingdom', *Geography*, 46 (1961), 139–55. A further factor was the neighbouring presence of the Tan-y-Grisiau pumped-storage scheme which was then under construction, together with 45 miles of overhead transmission line to the coal-fired power station at Connahs Quay. It is one of the ironies of the Trawsfynydd decision that a further nuclear-powered station may now be sited alongside the existing conventional plant at Connahs Quay, catering for the same base-load demand as Trawsfynydd itself

40 *Ninth Report of the National Parks Commission* (HMSO, 1958), 25, 75

41 Letter to *The Guardian*, 17 March 1969, by W. Eglan Shaw

42 The arguments for both sides are forcefully put in The Exmoor Society, *Can Exmoor survive?* (1966) and the Country Landowners Association and the National Farmers' Union, *Reclamation in Exmoor National Park* (1967) from which the quotation is taken. See also Capner, G., 'Exmoor: response to change', *Town and Country Planning*, 37 (1969), 262–9

43 The Council for Wales and Monmouthshire, *Report on the*

Welsh Holiday Industry (HMSO, Cmnd 1950, 1963), 75. The top four parks were the Peak District, the Lake District, Dartmoor and Snowdonia, named by 13, 12, 9 and 8 per cent respectively. Of those who had holidayed in Wales, 29 per cent knew of Snowdonia, 16 per cent the Lake District and 15 per cent the Peak District suggesting that these holidaymakers included more people with a love and knowledge of countryside. But even of those who lived in Wales and took their holidays there, only 37 per cent knew Snowdonia, 21 per cent the Pembrokeshire Coast and 13 per cent the Brecon Beacons. The sample is too small for much store to be placed on exact proportions, but the lack of basic knowledge is evident enough

44 The Ramblers' Association, *National Parks and what they are* (1966), 6

45 Blenkinson, A., op cit, 39

46 Ibid, 37

47 The first figure does not include grants to the National Parks themselves, but only the actual expenses of the Commission. The second figure includes £180,936 of Exchequer grants and contributions from the Commission. *Nineteenth Report*, op cit, Appendix D, 54–5. The exact expenditure by the Park authorities is confused by the degree to which administrative costs are absorbed by the constituent councils, but one measure is the expenditure incurred by the vigorous Peak Park Planning Board with its own separate planning staff. In 1967–8 its administrative costs were £86,293 (including £57,193 for wages and salaries) and its expenditure on positive action under the National Parks Act a further £58,688. Under the last-named head, the major items were publicity work and information centres (£12,706); provision of accommodation, camping sites and car parks (£17,579), tree planting and tree preservation (£5,863) and warden service (£20,274). Peak District National Park *Sixteenth Annual Report of the Planning Board* (1968), 52–3

48 Gilbert, E. W., *Vaughan Cornish and the advancement of knowledge relating to the beauty of scenery in town and country* (Oxford Preservation Trust, 1965), 5

49 *East Hampshire Area of Outstanding Natural Beauty: a study in countryside conservation* (Hampshire County Council, 1968)

50 Ministry of Housing and Local Government *The Green Belts* (HMSO, 1962), 2
51 Ibid, 2. See also Thomas, D. L., *London's Green Belt* (Faber, 1970)
52 For a most valuable discussion, with maps, of the recreational use of London's Green Belt see Lovett, W. F. B., 'Leisure and land use in the Metropolitan Green Belt', *Journal of the London Society*, 358 (1962)
53 Countryside Commission *The coasts of England and Wales: measures of use, protection and development* (HMSO, 1968). All factual data relating to the coast have been derived from this source unless otherwise stated
54 A National Trust survey, relating to 1964, showed 217 miles of coast belonging to the three armed Services, but was based on measurements to the nearest mile from 1 inch Ordnance Maps
55 Five coastal authorities had 36 per cent or more of their population of pensionable age in 1961 (Budleigh Salterton UD 36·0; Sidmouth UD 36·0; Worthing MB 36·5; Bexhill MB 37·0; Grange UD 38·0) compared with a national average of 14·8 per cent. Six coastal authorities registered an increase in the proportion of people of pensional age of more than 7·5 per cent between 1951 and 1961 (Sidmouth UD 7·5; Sandwich MB 7·7; Llandudno UD 8·0; Frinton and Walton UD 8·2; Bexhill MB 9·2; Kingsbridge RD 10·6) compared with a national average of 1·5 per cent
56 Rawnsley, C., 'The Preservation of the Coast', in *Proceedings of the Countryside in 1970, Second Conference* (Royal Society of Arts, 1965), A8
57 Ibid, A5
58 These figures include properties in Northern Ireland
59 The Benson Report recommended that Enterprise Neptune be phased out and a new General Appeal launched
60 An excellent summary of existing legislation is appended to each volume of the Reports of the Regional Coastal Conferences (note 61)
61 At the time of writing, all the regional reports had been published, but not the summary and policy proposals. The National Parks Commission was responsible for compilation, and each includes a map at a scale of ¼ inch to the mile showing categories of land committed for development; of land

U

protected from development; peak number of visitors at 'resorts, beaches and regularly frequented places'; peak use of
beaches; and boating facilities. Individual volumes are as
follows (HMSO is the publisher in each case):

The coasts of Kent and Sussex (1967);
The coasts of Hampshire and the Isle of Wight (1967);
The coasts of South-West England (1967);
The coasts of South Wales and the Severn Estuary (1967);
The coasts of North Wales (1968);
The coasts of North-West England (1968);
The coasts of North-East England (1968);
The coasts of Yorkshire and Lincolnshire (1968);
The coasts of East Anglia (1968);
Coastal recreation and holidays (1969)

62 Excluded from this are such counties as Gloucestershire,
where the frontage is estuarine rather than coastal

63 Furmidge, J., 'Planning for recreation in the countryside',
Journal of the Town Planning Institute, 55 (1969), 65

64 Ibid, 62

CHAPTER SEVEN

1 Rubinstein, D. and Speakman, C., *Leisure, transport and the
countryside*, Fabian research series, 277 (Fabian Society,
1969), 16

2 In 1967, the population of England and Wales was estimated
as 58,390,000 and that of the South-east standard region as
17,185,600

3 Coppock, J. T., 'The recreational use of land and water in
rural Britain', *Tijdschrift voor Econ. en Soc. Geografie*, 57
(1966), 93

4 Unpublished estimate by D. C. Nicholls

5 Brands Hatch, Kent; Crystal Palace, London; Goodwood,
Sussex; Mallory Park, Leicestershire; Oulton Park, Cheshire;
Silverstone, Northants; Snetterton, Norfolk

6 Wiltshire County Council, *Leisure in the countryside—survey of the use of selected public open spaces* (1967), 14

7 Burton, T. L. and Wibberley, G. P., *Outdoor recreation in
the British countryside* (Wye College, 1965), iii

8 The problems at county level are illustrated in Cheshire

County Council's *Cheshire Countryside, an interim report on recreation* (1968), which attempts to map facilities at county level but for 'Outdoor water recreation' and 'Open country recreation' necessarily resorts to pictorial symbols of a very generalised nature in showing distributions. It is perhaps optimistic to suggest that 'the present state of knowledge at least permits accurate inventories to be made' as the County Planning Officer for Gloucestershire recently claimed (*Planning for recreation*: Proceedings of the conference of the West Midlands Branch of the Regional Studies Association, 3 May 1969, 9) if such inventories are to be more than records of formally recognised facilities

9   For an invaluable summary of the work of the Commission, and for county lists of commons and detailed comments on the features of their distribution, see Hoskins, W. G. and Stamp, L. D., *The common lands of England and Wales* (Collins New Naturalist, 1963)
10 Ibid, 96
11 Ibid, 226–7 and Mattingly, A., 'Work in the field', *Journal of the Commons, Open Spaces and Footpaths Preservation Society*, 18 (1968), 7
12 Mattingly, A., op cit, 8
13 Hoskins, W. G. and Stamp, L. D., op cit, 200
14 Wager, J., 'Outdoor recreation on common land', *Journal of the Town Planning Institute*, 53 (1967), 398
15 See Swann, B., *The registration of common land and rights of common* (Central Committee on Commons Registration, not dated), for full description of procedures and definitions
16 Denman, D. R., 'Five crucial years in the destiny of common land, 1965–1970', *Report of the proceedings of the Countryside in 1970, second conference* (Royal Society of Arts, 1965), 37. This paper contains an excellent outline of the varied problems of commons management
17 Hoskins, W. G. and Stamp, L. D., op cit, 4
18 Ibid, 139
19 Ministry of Land and Natural Resources, *Leisure in the Countryside in England and Wales* (Cmnd 2928, HMSO, 1966), 12
20 Coppock, J. T., 'Changes in rural land-use in Great Britain', *Institute of British Geographers Special Publication No 1* (1968), 115. This paper contains some very useful maps and

diagrams of forest growth and distribution with data up to
1967. See also Edlin, H. L., *Forestry in Great Britain, a review of progress to 1967* (Forestry Commission, 1967)

21 Matthews, J. D., 'Forestry and the landscape', *The
Advancement of Science*, 23 (1966), 366–7

22 Hoskins, W. G., *The making of the English Landscape*
(Hodder & Stoughton, 1955), 143

23 Ibid,150

24 Ibid, 149–50, Hoskins' masterly description of the creation
of the rural scene is an incessant reminder of the transient
nature of fashion in beauty and landscape

25 Locke, G. M., 'A sample survey of field and other
boundaries in Great Britain', *Quarterly Journal of Forestry*,
56 (1962), 137–44

26 Moore, N. W., Hooper, M. D., and Davis, B. N. K., 'Hedges,
I Introduction and reconnaissance studies', *Journal of
Applied Ecology*, 4 (1967), 201-20

27 Ibid, 215. The paper contains material on the rate of loss of
different species in differing areas

28 Lowenthal, D. and Prince, H. C., 'English landscape tastes',
The Geographical Review, 55 (1965), 197

29 Wood, R. F. and Anderson, I. A., *Forestry in the British
Scene* (Forestry Commission Booklet No 24, HMSO, 1968), 5

30 Edlin, H. L., *Trees, woods and man* (London, 1956), 168.
Quoted in Lowenthal, D. and Prince, H. C., op cit, 198–9

31 *Forestry in Wales* (Forestry Commission, 1967), 6

32 Burton, T. L. and Wibberley, G. P., op cit, 13

33 Elliott, G. K., '50 years of state forestry', *New Scientist*, 42
(1969), 516

34 Forestry Commission, *Forty-eighth annual report and
accounts, 1966–67* (HMSO, 1968), Tables 4, 21 and 22

35 These figures refer to the acreage planted or proposed for
planting, not to the total land owned by the Commission
in each area

36 *The Yorkshire Evening Post*, 18 September 1969. The
scheme is to proceed though opposed by the Yorkshire
Dales National Park (West Riding) Planning Committee

37 For fuller details, see the individual park guides, or the
summary in Edlin, H. L., *Forest Parks* (Forestry Commission Booklet No 6, HMSO, 1961)

38 For a readable summary, see Elliott, G. K., op cit

39 For an illustrated discussion of problems and achievements see Crowe, S., *Forestry in the landscape* (Forestry Commission Booklet No 18, HMSO, 1966)

40 *The Guardian*, 1 July 1968

41 For a much fuller survey, see Tinker, J., 'Marrying wildlife to forestry', *New Scientist*, 42 (1969), 518–20

42 The Countryside Act, 1968, section 23, formally conveys powers to the Forestry Commission to 'provide or arrange for or assist in the provision of, tourist, recreational or sporting facilties' but equally makes it clear that 'all expenses incurred . . . in the exercise of their powers under this section shall be paid out of the Forestry Fund'

43 A survey of public use and attitudes in selected forests was carried out by W. E. S. Mutch in 1963–4 and reported in *Public recreation in National Forests: a factual study* (Forestry Commission Booklet No 21, HMSO, 1968)

44 The last total should be virtually doubled to give a fair comparison with the other two, for it relates to tickets sold rather than passenger journeys booked. The other lines count one return ticket as two journeys

45 Lowenthal, D. and Prince, H. C., op cit, 205

46 Personal communication, 26 March 1968. The BTA estimate that in 1968, stately homes and castles of all kinds received some 20 million visits (*The Guardian*, 15 May 1969)

47 *Sunday Times*, 14 April 1963

48 Lees-Milne, J., 'Don't kill the goose or hints to owners', *Historic houses, castles and gardens in Great Britain and Ireland, 1968* (Index Publishers, 1968), 4

49 Countryside Commission *Policy on county parks and picnic sites* (HMSO, 1969), 3

50 'A taste of honey', *Parish Councils Review*, 19 (1969), 195

51 Countryside Commission, op cit, 4-5

52 Cheshire, Derbyshire, Gloucestershire, Lancashire and Wiltshire

53 *Cheshire Countryside: a scheme for a Wirral Country Park* (Cheshire County Council, 1968)

54 Quoted from a statement prepared by the Technical Advisers to the Joint Management Committee when the project was submitted to the Countryside Commission for approval

55 *The Guardian*, 20 May 1969

56 Lowenthal, D. and Prince, H. C., op cit, 198
57 Rt. Hon. Anthony Greenwood MP, in an address to the annual meeting of the CPRE, 6 July 1967
58 Ministry of Housing and Local Government Welsh Office, *Report of the Footpaths Committee* (HMSO, 1968), 3. This is generally referred to as the Gosling Committee, after its chairman Sir Arthur Gosling, KBE, CB
59 Ibid
60 For a recent full account see Millar, T. G., 'Britain's long-distance paths', *Town and Country Planning*, 37 (1969), 103–7
61 See page 134
62 *Footpaths and bridleways, a plea for their protection* (Ramblers Association, 1967), 1
63 *The Guardian*, 22 July 1968
64 Society of Sussex Downsmen *Forty-fourth annual report and balance sheet 1967–8*, 29, 33–9
65 'Roads used as public paths', *The Parish Councils Review*, 19 (1968), 172
66 Rubinstein, D. and Speakman, C., 'Leisure and transport', *Journal of the Commons, Open Spaces and Footpaths Preservation Society*, 18 (1968), 29
67 Ibid
68 See, for example, *The Guardian*, 5 and 28 September 1968
69 Water Resources Board *Fifth Annual Report* (HMSO, 1968), 6. No figures were available for *actual* as opposed to *authorised* abstractions. Of the total, 905 thousand million gallons were from ground water sources as opposed to surface water. The principal categories of user were (in thousand million gallons authorised annually)

Public water supply	1,684
Central Electricity Generating Board	5,098
Other industrial use	1,655
Agriculture	103
Miscellaneous	260

See also Speight, H., 'Britain's water resources', *Town and Country Planning*, 34 (1966), 314–322. Other papers in this (June) issue are also invaluable in this respect
70 This point is particularly well illustrated by Figure 8, Coppock, J. T., op cit 1966, 92
71 The lower figure is that quoted by J. T. Coppock, op cit

1966, 93, but 'excludes small patches of water and the lesser rivers': the higher estimate is based on a calculation by the Ordnance Survey and quoted by T. L. Burton and G. P. Wibberley, op cit, 17. Both estimates include reservoirs as well as natural water bodies, but there are obvious problems of definition: the higher estimate seems the more realistic and is substantiated from other sources

72 In *The Old Vicarage, Granchester*, written in 1912
73 *The Guardian*, 18 September 1969
74 For a much fuller treatment of this theme see CCPR *Inland Waters and Recreation* (1964), 46–51. This whole volume is particularly relevant to the theme of this section.
75 These are the requirements quoted in Gloucestershire County Council *Outdoor Water Recreation* (1968), Table 1
76 Hadfield, C., *British Canals* (Phoenix House, 1950), 26
77 Ibid, 15
78 For fuller details of the particular problems of the Broads, see The Nature Conservancy, *Report on Broadland* (1965)
79 Norfolk County Council, *Report of the Broads conference on the problems and requirements of the Broads area* (1946)
80 Norfolk County Council, *Report on the Norfolk Holiday Industry* (1964)
81 Ives, W. L., *The problem of our inland waterways* (British Transport Commission, 1957), 17
82 Ministry of Transport, *British Waterways: recreation and amenity* (Cmnd 3401, HMSO, 1967), 3
83 British Waterways Board, *Leisure and the waterways* (1967), 9
84 Ibid, 7–9
85 British Waterways Board, *Annual report and accounts 1968* (HMSO, 1969), 14
86 *Basic Road Statistics 1969* (British Road Federation), 12
87 *Fifth annual report of the Water Resources Board* (HMSO, 1968), 37
88 British Waterways Board, *The facts about the waterways* (1965), 35. Appendix 9 of this report contains a full list of all reservoirs and their recreational use
89 *What price water?* (The Voluntary Joint Committee for the Peak District National Park, 1969), 5
90 *The Guardian*, 9 November 1968
91 Ibid, 20 September 1969

92 Water Resources Board, op cit, 45
93 Ministry of Land and Natural Resources (3/66) and Department of Education and Science (19/66) *Use of reservoirs and gathering grounds for recreation* (HMSO, 1966), 1
94 Ibid
95 Water Resources Board, op cit, 1
96 *The Guardian*, 7 March 1968
97 J. G. Lloyd at the Institution of Water Engineers. Quoted in *The Guardian*, 16 May 1968
98 Derbyshire County Council, *Sailing on reservoirs* (1967), 3. For a specific management study and recommendations see Rugby Joint Water Board, *The use of Draycote Water and Stanford Reservoir for recreation* (1967)
99 *Concrete evidence: facts about sand and gravel* (Sand & Gravel Association of Great Britain, 1965), 5, 8. This includes 'dry' as well as 'wet' pits
100 Ibid, 15
101 Gloucestershire County Council, op cit, G1. See also Cotswold Water Park Joint Committee, *Cotswold Water Park Draft Report* (Gloucestershire County Council, 1969)

CHAPTER EIGHT

1 Hutchinson, Sir Joseph, 'Land and human populations', *The Advancement of Science*, 23 (1966), 242
2 Ibid, 241
3 Rodgers, H. B., 'Leisure and recreation', *Urban Studies*, 6 (1969), 381–2. This paper is one contribution to a most valuable symposium 'Developing patterns of urbanisation'
4 Ibid, 375
5 Ministry of Land and Natural Resources and the Secretary of State for Wales, *Leisure in the countryside in England and Wales*, Cmnd 2928 (HMSO, 1966), 3–4
6 Outdoor Recreation Resources Review Commission, *Outdoor Recreation for America* (Washington, 1962), 96–120
7 A wide variety of these have been propounded. At one end of the scale are attempts at a detailed assessment of landscape quality as a prelude to more effective development control, eg Fines, K. D., 'Landscape evaluation: a research project in East Sussex', *Regional Studies* (1968). The East Hampshire

study—*East Hampshire Area of Outstanding Natural Beauty: a study in countryside conservation* (Hampshire County Council et al, 1968)—attempted to 'devise methods of establishing a technique for the promotion of the conservation of the countryside' and to 'produce a plan for a particular rural area . . . in which the issues relevant to that area may be analysed and reconciled, and which . . . is clearly related to the interests of the users and owners of rural land, the public at large and local residents'. At the other end of the scale are the rural strategies prepared by counties as a prelude to a County Structure Plan as envisaged by the 1968 Town and Country Planning Act. See, for example, *Cheshire Countryside, an interim report on recreation* (Cheshire County Council, 1968); *Hertfordshire: countryside appraisal, 1969* (Hertfordshire County Council, 1969)

8   The Peak Park Planning Board has been particularly to the fore in encouraging such sympathetic development. See, for example, *Building in the Peak* (Peak Park Planning Board, 1964)

9   The sum initially allocated was only £2,750, but the principle is a highly interesting one. 'Experiment in upland management', *Recreation News*, 12 (November 1969)

10 Lancashire County Council, *Forest of Bowland recreational study (summary report)*, (1967), 3

11 Mansfield, N. W., 'Traffic Policy in the Lake District National Park', *Journal of the Town Planning Institute*, 54 (1968), 263

12 For a fuller discussion of these restraints, see Rodgers, H. B., op cit, 376–9

13 See, for example, West Riding County Council *Traffic in the Yorkshire Dales* (1969), 31: 'attractive opportunities must be available outside the National Parks, so siphoning off as much as possible of the growing pressures'.

14 For an excellent summary of both problems and prospects, see Christian, G., *Tomorrow's countryside* (John Murray, 1966)

15 Brancher, D. M., *Scenery, roads, cars and cost*, Proceedings of the third annual study conference of the Council for the Protection of Rural Wales (1969), 3

16 Gloucestershire County Council, *Outdoor Recreation and the Gloucestershire Countryside* (1968), 16–17, Map 7

17 Ibid, 9
18 Brancher, D. M., op cit, 13
19 Countryside Commission Goyt Valley traffic experiment (1970)
20 Chas. T. Main Inc, *Preliminary Report and Master Plan, Dillon Reservoir State Park* (State of Ohio Department of Natural Resources, 1965), ii
21 Heytze, J. C., *Recreation in the Forest of Nunspeet* (The State Forest Service of the Netherlands, 1969), 2. See also, for a more detailed study, Heytze, J. C., *Bos en Recreatie* (Staatsbosbeheer, 1968)
22 Friends of the Northern Regional Open Air Museum, *Living History, an open air museum for the North of England* (c 1967). By January 1970, the Joint Regional Committee of Local Authorities had appointed the first two full-time members of staff, and the possibility of the formal opening of the museum in July 1970 had been discussed
23 Pritchard, T., et al, *Nature Trails* (Nature Conservancy, 1967), 4
24 *The Yorkshire Post*, 13 July 1968
25 Undertaken by J. H. Appleton of the University of Hull in 1969, but not published at the time of writing
26 Huron-Clinton Metropolitan Authority, *1965 Park Users Survey* (1965)
27 Huron-Clinton Metropolitan Authority, *Eleventh Biennial Report as of December 31, 1963* (1964), 13
28 Quoted in Tunnard, C. and Reed, H. H., *American Skyline* (Mentor, 1956), 153

INDEX

328 INDEX

National Parks, 39, 41, 122, 171, 176, 193-207, 221-2, 238, 273-6; private parks, 29; Royal Parks, 33; use of, 101-6; Victorian parks, 33-7, 100, 285
Participation rates, 48-73, 91-3; activity growth rates, 67-73; factors affecting, 62-6; female participation, 64-5; in outdoor recreation, 52-62; in team games, 91-3
Passive recreation, definition of, 52
Peak District National Park, 115, 123, 196, 200-1, 207, 225, 263
Peak periods, 123, 131, 161-4, 166
Pembrokeshire Coast Path, 247
Pembrokeshire, oil refinery, 202
Pennine Way, 247, 249
Pilot National Recreation Survey, 44, 114, 119
Planning for Leisure, 44
Playgrounds, 80-1, 100-11
Pony Club, 143
Population density, 21, 267
Population predictions, 16, 267-8
Potash mining in National Parks, 202-3
Private sports grounds, 92-4
Provision of Facilities for Sport, 78

R

Railways and recreation, 24-7, 239, 251, 284
Ramblers Association, 143, 196, 249, 250
Rambling, 27, 143
Regional parks, 284-90
Reservoirs, 201, 260-5, 279-82
Resource-based land, 175, 222, 223, 238
Riding, 143
Rights of way, 247-50
Rivers, 254-7
Roads, 251-3, 277-9
Route networks, 223, 246-53
Royal Commission on Common Land, 179, 224, 228-9

Royal Parks, 33
Rugby football, 91-3
Rural parks, 223, 238, 246; *see also* Country Parks

S

Sailing, 148-9, 218-20
Sand dunes, 33, 181, 212
Savernake Forest, 120
Scott Report, 178, 195
Seaside holidays, 31-3, 155-61, 169, 218; seaside resorts, 31-3, 218, 289
Seasonal fluctuations, 126-9, 161-4, 269-70
Second homes, 154-5
Sefton Park, 34
Shooting, 145-6
Site studies, 119-31
Ski-ing, 143
Snowdonia National Park, 198, 200, 202
Snowdonia Forest Park, 236
Society for the Promotion of Nature Reserves, 178
Society for the Protection of Birds, 177
Society of Sussex Downsmen, 250
Spas, 31-2
Spectator sport, 25
Speke Hall, 125-7, 129
Sports Council, 41, 78, 92
Sports halls, 78-9, 88
Staffordshire and Worcestershire Survey, 125-6
Stamp, Sir Dudley, 224, 228-9
Stanage Edge, 143
Standards of open space, 84-6, 92
Stately homes, 29, 183, 189, 239-41
St James Park, 33
Studley Park, 129
Sunday trips, 112, 123-6, 164, 269-70
Surveys: of park use, 100-6; of recreation demand, 143-4; of recreation sites, 119-31; Sports Council 'initial appraisals', 78-82